The Not So Silent Merger

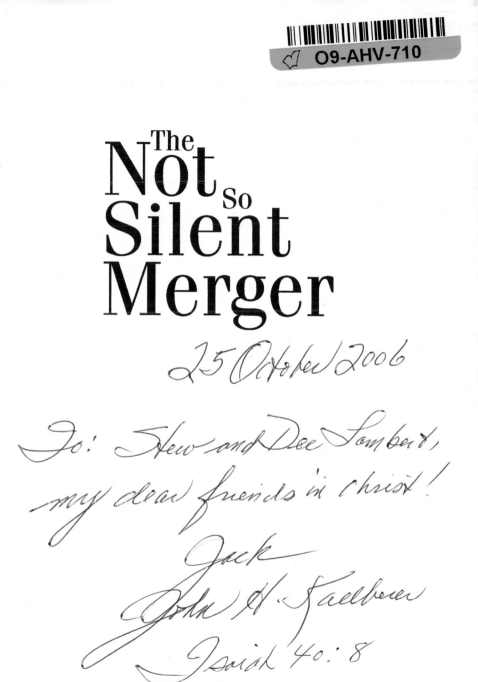

25 October 2006

To: Stew and Dee Lambert,
my dear friends in Christ!

Jack

John H. Kaelberer

Isaiah 40:8

The Not So Silent Merger

The World in the Church

Captain John H. Kaelberer, CHC, USN, Ret.

ISBN 1-4141-0241-0
Library of Congress Catalog Card Number: 2004095189

Dedicated to

Barbara Gay Moyer Kaelberer

My beautiful wife, and mother of our three children, who is the love and joy of my life. Her depth of Christian love has been a wellspring of support, comfort, and life fulfillment. She is God's great blessing to me!

Table of Contents

About the Author

John (Jack) Herbert Kaelberer was born on 2 October 1929 in Philadelphia, Pennsylvania, to Emma and Herbert W. Kaelberer. He is a graduate of Muhlenberg College, Allentown, Pennsylvania, and The Lutheran Theological Seminary at Philadelphia. He was ordained by The United Lutheran Church in America on 20 May 1954. He also holds masters degrees from The Lutheran Theological Seminary at Philadelphia in divinity, and from The United States International University, San Diego, California, in human behavior.

His civilian pastorates were at St. Paul's Lutheran Church, Allentown, Pennsylvania from 1954 to 1956 and at St. John's Lutheran Church, Hatboro, Pennsylvania from 1956 to 1965. He entered active duty in the Chaplain Corps, United States Navy, in 1965 and retired from active duty in the rank of Captain on 1 September 1989.

Among his duty assignments were:

- Destroyer Division 212
- Naval Hospital, Oakland, California
- 1st Marine Division (FMF), Vietnam
- Naval Station, San Diego
- Duty under instruction: The United States International University, San Diego
- USS Chicago (CG-11)
- Naval Postgraduate School, Monterey, California
- Force Chaplain, Fleet Marine Force, Pacific, Hawaii
- Assistant Chief of Staff for Religious Ministries, U.S. Marine Corps Recruit Depot, San Diego
- Fleet Chaplain, U.S. Atlantic Fleet, Norfolk, Virginia

Among his awards are:

The Legion of Merit Medal, The Bronze Star Medal with Combat V, The Meritorious Service Medal, The Navy Commendation Medal, The Vietnam Cross of Gallantry, The Combat Action Ribbon, and various Vietnam campaign ribbons.

In 1985, Chaplain Kaelberer entered the ministerium of The Lutheran Church-Missouri

Synod, after twenty-nine years of serving The United Lutheran Church in America, which became the Evangelical Lutheran Church in America. He is married to the former Barbara Gay Moyer of Bloomsburg, Pennsylvania. They have three children: John H. Jr., Rev. Eric V., and Mrs. Mary Joan Moulton.

Acknowledgments

I wish to express my appreciation to The Rev. Dr. James E. Shaw, Captain John C. Wohlrabe, CHC, USN, The Rev. Joel Wood, The Rev. Richard W. Andrus, and The Rev. Robert J. Merz for reviewing the manuscript and for their wise counsel. Special appreciation is extended to my son, The Rev. Eric V. Kaelberer, for his many suggestions and for writing the Foreword. Special appreciation also to my creative daughter, Mary Joan Moulton, who took my idea for the cover of this work and made it real; and to my wife, Barbe. She has been my right hand in editing and proofreading the manuscript. Above all, my greatest appreciation is for her love and for her prayers that this work might be to God's glory and for God's people that they may enjoy forever the honor and blessing of God's Word, His love message in Jesus.

Foreword

Every day in the media we see attacks on Christians and our beliefs. These are beliefs which are centered in God's Holy Word. Yet these attacks, though hurtful, are not as damaging as the scriptural betrayals which come from liberal Christian theologians and other scholars within the Christian Church itself. Attacks from outside never hurt as much as those from within the family. When those who claim faith in Jesus as Lord, attack His Word, His love message, then our eyes tear and our hearts break. That you have picked up this book may suggest that your heart may already be broken by such assaults.

Most writings of this nature deal with questions of how far the Christian Church has fallen in its ability to address the post-modern culture. They take a defensive and accusatory position because

15

the position they defend is their personal position, not the truth flowing from God's inerrant and infallible Word.

What is different about this book is the "Here I Stand! I can do no other, may God help me!" statements in accord with God's Word, words which came from Dr. Martin Luther. In such a statement we find the bedrock upon which truth stands and the clarity to address scriptural truths under attack. This book is far from soothing or fun reading. Naming the historical-critical method of biblical interpretation as the weapon of choice, my father lays out for you how the world has been invited into the Christian Church to bring deception, confusion, and yes, spiritual death upon God's beloved. When, in fact, the church is called to "go into all the world with the Good News." It is essential reading for understanding what is happening in the Christian Church today wherein betrayal has come from within. Of course, the main enemy of God has been and is the *god of this world,* but he has not been a "lone ranger." He has enticed theologians and other scholars within the Church to dance to his main tune: the destruction of the authority of God, especially His Holy Word. With that Word weakened and decimated, the sacraments of Baptism and the Lord's Supper crumble.

It is also from within, through the power of the Holy Spirit, that God's Means of Grace, His Word and Sacraments, will restore Christian spirituality

16

based upon God's authority, not upon the imaginings and musings of mortal theological scholars. I hold great hope for the Christian Church, because the *god of this world* is not the God who redeemed this World with His very blood. Our true and loving God of the Cross and the Empty Tomb will win, for as Holy Scripture proclaims: "The gates of hell shall not prevail against it!" (Matthew 16:18)

Pastor Eric Vance Kaelberer

Introduction

You search the Scriptures, because you think in them you have eternal life: and it is these that bear witness of Me.

(John 5:39)

Some years ago as Fleet Chaplain, U. S. Atlantic Fleet, I called on U. S. Navy commands in England and Scotland. One afternoon when I had some free time, I visited several Anglican churches in London and talked to their rectors. The familiar theme from both clergymen was the demise of Christianity in England. They recounted how beautiful churches, now filled with a handful of aging worshipers each Sunday, were thrashing like drowning non-swimmers trying to keep their churches financially afloat while all around them was a frivolous culture that could care less.

From what I remembered of the reports coming to America during the "Blitz of London," from September of 1940 to May of 1941, when conventional bombs and incendiary bombs were reigning their terror, I remarked to one of the rectors that I heard how Londoners overflowed their churches seeking God's intervention. He was too young to personally remember although he had heard such reports. However, he said that because the older generations had forgotten and turned their backs on God in Whom they had sought refuge during the war, that his congregation was turning their attention to the youth of London. From a benefactor they had received fifty thousand pounds to restructure their ministry to the youth.

Sadly, that "London Tale" is being played out in many churches of America where liberal changes have occurred. The churches that have stood for decades as the "mainline" denominations of America, have drastically changed. Methodist, Episcopal, Congregational, and the United Church of Christ, along with some liberal denominations within the Presbyterian, Baptist, and Lutheran mix as well as many others, no longer stand doctrinally where they stood just fifty years ago. Following the lead of liberal theologians who have demythologized the Bible, abandoning its authority, denying the miracles of the Virgin Birth and the Resurrection, and trashing as uncongenial any biblical doctrine contrary to the modern day liberated lifestyle, these denominations have betrayed their divine calling to be the true Body of Jesus Christ, the Christian Church which God brought into being at Pentecost. Their membership and finances are no longer where they were even twenty years ago. Christian spirituality vanishes as well and for those old timers who remain within those denominations there are the ever haunting questions: "What is going on in my church? What has happened?"

What is going on is this: it is the theological adaptation of Isaac Newton's Third Law of Motion: "For every action, there is an equal and opposite reaction." More simply stated: "For every action, there is a reaction."

The "London Tale" told above is reaction. It is negative reaction. Worshipers have left the pews of Anglican congregations in London just as they have left many of the "mainline" denominations in America. Some type of theological action caused this reaction. Just as Newton maintained, whenever objects "A" and "B" interact with each other, they exert forces upon each other.

The Not So Silent Merger: The World in the Church, while it may be the title of this work, describes the action which has resulted in the negative reaction of spiritual demise occurring in many "mainline" denominations today. The spiritual football which is being kicked around is the Word of God in Holy Scripture. It is the action against the authenticity of that Word which has brought about the reaction of spiritual apathy and demise. Abandonment of the authority of God's Word by way of the historical-critical method of biblical interpretation has proven to be Force "A" which has interacted with Force "B," the inerrant and infallible Word of God in Scripture, and has brought spiritual disaster on God's people who have been subjected to it, the number of whom is known only to God.

It is not that Force "B" is impotent. Rather, God's Word wrongly honored, proclaimed, and taught, results in God's withdrawal of the power of His Word. Nowhere in Scripture will you ever find God blessing what He cannot honor. Please see Isaiah 40:8, John 17:17, Hebrews 4:12, 1st Peter 1:23–25, and 1st John 2:5 as representative passages of the power of God's Word.

The well-worn excuse that times change should not be permission for the Christian Church to change also. Douglas A. Walrath explains the exodus from the church in sociological terms. He maintains that when neighborhood and social change take place, so follows the church like a helpless carbon copy. That sociological explanation fails to incorporate the theological implications.[1]

Howard B. Kuhn, in writing about secular theology and the reaction of some young theologians about what was going on in post-World War II theology, states that theologians in the liberal tradition were more apt to accentuate and accept scientific judgments and findings as having more authority than the revelation of God's truth in Scripture. They leaned toward man's faulty scholarship rather than to God's Word for eternal spiritual truth, truth from God. Kuhn further states:

> Although the younger theologians contended that historic Christianity had failed to meet the basic problems of modern life, it would be more accurate to say (and some of the younger theologians themselves recognized this) that historic Christianity had been abandoned by major religious bodies. Thus, Christianity was applied to the issues and problems of modern life in a deformed and defective manner.[2]

Wade Clark Roof underscores the inability of liberal "mainline" churches "to fashion a meaningful and compelling faith congruent with modern culture."[3] That there is a disconnect signifies that the culture of the world appears to hold dominance over the power of God's living Word, Jesus, and His written Word, the Holy Scriptures.

David F. Wells hones in on the loss "of biblical fidelity, less interest in the truth, less seriousness, less depth, and less capacity to speak the Word of

God to our generation in a way that offers an alternative to what it already thinks." He sees the new evangelism of our day not being driven by the "same passion for truth" as the reason why it is "often empty of theological interest."[4]

What unfolds within these pages is the exposure of the *god of this world* who attempts to merge with and take over the Christian Church in a worldly context, because he has nothing to say beyond this world about life . . . only spiritual death disguised in appealing concepts not of the God of Holy Scripture. The design to do so is simple. In a series of subtle and deceptive maneuvers, making use of traditional Christian terminology while changing the truthful doctrine of God contained in His Word, liberal theologians seduced by the *god of this world,* present an "up to date" version, to fit the prevailing culture. As self-appointed theological engineers they attempt to re-design Christianity, presenting new *spins* which mirror the culture. What they conveniently omit and want you to omit is the authority of God's Word. The *god of this world* denies that the God of Holy Scripture is both *Creator* and *Redeemer* and you, dear people of God, are the target of this spiritual deception which leads to spiritual death.

Using theological *spins* which are spiritual roadblocks and theological minefields, the *god of this world* threatens Christian spirituality, which I define as life in Jesus Christ through the Means of God's Grace: His inerrant and infallible Word in Scripture and the Sacraments of Baptism and The Lord's Supper. The flow against Christian spirituality is from "on high," from liberal theologians who have negatively influenced many old "mainline" denominations through their devotion to a theology based on the historical-critical method of biblical interpretation, the weapon of choice used by the *god of this world*. This method will be discussed in Chapter 2. Congregations who are solidly faithful in living according to God's Means of Grace, are not exempt from these false theologies and ideologies which can threaten the spiritual lives of some of their members. These theologies and ideologies come dressed in the appealing garb of the world, gussied up with "new world" glamor to seduce the least suspecting, impressionable members of Christian congregations who are led to view these theologies and ideologies as "interesting and reasonable ideas," all the while not aware of how they can and will infect and topple their Christian spirituality.

Recently a deadly virus has spread from Hong Kong and Guangdong province, China, to other countries around the world. It is known as Severe Acute Respiratory Syndrome (SARS). This virus has been initially identified as a new coronavirus, a relative of one of the many viruses that causes the common cold.[5]

Anything that threatens the health and life of humans causes great alarm and panic. Unfortunately, threats to the spiritual health and life of God's people are not taken as seriously. Human spirituality has become a private, no trespassing area of human life to the degree that threats to healthy spirituality are ignored or passed off as trivial, of no real importance. In reality, these threats have been with man since Adam and Eve. They can be grouped under one common spiritual virus which I name as: *Spiritual Arrest Religious Syndrome*—also (SARS).

We have witnessed the impact of this spiritual virus via world history. Indeed, it is vividly described in Holy Scripture as *sin*—an offense against God's law and love as well as a offense against moral law—where God's will and way for abundant spiritual and human life have been arrested and imprisoned in a *god of this world* oriented culture. So, added to the spiritual roadblock, theological minefield analogy, is the SARS theological virus. They are of the same origin. All of these words focus on the current spiritual illnesses facing the entire spectrum of the Christian Church, illnesses contrived and spread by the *god of this world*. No Christian denomination is immune from attack and for that reason it is systemic, meaning it affects the entire body rather than only one part of the body of Christ, The Christian Church. It is a spiritual life and death issue. Only a fool will argue otherwise. However, if arguments arise, be

26

assured these arguments will always focus on this world and its culture and not upon Christian spirituality, a force from God that gets in the way and must be ignored or attacked as "out-dated."

Those who face the greatest threat to their spirituality are youth, both inside and outside the Christian Church. With eyes wide open they are witnessing spiritual decline all around them while the *god of this world* seduces Christians and non-Christians to follow his path to spiritual chaos and death. As an astute war-planner, he has strategically positioned spiritual roadblocks, has spread the SARS virus, focusing on this world where he still tries to out-wrestle God.

These roadblocks, these theological minefields, infected with the SARS spiritual virus, are discussed in the following chapters. You will see by the range of topics covered that their systemic quality originates in the historical-critical method of biblical interpretation wherein the authority of God's Word is neutered. The roadblocks that flow from this method are evidence of the willing duplicity of liberal theologians and scholars in other disciplines to be in lock-step with the *god of this world* to put God in the caboose of post-modern culture. Each one takes aim at the spiritual life of the Christian man, woman, or child in our churches. Where they have been successful, surrender to the world and its culture occurs faster than a former Iraqi soldier with a white flag.

In no way am I advocating a retreat of Christ's Church from the secular world. Our God has placed His Church in the world with the love mission of Jesus Christ for the salvation of sinners like you and me. When the secular rules the sacred, the Christian Church is derailed from its appointed work of powerfully preaching God's inerrant and infallible Word and faithfully administering the Sacraments of Baptism and The Lord's Supper.

Spiritually infected roadblocks and minefields, while in abundance today, will never prevail! This assurance comes from Jesus in response to Peter's confession that Jesus is "the Christ, the Son of the living God." in Matthew's 16th chapter. Our Lord then tells Peter in the 18th verse of that chapter that He will build His Church upon that confession of faith when He said: "And I say to you that you are Peter, and upon this rock I will build My church; and the gates of Hades shall not overpower it." So it will ever be! Authenticating that truth is Dr. Martin Luther in a sermon preached in 1543:

> God is still wise and mighty enough to know very well how to sustain His church without the help of the world and the devil. Therefore the challenge: As you please, devil; come on with

all your henchmen; Christ will not only continue to exist in spite of you but will finally crush your head. Of this we are confident. To Him be praise and honor throughout eternity, together with the Father and the Holy Ghost, the one true God and Creator of all things. Amen.[6]

This book is written for the Christian laity as well as for those who have no ties to Christian fellowship and nurture found in churches where Jesus Christ is Lord and where God's Word is honored as true Word of God. My prayer is that what is written herein may be to the glory of God and in honor of His powerful and authoritative Means of Grace, His Word and the Sacraments of Baptism and The Lord's Supper.

This book is a sequel to my previous book, *Blessing & Honor/Honor & Blessing: Understanding The Confusion/Deception of Biblical Spin*. Some of the material in Chapter 2 of this work duplicates what is written in *B&H/H&B*. This is necessary to set the stage for all that follows.

NOTES

1. Douglas A. Walrath, *Understanding Church Growth And Decline,* Dean R. Hoge and David A. Roozen, eds.,(New York: The Pilgrim Press, 1979), 251.

2. Harold B. Kuhn, in *Tensions In Contemporary Theology*, Stanly N. Gundry and Alan F. Johnson, eds., (Chicago: Moody Press, 1976),158.
3. Wade Clark Roof, *Community and Commitment*, (New York: Elsevier,1978),7.
4. David F. Wells, *No Place For Truth*, (Grand Rapids: Wm. B. Eerdmans Publishing Co., 1993), 12.
5. Reuters news release, 10 April 2003: "Scientists Identify Virus Behind Deadly SARS."
6. Martin Luther, *What Luther Says,* ed. Ewald M. Plasss, 3 vol. (St. Louis: Concordia Publishing House, 1972), vol. I, 284, #835.

CHAPTER 1

An Enemy Has Done This!

Declare and set forth your case; Indeed, let them consult together. Who has announced this from old? Who has long since declared it? Is it not I, the Lord? And there is no other God besides Me, A righteous God and a Savior; There is none except Me.

Turn to Me, and be saved, all the ends of the earth; For I am God, and there is no other.
(Isaiah 45:21,22)

Even before 11 September 2001, the war of terrorism against the United States of America was in progress. 23 October 1983 witnessed the bombing of the Marine Corps barracks in Beirut, Lebanon. In 1998 embassies of the United States were bombed in Nairobi, Kenya, and Dar es Salaam in Tanzania. On 12 October 2000, the USS COLE was attacked in

Yemen. It was not until 11 September 2001 that America came to the full realization that "an enemy has done this!" An old Pennsylvania Dutch proverb applies: "We grow too soon old and too late smart."

Some denominations in the Christian Church have also been "slow on the draw" in recognizing its enemy, even welcoming him into their midst. The enemy is Satan, the *god of this world.*

Around 1200 B.C. the Trojan War occurred. It pitted young Doric Greeks of Troy against the Aegean Greeks. From this war has come a legend famous for the tactic of the Wooden Horse which was offered by the Aegeans to the Trojans as a gift. Supposedly, the Aegean Greeks had departed, leaving only a gift. However, inside this hallow and huge horse were soldiers. Sinon, an Aegean Greek spy, convinced the Trojans to accept the gift because it would make Troy invulnerable. The Wooden Horse was brought into the city. Later that night Sinon released the warriors, who took and burned Troy, thus prevailing against the Trojans.

Historians seem to make the conclusion that this story of welcoming the enemy is mere legend. Whether fantasy or reality the point of the existence of an enemy or enemies cannot be denied. Holy Scripture clearly points out who is God's enemy. He is happiest when he can be hidden within the camouflage of darkness and intrigue and welcomed as a friend. His greatest joy is to penetrate Christian theology while masking his deception as believable truth. He is a cunning enemy whom Jesus knew very well.

Jesus shows the work of the enemy in the "Parable of the Tares among the Wheat" in Matthew 13:24–30. There we read how a man directed his servants to sow good seed in his field. While his servants were asleep, his enemy came and in that same field sowed tares, an undesirable and degenerate form of wheat.

When both types of seed germinated, began to grow, the evidence was plain to see. While the servants questioned how this could have happened, since they believed only good seed was sown, the owner of the land was quick to diagnose the situation. His reply: "An enemy has done this!"

The servants wanted immediately to do some weeding to rid the field of the darnel, the degenerate wheat. This action was negated as the land owner didn't want the good wheat to be destroyed in that early process. Both types of seed were allowed to grow together until harvest time when the fruit from both seeds could be discerned and separated. The good wheat was to be kept while the degenerate wheat was to be destroyed by fire. Jesus explains in verses 37 to 40:

> The one who sows the good seed is the Son of
> Man, and the field is the world; and as for
> the good seed, these are the sons of the king-
> dom; and the tares are the sons of the evil *one*;
> and the enemy who sewed them is the devil, and
> the harvest is the end of the age; and the reapers
> are angels. Therefore just as the tares are gath-
> ered up and burned with fire, so shall it be at
> the end of the age.

Today, *the sons and even the daughters of the evil one* are active in their schemes and attempts to sow the world with their *renditions* of Christianity. Jesus, in the Sermon on the Mount, Matthew 7: 16,17, did not hold back any semblance of tolerance toward those who would sow His Kingdom with spiritual darnel when He said:

> Beware of the false prophets, who come to
> you, in sheep's clothing, but inwardly are rav-
> enous wolves. You will know them by their
> fruits. Grapes are not gathered from thorn
> bushes, nor figs from thistles, are they?

That statement and question of Jesus resounds mightily today as conflicting theologies or ideologies posing as theology, are preached as being more relevant to modern society than God's inerrant and infallible Word in Scripture. Confusion and deception rain down upon God's people when the clear Word of God's truth in Scripture is compromised and ignored. When this happens, it is to the delight of the *god of this world*, an enemy that Jesus knew very well from His temptation in the wilderness. You will recall that Jesus knew him well enough to give him the name "Satan" (in Matthew 4:10) after His third temptation when He said: "Begone Satan!"

In the 16th chapter of Matthew, Jesus reveals to His disciples that He had to go to Jerusalem to suffer, to be killed, and to be raised up again on the third day. He was pointing to the way of the cross, His perfect sacrifice for the sins of man. He was going to pay the full debt of sin. Rambunctious Peter rebuked Jesus by saying: "God forbid it, Lord! This shall never happen to You." Jesus' response was : "Get behind me, Satan! You are a stumbling block to Me, for you are not setting your mind on God's interests, but man's." Here was impulsive, but beloved Peter being used in the camp of "Satan," a tool of Satan. Peter's thoughts and intentions were being used by Satan against that which God, the Father, had ordained for His Son as Savior of the world. Peter was speaking his own ideas which were not in harmony with God's will. In that instant and context, Peter stood as an enemy to all that the Father had planned for mankind's salvation.

In the context of Peter's spiritual blindness, the forces of Satan can be seen as influencing liberal theologians of centuries past and of this day. The world is Satan's battlefield, infected by the spiritual

SARS virus. The words of Jesus in John 15:18–19 are very clear.

> "If the world hates you, you know that it has hated Me before it *hated* you. If you were of the world, the world loves its own; but because you are not of the world, but I chose you out of the world, therefore the world hates you."

Again, in John 18:36–37, Jesus said:

> ". . . My kingdom is not of this world. If My kingdom were of this world, then My servants would be fighting, that I might not be delivered up to the Jews, but as it is, My kingdom is not of this realm." Pilate therefore said to Him, "So you are a king?" Jesus answered, "You say *correctly* that I am a king. For this I was born, and for this I have come into the world, to bear witness to the truth. Every one who is of the truth hears My voice."

Any activity of man that is against God and the revelation of His Son, Jesus, in Holy Scripture, comes from the hostile domain where Satan has his camp. Satan's camp is the world. This does not mean that God no longer loves the world He created and called "very good" in Genesis 1:31. It does mean that in the world there are forces of alienation and opposition to all that God has revealed as His truth, His love message in Jesus, which is centered in Holy Scripture. Nor does this mean that God has abandoned the world. John 3:16 is proof of this and stands as God's love message to the world.

> For God so loved the world, that He gave His only begotten Son, that whoever believes in Him should not perish, but have everlasting life.

It should never be forgotten that God, through St. Paul, named Satan as the *god of this world* when he wrote:

> . . . the god of this world has blinded the minds of the unbelieving that they might not see the light of the gospel of the glory of Christ, who is in the image of God.
> (2nd Corinthians 4:4)

In the New Testament, the Greek word for the world is *kosmos*, and it is used to denote the earth as well as the contrast between heaven and earth. It also is used to point to the human race, mankind in general and also the sum of temporal possessions.[1] While the Christian Church must always address God's love message in Jesus to the world, it dare not become so influenced and swayed by the world's attractions and cunning half-truths that it begins to take on the appearance and mind set of the world. To do so would compromise the truth of God for Satan's subtle suggestions of spiritual chaos and ruin. God and the world, in the biblical view, are always seen as opponents. For that reason, God inspired John to write:

> Do not love the world, nor the things in the world. If any one loves the world, the love of the Father is not in him. For all that is in the world, the lust of the flesh and the lust of the eyes, and the boastful pride of life, is not from the Father, but is from the world.
> (1st John 2:14–15)

> We know that we are of God, and the whole world lies in the power of the evil one. And we know that the Son of God has come, and has given us understanding, in order that we might know Him who is true, and we are in Him who is true, in His Son Jesus Christ. This is the true God and eternal life. Little children, guard yourselves from idols.
> (1 John 5:19–21)

Sadly, today, as in past centuries since God created the world, there are men and women who question God and the truthfulness of His revelation in Holy Scripture, His love message in Jesus. They are the liberal theologians, historians, and scientists who postulate their own ideas and research as impeccable truth which they place above or in place of that which God has revealed. This is the conflict of authority which will be discussed later in Chapter 3.

This conflict comes from the world of man and as such, represents the intrusion, the invasion, the "not so silent merger" that the world is making in some denominations of the Christian Church. Any similarity of their theological conclusions being completely in harmony with God's revealed Word in Holy Scripture is purely coincidental. Exactly at this juncture, God's Word in Genesis, the first chapter, comes into play. If the account of God's creation cannot be accepted as truth, then all that follows in Scripture must be down-played and questioned. Therefore, in our day and age when evolutionary thinking permeates the minds of those influenced by liberal education, mind barriers against a *Creator* and *Redeemer* God have been erected. Indeed, the truth is that God has been removed from liberal education, whether education in public schools, state sponsored universities, or Christian colleges and universities which have compromised the authority of God's Word. More about this appears in Chapter 8.

It wouldn't be quite so bad if it were only an exchange of ideas as in a debate. It is so much more. The salvation of human lives is the issue. Either what God has revealed from the book of Genesis to Revelation, is truth, or it consists of fantasies and lies. Even to do what Peter did in trying to derail Jesus from His mission of salvation was not of God, but of Satan, the *god of this world.*

Yes, the enemy cunningly and deceitfully uses the God-given abilities of the human brain to challenge that which our God has decreed. Often it is the situation of one critic speaking to another critic of God in the academic sphere of the mind, all the while oblivious to or blatantly ignoring the working of the Holy Spirit in and through God's Word. The ultimate enemy, Satan, has skillfully enlisted theological cohorts in his hostile cause, many of whom have professed a love for God and who willingly and with solid dedication, try to serve the Church of Jesus Christ their way according to their union with 21st century culture. However, when faced with the inerrant and infallible Word of God in Holy Scripture, they waffle as they question its truthfulness, its ability to speak to the world of today, and even question whether or not all of Holy Scripture can be regarded as coming from God. Many times their attention to God's truth in Scripture has been diverted toward an inclusion of other "truths" as being co-equal, even superior, coming from man and not from God. Christian spirituality, life in Jesus through God's Means of Grace, takes it on the chin. And that is why many liberal denominations today are floundering. They have lost their spiritual foundation in God's revelation in Scripture. Shifting theological sands are their impotent foundations and there are many types of sands. These sands appear in the following chapters.

Just as our Lord prayed for those who were crucifying Him with these words from Luke 23:34:

"Father forgive them; for they do not know what they are doing." Therefore, I question whether or not liberal theologians of times past and of today really know what they are doing as they heap critical doubt upon the truth of God's Holy Word. In so doing, they bring confusion and deception upon God's people who need God's love and truth for their lives.

Our Lord put it quite plainly when He stated in Matthew 12:30:

He who is not with Me is against Me, and he who does not gather with Me scatters.

To scatter the people of God in diverse directions of life where Holy Scripture's authority is questioned and down-played as the authentic Word of God, is certainly not the will of God. Jesus revealed His Father's will for all His beloved people in the invitation He issued in Matthew 11:28–30:

Come to Me, all who are weary and heavy-laden, and I will give you rest. Take My yoke upon you, and learn from Me, for I am gentle and humble in heart; and YOU SHALL FIND REST FOR YOUR SOULS. For My yoke is easy, and My load is light.

I believe that theologians, historians, and scientists are made, not born. Certainly they have innate abilities and talents which direct them in certain vocational directions, but the formulation in the direction of their disciplines comes from their academic training. This is the unknown factor, until it impacts upon the people of God.

Many will graduate in the fields of the arts and sciences from colleges and universities that have abandoned acknowledgment of God as He is known in the Judeo-Christian sense.

Their indoctrination is into a world where evolution is hyped as "true science," attempting to disprove God as Creator. Relativity becomes the norm, resulting in moral and spiritual surrender. The results of their learned moral and spiritual relativity impacts our culture which applauds them for being in step with the day in which we live. From the compromising world, this relativity has crept into liberal Christian denominations. This fact is easily established. Just listen to the sermons coming from liberal pulpits and read the writings in their journals, and you will not find the centrality of God and His Means of Grace as their focus. Social issues of the culture abound *ad infinitum* (without end) as God's Word is deconstructed and reconstructed along the lines of moral and spiritual relativity wherein man becomes the definer and God becomes a mere decoration. It is liberalism unbridled.

The *goose step* of liberalism was taught and learned beginning with the Enlightenment of the 18th century which held that the questioning of God's Word as true revelation from God was an academic right and obligation. Its foundation can be seen in the Renaissance which began in Italy in the 14th century and spread throughout Europe. The Renaissance brought with it a new appreciation for the world of nature, accompanied by a fresh delight in man and who he is. There was a revival of classical learning and art, with painters and sculptors popularizing a humanist orientation that man, beginning with himself, was the center of knowledge and had the ability to solve every problem. The place of man as a definer of *his world* in a secular sense characterized the culture of the Renaissance. God wasn't completely abandoned, but He was in the dim shadows.

It wasn't a big leap from the Renaissance to the Enlightenment, but a gradual movement and development, with man occupying center stage so that when the Enlightenment invaded Europe in the 18th century, it did so by highlighting and emphasizing the *individual and his reason* as authority in a subjective way, rather than an objective way. Objectivity and subjectivity will be discussed later in Chapter 3.

Because of its subjectivity, the Enlightenment has been called "The Age of Reason." Man's reason stood as the supreme authority while the Church of Jesus Christ, the Bible, and the state were questioned and down-played as competent authorities.

I have chosen the Enlightenment of the 18th century as the point of departure to begin an understanding of how and why "the not so silent merger" of the world with the church occurred and with it an unending assault on Christian spirituality which is based on the working of God's Holy Spirit through God's Means of Grace.

The Enlightenment pushed man's reason as supreme authority over and above God's revelation of His love message in Jesus. Prior to the Enlightenment, Holy Scripture, as the inerrant and infallible Word of God, was not held in question. The church had the fruits of the "sown Word of God" and theology had its source in that Word. Interpretations of that Word could be debated by theologians, but the debates rarely questioned the authority of God as the source of His revelation in Scripture. The Enlightenment changed that scenario.

One of the clearest and most concise definitions of the Enlightenment is given in *The Dictionary of the Christian Church.*

> The Enlightenment combines opposition to all supernatural religion and belief in the all-sufficiency of human reason with an ardent desire to promote the happiness of men in this life . . . .

Most of its representatives . . . rejected the Christian dogma and were hostile to Catholicism as well as Christian orthodoxy, which they regarded as powers of spiritual darkness, depriving humanity of the use of its rational faculties . . . . Their fundamental belief in the goodness of human nature, which blinded them to the fact of sin, produced an easy optimism and absolute faith of human society once the principles of enlightened reason had been recognized. The spirit of the Enlightenment penetrated deeply into German Protestantism (in the 19th century), where it disintegrated faith in the authority of the Bible and encouraged Biblical criticism on the one hand and an emotional "Pietism" on the other.[2]

At this point, it must be emphasized that some Christian theologians, holding respected academic positions in seminaries, mainly in Germany, played into the attractive seduction of Enlightenment thinking. Theological debates of all kinds were now in process and out in the open. Protestant theologians were debating Roman Catholic theologians about justification and the primacy of the Pope. Debates among Protestant theologians of the Lutheran, Reformed, and Anabaptist persuasions were in progress concerning authority, the interpretation of Scripture, the Sacraments, and church reform as representative issues.

While they were in heated theological debate, the Enlightenment force of reason continued to roll on and gather steam. Some liberal Protestant theologians got a whiff of the seductive odor of reasonable thinking, thinking that did not have the constraints of authority from God in His revelation of Jesus as Son of God, nor Holy Scripture as His true Word. Thus, their reason stood as a rebellious means to bring God and His Word under their control. With the scent of reason in their nostrils and its elixir invading their theological blood streams, they were empowered to turn their theories in the direction of the winds emanating from the unrestrained freedom of rebellious reason. Aided and abetted by the academic drive to "publish or perish," liberal theologians attempted to step into theological "glory." They became like kittens, entwined in balls of yarn, wrapped in their own reasonableness, a tool of devilish delight. Who was now in control of theology? Was it God or was it man under the control of the *god of this world?* And the beat goes on!

Some leading theologians, who will be discussed in the next chapter, turned their attention to Enlightenment issues, impending spiritual roadblocks and minefields. Instead of standing tall and rejecting the fallacies of rational thought about God, His Son, and His Word, they embraced Enlightenment reason and capitulated, surrendered, and gave God up as a hostage to man's reason, reason that denied *God The Creator* and *God The Redeemer.*

The beat of a different drummer had been sounded as cadence for the march of liberal theology for many of God's beloved in this world. Its source of authority was not in God's revealed Word in Scripture, but in the *reasonable* trends of culture. As the whims of culture change, liberal theology changes with it and a Christianity, in name but not in essence, appears. It is one that questions both the supernatural power of God to create the world and the power of God through His Son, Jesus, to bring salvation to the world. The spiritual lives of God's people in liberal denominations are adversely affected as the God ordained foundations are shaken and discarded. The spiritual SARS virus has reached epidemic proportions.

In trying to be relevant to a post-modern culture, many "mainline" denominations now view homosexuality and abortion as normal moral behaviors. Theistic evolution is featured wherein the trustworthiness of Scripture is admitted, but also the process of organic evolution as championed by Charles Darwin is allowed to stand alongside the Genesis account as believable. Chapter 5 discuses the evolution problem, an all-out attack against God.

Further, sin is recast in a different mold and comes out as oppressive intolerance and lack of understanding by the "radical religious right." What these denominations fail to see is that post-modern culture, under the rule of the *god of this world,* is now in control of liberal theology. Christianity defined and normed in Holy Scripture has not only been compromised, but changed. It has been a "not so silent merger," one that has been accepted as normal because the post-modern culture of the world defines and determines what is normal. Biblical Christianity is left adrift and has to be towed to a foreign harbor of a liberal culture for repairs or the scrapheap. The drum beat of liberal theology is not one of urgency for God, but accommodation to an out of step, sinful world. God and His Word are presented as archaic ideas. Only one conclusion can be made: "An enemy has done this!"

Martin Luther knew this situation very well when he wrote:

> The devil does not so storm and rage against other ways and views of men, against adulterers, thieves, murderers, perjurers, the godless, sacrilegious, and unbelieving. In fact, he keeps them in peace in his court, pampering and indulging them in everything. Likewise in the earliest days of the church he not only let the idolatries and religions of the whole world remain intact and undisturbed but splendidly nurtured them. The church and religion of Christ alone he harassed . . . . So it is today. He has no other concern than the one that has ever been peculiarly his own: to persecute our Lord Christ

(who is our Righteousness without any works of our own). As it is written: "Thou shalt bruise his heel. (Gen. 3:15)[3]

NOTES

1. See W.E.Vine, *Expository Dictionary of New Testament Words,* (Grand Rapids: Zondervan Publishing House, 1952), 233.
2. F. L. Cross, ed., *The Dictionary of the Christian Church,* (London: Oxford University Press, 1958), 104, 105.
3. Martin Luther, *What Luther Says*, op. cit.,vol. III, 1207,#3840.

CHAPTER 2

The Wedge: The Historical-Critical Method

And for this reason we also constantly thank God that when you received from us the Word of God's message, you accepted it not as the word of men, but for what it really is, the Word of God, which also performs its work in you who believe.

(1 Thess. 2:13)

The rebuke that Jesus gave to Peter in Matthew 16:23: "You are a stumbling block to Me, for you are not setting your mind on God's interests, but man's." applies to the historical-critical method of biblical interpretation. This method boldly asserts that enlightened man, a product of the power of reason which ascended in the 18th century, can be the judge and jury of Holy Scripture, rather than our God Who inspired it to be written. This method, without a shadow of a doubt, elevates and extols man's theological insights and conclusions, his scriptural interests, as greater and more *believable* than the God of the Scriptures. It also shapes its theological conclusions about God and His Word from various culture conditioned perspectives and not from God's authority in His Holy Word.

Anyone entering the arena of biblical interpretation is in the field of hermeneutics, a theological free-for-all where interpretation of God's Word is up for grabs. The word *hermeneutic* comes from the Greek word, *hermeneuein,* used with variations to mean "translate," "explain," and "interpret." It tries to shrink or diminish the distance between the writer of Scripture, and you, the readers. The historical-critical method of biblical interpretation falls within this field of theological study.

How did it happen? The Enlightenment opened the door of doubt, the seeds of which had already been sown some years earlier by René Descartes regarding what could be considered reasonable in man's thinking and believing. In so doing, it nurtured the historical-critical method which became the wedge to maintain the opening through which man's authority over Holy Scripture could slip into the Christian Church. Descartes held all knowledge open to doubt except the reality of self.

The seeds of this method, much like the darnel seeds in the "Parable of the Tares Among the Wheat," were first sown by Johann Salomo Semler. Semler came under the influence of Descartes. Born in 1725, the son of a Lutheran pietist pastor, Semler rose to become the head of the theological faculty at Halle, Germany. He challenged the divine inspiration of the Bible and maintained that the Bible was no different than any other book.

Gerhard Maier pointed out the central principle of thought that Semler advanced, which became the motivational heart of the historical-critical method. It is found in one sentence. He wrote: "The root of evil (in theology) is the interchangeable use of the terms 'Scripture' and 'Word of God.'"[1]

Semler could not equate these terms or words as being equal. His thesis was that not all of Scripture was the Word of God. He saw as his task the challenge of finding out what could be the Word of God in Scripture.

With the "ripe" academic and theological arena now in place, thanks to the Enlightenment, Semler's pronouncement came as a forceful attempt to shatter the authority of Scripture. He placed a wedge or a divide between Scripture and Word of God and opened the floodgates of theological reasoning for other enlightened theologians to pour through, and they didn't need an invitation to perform on the theological stage. The Enlightenment climate of the superiority of man's autonomous reasoning capabilities was well in place. Man now stood as the *believable* authority on the theological stage, while God and His script (His Word) were an echo of the past that could be picked apart, portions negated, corrections made, with scraps heaped upon the cutting room floor. God's Word stood as a guilty victim of *unreasonableness* which *enlightened* theologians could make *reasonable*.

To this cast were invited, not only theologians who could "mouth" theories about God's Word not being God's Word, but also historians and scientists. The historical-critical method, while having its birth in the 18th century, lingers to this day and will go on for years to come as most liberal biblical scholars have joined its academic fraternity/sorority. Standing as the main weapon against the authority of God's Word, it infects every area of Christian spirituality. Liberal theologians of the past and of the present have one common trait, one agenda—the placement of their reason, their theological acumen as superior to God's revelation in Holy Scripture. It is the question of authority which never disappears from the theological scene. Does it belong to God or to man?

In a thumb-nail sketch, we can see contributors to this method, this rebellious child of the Enlightenment. Briefly, some are:

Immanuel Kant who lived from 1724 to 1804. He was a catalyst who put the spotlight on man as the interpreter of authority according to his reason. Kant followed the lead of Descartes. He saw no need to look to God and His revelation in Scripture. Man had all that he needed in himself. By use of reason, man could ascend the throne of truth as the definer of truth. This truth found its base not in the revealed Word of God as objective truth, but in the subjective findings of man. Riding on the authority of reason, man could authenticate himself by his own autonomy. Kant never allowed any thought of God being transcendent, meaning that He is the Almighty God, the creator of the world, uniquely different from His creation, eternal, unchanging, holy, righteous, and the epitome of love.

Gotthold Ephraim Lessing lived from 1729 to 1781, and was a contemporary of Semler and Kant. Again, this theologian's premise was the dominance of man's reason as the road to truth. He made two statements which gave explosive ammunition to the historical-critical method. They are known as "Lessing's broad, ugly ditch." His statements: "There is a broad, ugly ditch of history that I cannot jump across." and "The accidental truths of history can never become the proof of the necessary truths of reason."[2]

For Lessing, in order to believe, one must see and verify. To him, if no historical truth can be demonstrated, because it is confined to past history, then nothing can be demonstrated by means of historical truth. He sowed doubt concerning anything the Bible revealed as being believable, such as the miracles of Jesus, His Resurrection, and as well, all that He did in ministry. His presupposition was that absolute truth cannot be grounded in history, let alone in Scripture. He was part of the liberal prelude to the discordant symphony of biblical attack.

George Wilhelm Freidrich Hegel lived from 1770 to 1831, and still his influence on theology through the historical-critical method lives on. He held that truth could not be objective, especially God's truth as absolute truth. Instead, it had to be fashioned through a *synthesis* of many sources. From many truths, a real and cogent truth could be found in a subjective way. He used the method of opposing opposites against each other, a method called the dialectical method. Reality, including the Scriptures, was seen as having no solid consistency, as it remained open-ended to any and all interpretation, because it had no fixed standards of right and wrong. Truth could no longer be objective as absolute truth that comes from God. As a result, any comedian or actor upon life's stage has *carte blanche* freedom to define his or her synthesis as truth, write his or her own script in a subjective way. Truth became a bobbing cork upon a restless sea of biblical subjectivity and uncertainty.

Freidrich Daniel Ernst Schleiermacher lived from 1763 to 1836 and is named as the father of modern Protestant theology. His main theological emphasis was to make religious experience (feeling) the criterion of theology and the method for interpreting Scripture. His emphasis upon man and his religious experience trumped revelation from God in Scripture. Here, once more, is the historical-critical method of biblical interpretation's insistence of the subjectivity of man over the objectivity of God's Word. He negated the power of the Scriptures to create faith through the power of the Holy Spirit. This theologian's doctrine of God shifted and moved thought from the transcendence of God to the immanence of God. He maintained that God could not be known as He reveals Himself in the doctrine of Scripture. He held that it is only through the self-conscious experience of feeling that a person could have the immediate experience of God. To see how far Schleiermacher wandered from the objective truth of God in Christ as revealed in God's Word, I refer to Bengt Hagglund's definition of Schleiermacher's position regarding Christ's work:

—or His suffering, death, and resurrection—has no bearing on salvation, but only His person, which represents the perfect consciousness of God . . . . Schleiermacher looked upon the Resurrection as resuscitation from apparent death, and he referred to the Ascension as Christ's actual death. Salvation refers only to "God being in Christ" (das Sein Gottes in Christo) and to the posthumous impact of His person—not to Christ's death and resurrection.[3]

David Freidrich Strauss lived from 1808 to 1874. He attacked the reliability of the Gospel accounts regarding Jesus. He maintained in his book, *Das Leben Jesus* (Life of Jesus), that the Gospel messages in Matthew, Mark, Luke, and John were purely myth, fashioned by the early and archaic Christian community. All the supernatural and messianic accounts in the Gospels were held to be only myth because they could not be regarded as historical. Thus, Jesus was merely an ordinary man, a teacher of religion and morality. In attacking the divinity of Christ, we see once more how the transcendence of God in Christ was reduced to immanence or an impotent immanence at best.

At this point, it is important for the lay person in the church to understand that before the Enlightenment influence and the historical-critical method of biblical interpretation came into prominence, the transcendence and the immanence of God were held in even balance. This was and is the way our God has revealed Himself in Holy Scripture.

Transcendence and immanence are theological words which the laity rarely encounter. They are part of the divine attributes of God. The transcendence of God refers to His exaltation above all the creatures of earth, His ability to enter time and space without becoming limited, and His unsurpassed holiness as majestic Creator far beyond the comprehension of man, the created. These are the bare essentials of God's transcendence. God's immanence refers to God being present in all his creatures and in the world, but never part of them. Liberal theology concentrates on God's immanence, His presence as dwelling within the world, not apart from or raised above the world as a transcendent holy being. As one dimensional theology which leads to panthcism, the exclusive focus on immanence only views God and the universe as one, totally destroying the God of Scripture and His redemptive act of love through His Son, Jesus. It is a myopic view of God, not the full picture when separated from God's transcendence.

In both, His transcendence and immanence, God sent His Son, Jesus, into the world. In His transcendence, only God can send His Son, born of a virgin, to this earth for man's salvation. God's transcendence is also seen in the Old Testament as a God Who reveals Himself objectively by breaking into history by way of His action in the affairs of His chosen people, Israel. In His transcendence as well as in His immanence, God is known in faith by those who believe in His Son as Lord and Savior. The Christian Church, the body of Christ, is living reality of His immanence here on earth. Most clearly this is shown in Jesus' words in Matthew 18:20: "For where two or three have gathered together in My name, there I am in their midst." This is the essence of spirituality that Christians have in their worship wherein the Means of God's Grace are proclaimed and administered. It is the Real Presence of Christ in both Word and Sacraments. True Christian spirituality honors both the transcendence and the immanence of God. Jesus Christ, as true God and true man, is both immanent and transcendent. His holiness in transcendence cannot be separated from His holiness in immanence. This is the witness of Holy Scripture.

To separate the transcendence of God from His immanence becomes for the liberal theologian another wedge through which the world can enter the Christian Church in a "not so silent merger." Then, God in Christ can be reconstructed, stripped of His holiness and made to be a user-friendly "pal" instead of the Savior of man. Theology can then be man-made for man's consumption, according to his sinful whims. "Anything goes!" becomes the watchword of liberalism, just so the name of Jesus can be plugged in to render authority to whatever endeavor appears on the horizon of culture, a most appetizing feature of liberal theology. When this happens, any and every trace of the Christian Church being the Christian Church disappears. This is another reason and a dominant reason for the liberal "mainline" denominations falling on their swords of historical criticism. In succeeding chapters, this will become crystal clear. Why? Simply because it is theology foreign to God's revelation in His Holy Word.

It was not only the theologians mentioned above who disrupted this revealed balance of transcendence and immanence, but others, as well, who came after them in the tradition of the *reasonableness* of the historical-critical method. Were they pulling the plug on God's authority in His Word? You bet they were!

Continuing along the trail of the thumb-nail sketch of some liberal theologians is Albrecht Ritschl who lived from 1822 to 1889. He played a major part in the history of the historical-critical method of biblical interpretation as his influence dominated liberal Protestantism in Germany. Ritschl contended that Christianity must be built on fact. He asserted that we find God in history, where positive values emanate in Jesus, who then becomes the hero of God. Thus, religion is to be based on value judgements as Jesus will lead mankind to discover the God of values. He wrote very little about the Resurrection and Ascension of Jesus. Ritschl pointedly reduced Jesus to a moral figure of integrity who continues to lead and build community in the Kingdom of God.

Adolf von Harnack lived from 1851 to 1930. He viewed the Scriptures as an historian wherein he saw the heart of Christianity as the ethical righteousness of God's Kingdom as taught by Jesus. As the historian, he took the liberty to pick and choose from the Scriptures whatever he deemed worthy of his liberal theology. The crowning point of his theology is seen in the way he viewed Jesus, as he summoned theology away from the religion *about* Jesus to the religion *of* Jesus. Internal experience, not biblical doctrine, was for him the essence of faith. His view of theology spread to America in the early 20th century when the preaching emphasis in many Protestant churches was: "Life, not doctrine." A social gospel evolved, devoid of the miraculous acts of God in Jesus. The values and ethics of the New Testament were in full bloom, while Jesus was placed back-stage. The doctrine or teaching of Scripture became buried in ethics.

The list of theologians who gladly adopted the historical-critical method of biblical interpretation goes on and on in the 20th and into the 21st centuries. It is very important to see theologians like Karl Barth (1886–1968) who had no use for the Bible as propositional truth from God, because according to him, the Bible does not have the authority of being true Word of God. He maintained that biblical authority can only reside in the true Word of God, Jesus, who comes as truth to encounter man in its proclamation. In discarding the rest of Scripture from what Jesus did and does, he crumbled once more the objectivity of God's revelation in all of the Scriptures. While Barth did much to bring back the transcendence of God to theology, one of his theological tumbles and fumbles was his insistence that Jesus did not "become flesh" as John 1:14 reveals, but only "assumed" flesh in His Incarnation.

Heinrich Emil Brunner lived from 1889 to 1966. As an advocate of the historical-critical method he had little use for Scripture that did not directly reveal an encounter with Jesus as an "I-Thou" existential encounter within the Christian community. Scripture could not stand as a norm or a rule for doctrine, as he believed the less the Scriptures are taken literally, the more room there is for freedom of exposition so that every single exposition of Scripture becomes a kind of pope who alone possesses the right key to its interpretation. Like Barth, he detached himself from "the theory of the Virgin Birth," while claiming Jesus assumed human nature.

Rudolf Bultmann lived from 1884 to 1976. His attachment to the historical-critical method can be seen in his belief that the New Testament was not concerned with the Jesus of history, only the Jesus of faith. To Bultmann, Jesus was merely the historical cause (das Dass), which initiates faith. He held that Jesus does not in any way inform the content of faith (das Was). Therefore, to insist on the historical accuracy of the Bible was to provide a support for faith that was illegitimate. Bultmann used the word *kerygma* as the message and proclamation of the early church, a proclamation that had to be disengaged from the myth of its New Testament form. He proposed to do this by demythologizing, interpreting the language of the 1st century into existential language, so that modern man could be confronted in his existence and make a decision of faith and so realize his authentic existence. To him, the Bible was not revelation from God. He regarded Advent, Christmas, Good Friday, the Resurrection, the Ascension, and Pentecost as occurring on the same day, the day of proclamation.

Paul Tillich lived from 1886 to 1965. Known as the "Father of Radical Theology," he tried to inter-connect theology, philosophy, religion, and culture. He believed that philosophy asks the questions concerning the existence of life, and that theology answers those questions. Revelation apart from the Word of God, whether casual human words or natural revelation, was very much a part of Tillich's theology. That Tillich detached himself from the authority of the Scriptures can be seen in how he regarded the birth, the Incarnation of Jesus. He believed the Incarnation needed to be reinterpreted to have the meaning that Jesus was "essential man appearing in a personal life under the conditions of existential estrangement."[4] As such, Jesus was not considered by Tillich to be divine or to have a divine nature. Instead, he brought out through his humanity an entirely new order of being, so that the original order of God and humanity was restored; this restoration stood as his Christhood, the New Being. The orthodox Christian doctrine that Jesus is both true God and true man was abandoned by this theologian.

Tillich, as the "Father of Radical Theology," gave ammunition to liberal theologians to abandon the transcendence of God. In its place was radical emphasis upon the immanence of God. They didn't view God as "up there" or "out there," because to them God as transcendent was dead; while God as immanent, God within the ground of being was alive and well. Bishop John A. T. Robinson, the Anglican Bishop of Woolwich, England, was one of the dominant leaders in the 1960s of the "Death of God" movement in liberal Christianity which called into question many of the basic assumptions and biblical doctrines held by Christians for centuries.

These thumb-nail sketches are merely tips of the iceberg of the theologies of the theologians mentioned above. They serve as a taste of the theological input which came after the Enlightenment as the historical-critical method of biblical interpretation made its way into some Protestant denominations that adopted the liberal leanings of that method in "the not so silent merger." In all of the above sketches, the place of Holy Scripture as the inspired, inerrant, and infallible Word of God has been superceded by the reason of man. *Reasonable* man through the use of the historical-critical method has usurped the authority of God. The impact of this method is squarely upon the people of God who are in churches where this method is employed as the means to God's truth. What is offered to them are the thoughts of sinful man in place of the absolute truth of God in Holy Scripture, His love message in Jesus. Their spirituality has been redirected so that they are lead into spiritual minefields, some of which are discussed in following chapters.

Edgar Krentz, a proponent of the historical-critical method, tells what this method has done (and what it is) as it developed from the 18th into the 19th century.

> It is difficult to overestimate the significance the nineteenth century has for biblical interpretation. It made historical criticism *the* approved method of interpretation. The result

was a revolution of viewpoint in evaluating the Bible. The Scriptures were, so to speak, secularized. The biblical books became historical documents to be studied and questioned like any other ancient sources. The Bible was no longer the criterion for the writing of history; rather history had become the criterion for understanding the Bible. The variety in the Bible was highlighted; its unity had to be discovered and could no longer be presumed. The history it reported was no longer assumed to be everywhere correct. The Bible stood before criticism as defendant before judge.[5]

The Bible, the Word of God, as the defendant? Man as the judge? Man standing in judgment over the Word of God? Clearly, this is the intent of those committed to the historical-critical method of biblical interpretation. Man now stands as the dispenser of biblical truth while God is labeled the "defendant" as though what He revealed in Holy Scripture is seen as an insult, an offense, perhaps a misdemeanor against *reasonable* human biblical scholarship. The work of the Holy Spirit is completely negated. The Word of God in 2nd Corinthians 4:4 applies:

the god of this world has blinded the minds of the unbelieving . . .

More simply put: *doubt* regarding the authenticity of Holy Scripture as the true Word of God, becomes a virtue; while *faith* in the Word of God as His true Word to man, is regarded as a sin.

To shed more light on this method of biblical interpretation, G. B. Caird writes about the New Testament scholar of today.

> The New Testament scholar, by using all the resources of modern critical scholarship, projects himself back into the first century, entering by sympathetic imagination into its life, its feelings, and its ways of thought, and learning to some extent at least to see the world through the eyes of the New Testament writers; and then comes back to the present to share with his contemporaries what he has discovered. What he discovers will be both the chief source and the norm of all theological thought.[6]

The New Testament scholar described above must be some sort of super-human being to be able by the power of "sympathetic imagination" to correctly and fully ascertain the "feelings" and "the ways of thought" of the writers of New Testament Scripture. Can any person today even fathom the feelings and the ways of thought of persons they have never met or known? Indeed, can anyone even do that with the neighbors on their street? And what about the male-female puzzle of thought, which asserts that "men are from Mars, and women from Venus?"

Can that scholar, by reading a text or words written some time ago, have indisputable findings so that his or her conclusions now become the norm or the rule for thought, for theology or any another discipline? Does this *imagination* now stand as the new-found authority above God Who caused the Holy Scriptures to be written? Only liberal theologians could ever come up with that absurd conclusion and it is a conclusion drawn from their starting point: God is *not* the author of His own Word. Man is! It is giving authority to man's imagination, a fanciful idea, while ignoring the rushing current of truth from God in His Word.

Yet, we must not by-pass a revealing clue where a new kid on the block of hermeneutics has emerged. In step with the method of biblical interpretation by Caird has come "the hermeneutics of expansion" which attempts to include both concepts of God and of the world as in *synthesis*, a product of Hegel. It operates in the semantic world, the world relating to the meaning of language. Free to roam in the meaning of words it becomes a "loose cannon" of theological thought. "Loose cannon" came from the days when sailing ships lost the moorings on a cannon and in high seas or merely normal rolling seas, the cannon ricocheted against the wooden hull and caused extensive damage. Here, it applies to a liberal interpretation of God's Word where the authoritative rug is pulled from beneath the Word of God in history, and made to apply to the liberal thoughts of theologians in a modern or post-modern age. The meaning and interpretation of God's Word is not, to those devoted to the hermeneutics of expansion, found in the established Scriptures of God's Word, but in the thoughts and conclusions of theologians who advance their theories, their musings, about what God really was saying in His Holy Word from their perspective.[7] The God of "yesterday," they academically maintain, is not as smart as the scholar of today.

What we are dealing with here is the word "presupposition" which is defined as "to suppose beforehand." While "suppose" is defined as "to lay down tentatively as a hypothesis, assumption, or proposal" or "to hold as an opinion." Webster's Ninth Collegiate Dictionary is most clear in defining "presupposition" in those terms. A presupposition can never be neutral. It always has a cause or position to defend or advocate. Neutrality can only be claimed if what is being considered is a neutral situation, but when one regards the Word of God and is concerned about it, neutrality cannot be an option.

It is evident from the above that Caird's presupposition is that God is not the author of His Word, but that human authors were. Thus, the New Testament scholar has *carte blanche* freedom to delve by the means of his or her imagination into the past and come up with a theological "plum" that trumps what our God inspired to be written as His Word. Then, theology can be re-written according to the New Testament scholar's imagination which is free to roam wherever the scholar directs. Theology, then, stands on shaky ground with theories upon theories being projected upon God's people by liberal theologians, theories which have as their foundation *imagination*. Can you ever *imagine* medicine, law, physics, chemistry, or any other discipline standing upon *imagination*? Yet, that is the foundation of liberal theology, as it stands in opposition to the verifiable facts of Holy Scripture.

Another illustration from Caird comes with the conditional word "If" so as to question God as the source of St. Paul's epistles.

> If God spoke through Paul, he spoke through Paul's mind, and I put myself under the authority of *this* Word only by exploring the mind of Paul with all the resources at my command.[8]

Once more it becomes a shift in authority with the scholar's mind assuming the exploratory means to arrive at the truth, using "all the resources at my command." And the word "my" stands tall as the final determining, subjective "stick." Jumping into St. Paul's mind—what a trick!

Marching in the same liberal parade as Caird is Peter J. Gomes. Gomes has been the Senior Minister in the prestigious Memorial Church at Harvard University since 1974. He is a classic example of "interesting and reasonable ideas" coming from a liberal theologian enamored by the historical-critical method and the attractive *spins* which emerge from that method. According to John Kenneth Galbraith (Professor of Economics at Harvard and former ambassador to India), Gomes ranks "Second only to the President of the University" . . . "as the best known member of the Harvard community."[9]

Gomes is a gifted writer and theologian, one who is ultra biblically critical, meaning he has abandoned the full authority of God's Word as the inerrant Word of God. Using critical filters through which he strains out traces of God's authority, he presents a man-made Bible, shackled by the antiquity of the ages, open for reconstruction according to the cultural needs of an ever-changing society wherein values are also changing so as to be acceptable and relevant to the needs of sinful mankind. Thus, a tepid, man-flavored spirituality evolves, to which a label can be attached which reads: "Modern Day Christian Spirituality."

His book, *The Good Book*, makes for interesting study as he holds the Bible gently in one hand while presenting well-worn *spins* which degrade the authority of Holy Scripture with the other hand. Gomes represents the deception and confusion which is present in liberal biblical scholars, an enticing combination of spiritual entrapment for unsuspecting people of God under liberal influence and for their children as well. The final tally of tears is known only to God. While swishing around the topic of evil in general, he places small emphasis upon salvation through faith in Jesus Christ, the loving work of God's Holy Spirit through His Word. Stridently he maintains: "The Bible, however, never speaks of curing evil, and nowhere does it speak of conquering evil."[10] Apparently in Gomes' view, Jesus came for naught. Even the words of our God in Isaiah 1:18 are by-passed: "Come now, and let us reason together," says the Lord, "Though your sins are as scarlet, They shall be as white as snow: Though they are red like crimson, They will be like wool." Gomes' eye and ear catching appeal is addressed to the mind even though he claims his words are aimed at the heart. He shows obvious bias against Holy Scripture as true Word of God:

> We trust the text not because it is true in the sense of fact, but because in its infinite variety it points to the truth and communicates truth because it comes from the truth which we call God.[11]

If God's Word is not true and merely a sign, a man-made communication vehicle of truth, distilled through fallible human writers, as the historical-critical method claims, where is the authority of God's Word? Gomes maintains:

73

It is not the Bible but the God of the Bible in whom we find someone, something, worthy of our loyalty, our ultimate concern, our trust.[12]

How many times I heard that same theme when I was a student at The Lutheran Theological Seminary at Philadelphia in the early 1950s! Conveniently, Gomes separates the Bible's authority from God while reconstructing God as "someone, something, worthy of our loyalty, our ultimate concern, our trust." As though God has to entice us to find Him worthy!

Where is the working of the Holy Spirit, or is it simply a matter of reason? How easy it is then to apply a rudder to God so as to steer Him, according to the theological whims of the day, away from orthodox Christianity. Once more the basis for true Christian spirituality is undermined.

Gomes' liberal position toward Holy Scripture can be seen in his open avowal of being a homosexual[13] and one who believes the Bible is silent about abortion.[14] It is important to note that Gomes also holds the Chair of Plummer Professor of Christian Morals at Harvard College.

I bring this liberal scholar to your attention because liberal preachers feed on his words and these *spins* impact upon the people in the pews, many of whom have left liberal "mainline" denominations because of such liberal hallucinations. Godly spirituality has been sacrificed for spiritual economics: "Accepting what the traffic will bear" according to prevailing theological wind currents. Liberal elastic theology always shows holes in its world-conditioned socks. It is interesting to note that kudos for Gomes and his theology have come from The Right Reverend Lord Runce, 102nd Archbishop of Canterbury; Marian Wright Edelman, President, The Children's Defense Fund; Thomas Long, Princeton Theological Seminary; Harvey Cox, and William H. Willimon, Dean of the Chapel, and Professor of Christian Ministry, Duke University.

Another revealing clue to the instability of modern biblical research can be seen in the opening words of Brian K. Blount in his book, *Cultural Interpretation, Reorienting New Testament Criticism.* He begins:

> IT IS NOW COMMONPLACE TO HEAR BIB-
> LICAL scholars admit that textual inquiry is in-
> fluenced by the contextual presuppositions of
> the researcher.[15]

Presuppositions, imagination, and all the resources at the command of the scholar, all shaky foundations of the biblical critic, are held as absolute theological methods for questioning the truthfulness and the absoluteness of Scripture. Hopefully, liberal theologians strive to gain a critical beachhead against the infallibility of Scripture. Then, with their foot in the door of theological debate, they try to posit their own man-made theories concerning God and His Word in Scripture as truth. Any survey of theological thinking since the Enlightenment is indisputable proof of the many directions and currents of thought which are at the mercy of the prevailing culture.

Blount closes his presentation:

> Therefore the only way to expand interpretation beyond the boundaries of a single interpretative move or a group of interpretive moves is to allow different approaches to engage each other analectically and therefore learn and be changed by one another . . . . Through such recognitions we can move toward a fuller interpretation, one that we must concede will always remain incomplete.[16]

Unfortunately, *incompleteness* is the domain of liberal biblical scholars. Perhaps, one of their major concerns is to try to close the loop so they can present a complete theological package, in accord with the prevailing culture, that can stand not only in competition to, but above God's revelation in Holy Scripture, all through academic thought interchange. The concern of all Christian theologians, however, should be in presenting the truthful completeness of God's revelation in His Word according to His will and purpose. At issue is God's people, their eternal salvation in Jesus Christ, their Lord and Savior; not how happy or well adjusted they might be by enabling them to adapt to a changing, decadent culture, or the fickleness of theologians. God is never incomplete in providing for His Means of Grace to enable Christian spirituality. He loves us so completely that His grace in Jesus Christ, our Lord and Savior, is complete for our salvation.

God's Word, His love message in Jesus, is an absolute Word and it is that absolute Word of Jesus which instituted Christian Baptism and The Lord's Supper. Any other message or theology not in accord with His inerrant and infallible Word only brings confusion and deception upon the people of God. Growth in spirituality is pruned as well as rooted out when God's Word is mutilated in an incomplete and liberal way, the way pleasing to the *god of this world.*

Relevant to the above quotes from Blount is a quote from Roland H. Bainton concerning the Elector Frederick of Saxony who in 1521

> wished to be enlightened as to the meaning of Scripture, and appointed a committee. But the committee could not agree.[17]

Martin Luther in his 1535 Lectures on Galatians stated:

Therefore let us learn that this is one of the devil's specialties: If he cannot do his damage by persecuting and destroying, he will do it under the guise of correcting and edifying.[18]

That is exactly the tactic of the historical-critical method of biblical interpretation. It takes what has stood for centuries as God's Word, and as a judge, brings "correction and edification" to it, as would a "reasonable scholar."

In all of the hodgepodge of varying interpretations of Scripture and ways to interpret Scripture, one common clue or theme rises supreme. It is the separation of the clear meaning within the text from the text itself in Semler-like fashion. Remember how Semler attempted to find out what could be the Word of God in Scripture? He ultimately drove a wedge between Scripture and Word of God, claiming that all Scripture was not Word of God.

Semler and the long line of liberal theologians who followed jumped at the opportunity to dismantle the authority of the text to speak for itself by transferring the interpretation of its meaning to man, to theologians of all stripes and theories. Either conferred upon them by others, or personally assumed, they believed, and still hold the notion, that the key to unlock the meaning of Scripture resides in the key they have uniquely, liberally fashioned. That is why, today, you see so many different and varying theologies.

Meaning has been detached from the text so that any theologian can attempt to create a theology, no matter how far off the wall it is from the original text in Scripture. The great fault of liberal theologians is not allowing Scripture to interpret Scripture which is acknowledging that Scripture has a clarity and a unity whereby less clear passages can be understood in light of the clear passages on the same subject. Regarding Scripture interpreting Scripture, Martin Luther wrote:

> I cannot bear it that they thus revile and blaspheme Scripture and the fathers. They accuse the Bible of being obscure, whereas all the fathers concede that it is the brightest light and take their own from it as David says (Psalm 119:105): "Thy Word is my light." But they ascribe to the fathers the light with which they illuminate Scripture, whereas all the fathers concede their own obscurity and illuminate Scripture by Scripture alone. And, indeed, that is the right method. Scripture should be placed alongside Scripture in a right and proper way. He who can do this best is the best of the fathers. And all the books of the fathers we must read with discretion; they should not be taken on faith. But see whether they quote clear texts and explain Scripture by other clearer texts.[19]

In a nut shell, liberal theologians have lost their foundation, God's Word. The scholar, not God and His Word, are to be believed. Ernie Bringas, a United Methodist scholar and author established this position as the bedrock of the historical-critical method when he wrote:

> When we view the Bible (or the Church) as the infallible instrument of God, we surrender our reason and intelligence.[20]

In the Introduction, I wrote about the numerical decline of the "mainline" churches in America. The historical-critical method of biblical interpretation has been the culprit tool or means because it has substituted the "word" of liberal theologians for the true Word of God. The historical-critical method, influenced by the ebb and flow of culture, has declared a different gospel, not the Gospel of Jesus Christ! In essence, it has declared war on God's Word. As such, it has declared war on God.

Then, when the "Death of God" theology was presented as truth, that God Who proclaimed His Word in Holy Scripture was dead, was it any wonder that church members beat a hasty retreat from their churches? The world was given place in the pulpits of liberal churches, not only in America, but in Europe also. The *god of this world* in a "not so silent merger," has scattered the sheep by deceiving the shepherds.

NOTES

1. Gerhard Maier, *The End of the Historical-Critical Method,* (St. Louis: Concordia Publishing House, 1974), 15.
2. Alisdair I. C. Heron, *A Century of Protestant Theology,* (Philadelphia: The Westminster Press, 1980), 19, 20.
3. Bengt Hagglund, *History of Theology*, trans. Gene J. Lund (St. Louis: Concordia Publishing House, 1966), 357.
4. Paul Tillich, *Systematic Theology,*(Chicago: The University of Chicago Press, 1967), I, 95.
5. Edgar Krentz, *The Historical- Critical Method*, (Philadelphia: Fortress Press, 1975), 30.
6. Daniel T. Jenkins, ed., *The Scope of Theology,* (Cleveland and New York: The World Publishing Company, 1965), 40.
7. See Paul Ricoueur, *The Conflict of Interpretation,* (Evanston: Northwestern University Press, 1974), 21
8. Daniel T. Jenkins, loc cit., 41.
9. Peter J. Gomes, *The Good Book,*(New York: William Morrow and Company, Inc., 1993), back cover endorsement by J. K. Galbraith.
10. Ibid., 246.
11. Ibid., 35.

12. Ibid., 191.
13. Ibid., 164.
14. Ibid., 44.
15. Brian K. Blount, *Cultural Interpretation, Reorienting New Testament Criticism,* (Minneapolis: Fortress Press, 1955), vii.
16. Ibid., 184.
17. Roland H. Bainton, *Here I Stand,* (New York-Nashville: Abingdon-Cokesbury Press, 1950), 203.
18. Martin Luther, *Lectures on Galatians -1533,* trans. J. Pelikan, *Luther's Works,* (St. Louis: Concordia Publishing House, 1963), vol.26, 50.
19. Martin Luther, *What Luther Says,* op.cit., Vol I, 88, #268.
20. Ernie Bringas, *Going By The Book,* (Charlottesville, Virginia-Hampton Roads Publishing Company, 1996), 42.

CHAPTER 3

Authority: Objective or Subjective?

Now to Him who is able to keep you from stumbling, and to make you stand in the presence of His glory blameless with great joy, to the only God our Savior, through Jesus Christ our Lord, be glory, majesty, dominion, and authority, before all time and now and forever.

(Jude 24, 25)

In the world of art, a recent development is deconstructionist art. A work of art can be labeled "deconstructionist" if it deliberately attempts to present a meaning, then turns around and fractures a meaning or a set of meanings. The deconstructionist artist presents his or her work as a painting or a sculpture in such a way that the meaning is incomplete. It can be a painting with an incongruent arrangement of shape, size, or color so that the meaning of the art will be left to the imagination of the observer. Strange shapes of steel, stone, or other materials will be erected upon front lawns of big corporations, government properties, hospitals, colleges and universities. Their shape seems meaningless: beams intersected at unexplainable angles, stone chiseled in jagged or smooth fashion without clear definition. Once more, it will be up to the observer to attempt to make sense of the art, have the work generate ideas and concepts, because the art in itself is incomplete. It is like the culture from which it springs.

Ravi Zacharias, a noted Christian author, in his book *Can Man Live Without God*, relates a story concerning his visit to a newly built deconstructionist arts building at Ohio State University in Columbus, Ohio.

> Its white scaffolding, red brick turrets, and Colorado grass pods evoke a double take. But puzzlement only intensifies when you enter the building, for inside you encounter stairways that go nowhere, pillars that hang from the ceiling without purpose, and angled surfaces configured to create a sense of vertigo. The architect, we are duly informed, designed this building to reflect life itself—senseless and incoherent—and the "capriciousness of the rules that organize the built world." When the rationale was explained to me, I just asked one question: Did he do the same thing with the foundation?[1]

What a question! Zacharias hits the nail on the head. Without an authoritative, strong foundation, everything that is built can tumble and fall, like the house built upon sand which is described by Jesus as part of The Sermon on the Mount in Matthew 7:26. The foundation for any theology is the authority from which it comes. Can a theology from God, stated in inerrant and infallible truth in His Holy Word, stand against what can be called "deconstructionist theologies," spiritual roadblocks, minefields, cunningly employed by the *god of this world*?

Deconstructionist theologies, built upon the sands of the historical-critical method, sands that are senseless and incoherent, abandon God's authority in His Word, and attempt to say: "No way can God's Word stand!" I use the word "sand" in the plural because they are upon many shores of theological interpretations referred to in this work. One beachhead suggested by G. B. Caird, in the last chapter, was sympathetic imagination. Theological theories, not in accord with God's authority will always bear the tag of deconstructionist theology, because they place truth at the mercy of the observer, the theologian, and not at the foot of the One making the revelation, God Almighty. Like deconstructionist art, their theories or theologies will always be incomplete.

God's authority, on the other hand, is a complete authority. It emerges in what He has done in Jesus to bring eternal salvation to sinful mankind. All of Holy Scripture is God's love message in Jesus, built upon God's acts in history: the Creation, the Exodus, the Incarnation, the ministry, the Crucifixion, the Resurrection, and the Ascension of Jesus. It is plenary, absolute inspiration from God that caused the Scriptures to be written by the servants of His Word. The Old Testament has authority as God's inspired Word, not only because God caused it to be written, but because it was the Scripture Jesus honored and used in His ministry, a ministry foretold in the Old Testament. The redemptive events of God, which the Scriptures declare, are the foundational authority of God's Word which witnesses to these events. God's Word will always stand! As such, Holy Scripture is the norm for Christian doctrine. Apart from God's action in the events of Scripture, there can be no Christian theology, only musings.

The word *authority* has been used repeatedly in the last two chapters. That word is at the heart of the major problem Christianity now faces. Ever since God's enemy was revealed in the 3rd chapter of Genesis, when he substituted his authority for the authority of God and convinced Adam and Eve they could be like God, knowing good and evil, the battle for authority was joined. Every culture has viewed remnants of this battle.

We can look back over the history of Christianity and see the many diverse directions this conflict has taken. Before the Renaissance, authority was the domain of the Christian Church. Whenever the Pope spoke *ex cathedra*, meaning infallible proclamations from the chair of St. Peter, authority was recognized. Then came the Reformation with the placement of authority in the Word of God, the Holy Scriptures. The Enlightenment soon challenged the Reformation position of authority and swiftly transferred authority to the reason of man. Like a prized sports trophy, the competition for authority, the power to *define* whatever is proposed as truth, has been the goal of mankind in regard to truth, now granting truth many facets. William James (1842–1910), a professor at Harvard University and one who is held as a prominent psychologist and philosopher, penned the following regarding the diversity of truth.

> It never occurs to most of us . . . that the question "what is *the* truth?" is no real question (being irrelative to all conditions) and that the whole notion of *the* truth is an abstraction from the fact of truths in the plural, a mere useful summarizing phrase like *the* Latin Language or *the* Law . . . . Truth grafts itself on previous truth, modifying it in the process, just as idiom grafts itself on previous idiom, and the law on previous law . . . . Far from being antecedent principles that animate the process, law, language, truth are but abstract names for its results.[2]

One might say the above conclusion of James regarding truth flows from the Enlightenment, and that finding has substance as Enlightenment authority. Yet, one must go back even further in time than the Enlightenment to a French Roman Catholic philosopher/mathematician priest named René Descartes (1596–1650) to see the seeds of diversity in truth which impact upon authority.

Descartes is held to be the father of modern philosophy and also a famous mathematician who originated analytic geometry. As a philosopher, his fundamental principle was the dominance of personal thought and reasoning. With that principle in mind, he reduced the search for truth to the level of self-consciousness. His famous Latin words, *"Cogito, ergo sum."* (I think, therefore I am.) enabled him to come to the conclusion that man is no more than his thought and that a man's reason is necessarily truth. Herein lies the seeds of academic freedom.

Descartes' conclusion placed knowledge at the mercy of doubt with the exception of the reality of the person doing the thinking. Doubt, then, becomes the launching pad for knowledge. Indeed, it is the authority in the search for knowledge. It has also become the main foundation for deconstructionist theologies which are spiritual roadblocks we will see later in pluralism, evolution, ecumenism, homosexuality, lesbianism, and abortion, and other "isms" of man.`

Doubt demands proof and until a proposition of any kind can be proven to be true and authoritative, it has no standing. So, when doubt is placed upon the Word of God in Holy Scripture, the authority of God's Word has question marks unlimited hanging over it. Since God's Word cannot be separated from God, Himself, He becomes a victim of doubt as well, and His authority tumbles in ruins unless He can prove Himself to be truly God, according to man's rules of reason. Then, the authority for truth begins and ends with man.

God is left hanging in the obscure shadows of antiquity, even though His mighty and loving acts in Scripture have been authenticated in the history of man, the present not excluded. From there, it takes little effort to shove the indisputable evidence of God's authority to the "ballpark" of doubt. God is looked upon as standing in a puddle of impotent authority. He is open to any and all assaults upon His authority. The history of liberal theology bears testimony that such assaults from the doubt of the past and present will continue into the future as long as liberal theologians have the ability to propel their liberal theories in competition with the absolute truth of God in His Word. Deconstructionism in theology is still alive, and the people of God who come under such theological influence bear the spiritual consequences.

With Descartes came the great distinction of objectivity being inferior to subjectivity, another wedge through which the world entered the Christian Church in a "not so silent merger." It came with the fire of doubt raging in liberal universities, colleges, and seminaries. It is still in evidence today. While its openness was in the academic world of theology, its partial silence was directed toward the laity, the people of God. Those who faithfully worshiped God, recognizing His authority in Holy Scripture, did so while all around them a liberal change was happening in American culture and academia with permissiveness and experimentation as the watchwords, taking the starch out of biblical truth. Liberal theologians and clergy cleverly latched on to this change in the culture and craftily began feeding worshipers in the pews bits and pieces of the historical-critical method of biblical interpretation, a method which shreds the authority of God's Word. It was a silent merger at first, but it gradually gathered steam until it became *fashionable* and *acceptable* to have theologians and clergy question the authority of God's Word in writings, sermons, and Bible study classes. It was trendy and appealing for those who followed the influence of Semler, Lessing, and their liberal posse of theologians.

To have made the laity party to what was being taught in liberal American seminaries prior to World War II, would have brought a revolt against clergy who espoused such liberal views. After that war ended, an *enlightened* clergy could now, under the guise of *reason* and *reasonableness,* skillfully maneuver the hearts and minds of the majority of their members to an acceptance of their liberal conclusions. Liberality was chic and in vogue! Not all of the laity in the "mainline" churches have fallen prey to such reasoning. It is mainly those who were born before World War II and who had received and still believe the authoritative truth of God in Holy Scripture, who are now the dissenters. Many have left the churches of their ancestors and have joined churches where the authority of God in His Word is central as it proclaims God's love message in Jesus. Some still maintain church loyalty while feeling uncomfortable with the liberality of their churches which dwells upon cultural subjectivity as the basis for their proclamation, rather than the objectivity of God's Word. Even though they are unable to come to grips with the deconstruction tactics applied to the authority of the Word of God in Scripture, they hang on.

Objectivity and subjectivity are words that have been used not only in this chapter but in the last two chapters as well. Here, we are applying these words to God's authority which results in objective truth which is completely opposite to subjective truth. Subjective truth results in many truths competing for top billing via the use of reason.

Objective truth, in the theological sense, is truth that can stand with firmness and certainty, because it comes from God as witnessed to in the Scriptures. This Word is the pure and constant Word of God which claims its perfect and inerrant unity because it was written by the inspiration of God. It is plenary, authoritative inspiration. The God of creation is also the God of salvation in His Son, Jesus, and the God of His body, the Church, which is empowered by the Holy Spirit to discern and believe the objective truth of God in His Word. It is propositional truth from God which is firm and does not waver according to the crosscurrents of history or the many competing alien theories of man regarding God and His Word. It is verifiable truth, as many witnesses testify to God's mighty acts in both the Old and New Testaments. There is no myth in God's Word. God's truth in Holy Scripture validates itself by interpreting Holy Scripture *with* Holy Scripture. It stands as rock-solid objective truth from our Triune God. The Word of God is truth independent of man's experience and reasoning.

Objective truth from God cannot be compromised or else the spiritual life of church members declines faster than the stock market on the verge of a depression. Objective truth will always point to the working of the Holy Spirit through the Word and the Sacraments. The Holy Spirit will provide the results as congregations devote themselves to the objective truth of God through worship, living in the power of the Sacraments, sound Bible studies, evangelism, and prayer. God is faithful to the promises made in His objective truth of Scripture.

Subjective truth, on the other hand, involves man's interpretation of events, past writings, qualities, relationships, and other present cultural influences which come forth as his own intellectual conclusions which can then stand as the subjective authority of his experience or investigation. It is man's reason, standing as supreme authority apart from God's Word, being expressed as truth. Subjective truth is the Enlightenment position, in that it is the subject's authority to make final determinations of truth because there now can be many truths on the horizons of man as well as truths embedded in mankind's history. All one has to do is study theology since the Enlightenment to see the plethora of theories of "truths" which have been promulgated. This subjective authority has been a landslide, born of the historical-critical method of biblical interpretation, which has *surfed* itself into theological prominence which does not honor God's authority in His Holy Word. The simple truth is that subjectivity rebels and demands to be free from the constraints of objectivity. For this to be accomplished, the immovable authority of objective truth must be termed as obsolete and thus abandoned.

The Bible, by losing its authority as coming from God, must now be the object of historical inquiry using science, psychology, sociology, secular literature, and the arts in order to reclaim any semblance of authority, indeed, if authority can be conferred at all. All the above disciplines have been and are used by liberal theologians in the deconstruction of the authority of God's Word. If authority can be conferred, just maybe it might come from the reinterpretation of God's Word using the disciplines named above. And that is full-blown subjectivity which is the method of liberal, post-Enlightenment theology—a fertile ground for spiritual SARS!

Sadly, many liberal congregations follow the lead of theological subjectivity in their "Christian education." The dubious conclusions of science, psychology, sociology, and liberal theology garner center stage as an appeal for "something different, something new" which will evoke interest and entertainment. The results soon become evident: dependence on God diminishes, spirituality evidenced in Bible study, private prayer, and corporate worship become non-essential and the church becomes a social organization rather than the Body of Christ where new life in Christ is a daily occurrence as the Sacrament of Baptism proclaims, as The Lord's Supper enables, and as God's Word empowers through the Holy Spirit.

With truth no longer objective, and truth no longer an absolute, as it is in God's Word in Scripture, it becomes a "Hegelian" synthesis of many sources. Thus, liberal subjectivity flourishes as it is nurtured by the influence of Descartes, Semler,

Lessing, and others in their negation of the truthful objectivity of God's Word. Hodgson puts it this way:

> Throughout the ages the Bible has proven to be a "wax nose" that can be twisted to many different agendas.[3]

The term "wax nose" was used by both Hegel and Lessing.

According to subjective authority, reality is viewed, especially the Holy Scriptures, as having no consistency. The Bible becomes the main target for liberalism. It remains an open-ended option for any interpretation because no fixed standards of right or wrong, no absolutes, can be attached to it by *reasonable* minds. With truth no longer objective and absolute, any critical theologian has *carte blanche* freedom to define his or her subjective synthesis as truth. It need not have any relation to God's Word in Scripture, only that it be relevant and acceptable to the prevailing culture.

At this point it is important to see what has happened in America since World War II in the way the authority of our culture and the changing theologies of liberal theologians define and dispense truth. Certainly, before World War II, there were theological debates, controversies, and movements in progress within American Christianity. The Social Gospel of Walter Rauschenbusch, The Social Ethics of Max Weber, Ernst Troeltsch, and H. Richard

Niebuhr, and the Neo-Orthodox Movement of Karl Barth, C.H. Dodd, and Emil Brunner—to name a few—were presented and contested within the parameter of Christianity.

However, since World War II, Americans have witnessed a revolution in the way truth is seen or viewed. Even before that second great "war to end all wars" began, there was in place the Judeo-Christian value system, which firmly held that there was truth in Holy Scripture, and this truth came from God. While this truth could be debated among theologians, family life was strong, the Sabbath worship of God was taken seriously and held in respect, and the Bible was read in the classrooms of America's schools. There was the presupposition that truth came from God and that His truth could be trusted for all of life. The authority of God to reveal His truth was rarely openly disputed in the churches of America. Quietly, in liberal Protestant seminaries, that authority was being seriously debated and many times abandoned.

Then came our participation in the Vietnam War in the 1960s and 1970s. Along with the turmoil that erupted in the universities and colleges regarding opposition to the war in the mid-1960s, there arose a world-view called secular humanism. Its main tenant, or belief, was the presupposition that man cannot know truth as an absolute from God because God doesn't exist. It held that man is the source of truth because man makes the definitions of what is and what is not truth. Truth was now on a slippery slope. Absolute truth from God in Holy Scripture was abandoned in favor of man's wisdom and worldly accommodations which gave homage to man and not to God. St Paul clarified this presupposition when he wrote by God's inspiration, in Romans 1:25:

> For they exchanged the truth of God for a lie, and worshiped and served the creature rather than the Creator . . . .

In the late 1980s, another different view of truth emerged and impacted American culture and the culture of the world. It is called post-modernism. While secular humanism abandoned God and His Word in Holy Scripture as the source of truth, post-modernism went a step further. It abandoned man as the definer of truth. It maintains there are no recognizable sources of authority. God doesn't exist, and truth cannot be known as coming from man because there is no truth, only moral relativism in which there is no such thing as right or wrong. Every concept, every proposition, every act of man is relative. God's authority in regard to truth is out in left field. Any kind of truth is held to be *mush*, pliable, according to the relativist definer.

When truth, especially God's truth in Holy Scripture reposes in ruins in a post-modern world, the only thing that remains is possibilities, which like shoes, have to be tried on until a good fit is obtained. What fits one person as truth in a post-modern world may or may not fit another. On and on the possibilities mount until confusion reigns. Where is truth, or what is truth, or who has the authority to speak truth? Has it evaporated as an illusive, slippery concept which holds no substance or meaning? Has truth disappeared completely, or is it now masquerading as a matter of personal choice, so that it means whatever a person wants it to mean, but it is not labeled as truth because that would presuppose that there *is* truth, that there *is* right and wrong, and that God just might be the author of truth?

Gordon D. Kaufman, Professor of Divinity Emeritus, Harvard Divinity School, Cambridge, Massachusetts, makes a passionate plea for one of those possibilities which is called pluralism, a subject that will be discussed in the next chapter. Kaufman is a prime example of liberal scholars who have abandoned the authority of our God to act and speak in His revealed truth in Holy Scripture. Kaufman contends:

> Conservatives may still wish to maintain that it is possible and necessary to give an authoritative and binding definition of Christian beliefs and praxis (action—my insertion), and that theologians should proceed on that basis, but such positions express a kind of romanticism about how things used to be. History has moved Christian faith beyond that sort of possibility,

willy-nilly, and theologies alert to their own historical situatedness can no longer proceed easily on such assumptions. Theologians can no
longer take it for granted that there is a fixed
body of beliefs simply to be interpreted and explained. On the contrary, a major task for theologians today is to ascertain just which beliefs
and concepts inherited from tradition are still
viable, and to determine in what ways they
should be reconstructed so they will continue
to serve human intellectual and religious needs.
To do their work properly in today's world, theologians must ascertain what is in fact going on
in the world, must see what directions the history of the churches and the history of religious
reflection are moving, and must seek to make
their work relevant to and appropriate for that
movement. Theology can no longer look simply
to authoritative or normative decisions or situations in the past for its principal guidance. It
must orient itself toward the future into which
we are (quite rapidly) moving, a future which is
open and indeterminate in many ways.[4]

In the above quote it is plain to see that authority rests with the theologian to ascertain what is
applicable from past history as well as what is applicable in the present culture with a hopeful-
ness of being relevant in the future. This authority
platform for theology is as stable as a bobbing cork
on a restless sea with truth at the mercy of the theologian to make the definition. The authority of God,

then, is no longer trustworthy. God now takes His final curtain call.

When theologians, such as Kaufman, throw a pall of doubt over the authenticity and the truth of God's revelation in Scripture as something of the past that must be overcome and reoriented by a new theology, one must question whether or not that theology can be considered Christian. If a theology is to bear the name *Christian*, it must faithfully adhere to and preserve the truth of God in Jesus Christ which is authentically presented in Holy Scripture, God's Word. Otherwise, it is simply another pseudo theology which cannot be labeled *Christian*. Perhaps it should more appropriately be called "deconstructionist religious ideology."

Charles S. McCoy of the Pacific School of Religion in Berkeley, California, fits into the deconstructionist mold where God's authority to speak in and through His Word in Scripture is seriously challenged. McCoy points to Eberhard Jungel of the University of Tubingen, Germany, who confesses to being overcome by great embarrassment in attempting to speak of God.[5] In regard to this embarrassment, McCoy reveals his own presupposition regarding God's authority as not being equal to the turbulent culture of the post-modern world which must now define its own theology apart from God's Word in order to be relevant to the prevailing culture. He states:

100

Speaking of God is perhaps embarrassing, therefore, for theologians who misunderstand their
task or their location, who may be under the
impression that their speaking of God means
speaking for God, or who regard their work as
addressed only to previous theological literature
rather than the lively landscape of human wrestling with reality.[6]

"Previous theological literature" fits into the
archaic file of past biblical revelation, meaning the
Holy Scriptures; while "human wrestling with reality" is authority. McCoy like Kaufman and other
pluralists, whose theories appear in the next chapter, bear one common trademark—the cancellation
of the presumption of God to speak and act with
authority. McCoy has it all wrong. He is not wrestling with his concept of reality, but with God.

Van A. Harvey, in his book *The Historian and the
Believer,* makes the point that there is no such thing
as a disinterested or objective historian. The same
can be said of liberal theologians.

Every historian's judgments reflect his interests, values, and metaphysical beliefs. There
are no "bare facts" in history, it is said; there
are only interpretations. [7]

Harvey indirectly gives a meaningful clue to
Kaufman's analysis of authority. If the word "theologian" is substituted for the word "historian" and

101

"theological" for "historical" in the following quote, one can easily understand Kaufman's position. Harvey writes:

> The historian, in short, is radically autonomous because of the nature of historical knowledge itself. If the historian permits his authorities to stand uncriticized, he abdicates his role as a critical historian. He is no longer a seeker of knowledge but a mediator of past belief; not a thinker but a transmitter of tradition [8]

Could it be that the use of the word *critical* which presupposes authority for any liberal theologian to do his or her thing which vaults their conclusions as unquestionable authority is at the root of this theological foolishness?

Harvey adds another insight into the critical arena of liberal thought where the ideal of the intellectual integrity of the scholar reigns supreme, yet at the same time giving a modest but non-authoritative nod of recognition to Jesus Christ.

> From liberal Protestantism to the new hermeneutic, (a new theory of historical interpretation wherein the self, not external facts, becomes the criteria for interpretation—a 20th century phenomena - my insertion) Protestant theology may be regarded as a series of salvage operations, attempts to show how one can still

believe in Jesus Christ and not violate an ideal of intellectual integrity.[9]

Ted Peters, Professor of Systematic Theology at Pacific Lutheran Theological Seminary and the Graduate Theological Union in Berkeley, California, sheds light on the use of critical thinking as *modern* as it employs doubt. He believes:

> The purpose of doubt in modern thinking is to serve the truth, and a person who genuinely doubts is paradoxically expressing faith in truth. Doubt is pressed into the service of faith as a tool for discovering and dispensing with idols, for unmasking and disempowering those images of God that make God only one more component of the mundane world. Modern or critical faith is courageous faith because it seeks radical obedience to the first commandment by incorporating doubt and leaping into the realm of the unknown and unknowable.[10]

Peters is "right on" in his use of doubt as the means of "leaping into the realm of the unknown and unknowable." He mirrors Kierkegaard's "leap of faith." One must certainly ask, "Why leap into the unknown and unknowable?" Is that where God's revelation in Christ takes us? If that is so, then the critic, by use of doubt, is pointing to the reality of confusion and deception. Focusing upon "critical doubt" as "courageous faith" is to me, a far stretch from obeying the First Commandment of

God. That Commandment calls for unquestioned faith in our God Who revealed His command for obedience to Moses in Exodus 20: 2, 3. It is God's voice of authority—objective truth, not some unknown subjective thinking. Being uncritical is not the same as being anti-intellectual. The person of faith is not the person of doubt.

Peters views man as judge over God and His Word, offering subjective truth in place of God's objective truth. Then, authority can be conferred on any entity of the liberal scholar's imagination, or conclusions of other liberal theologians, with the exception of God Himself.

Darrell Jodock, former head of the religion department at Muhlenberg College, Allentown, Pennsylvania, my alma mater, joins with some of his contemporaries who espouse the historical-critical method of biblical interpretation, in accentuating the place of the Christian community of faith as authority in dealing with God's Word in Scripture. He argues:

> Scriptural authority is not foundational . . . . Far more important than specific teachings or beliefs *about* the Bible is an actual, active engagement with the Bible's contents and the claims it makes on the lives of persons in the community of faith . . . . A worked-out view is important in order to discern appropriate impli-

cations and explain them to others but is not required in order to make the Scriptures significant for Christian living. On the contrary, individuals or groups can experience the claim of the scriptural message without thinking through all the ramifications involved in their approach to the Bible; they need not, in this sense, possess any *theory* of biblical authority. If persons can find the Bible useful without having any theory of its authority, then surely agreement among Christians about a single theory is not necessary either.[11]

Jodock's aim is to bring:

. . . a contextual interpretation of scriptural passages within the community of faith . . . toward a productive focus on the recontextualized meaning of texts.[12]

Recontextualization of Scripture is nothing more than the deconstruction of the authority of God's Word. Jodock placed recontextualization within the post-modern setting. It was the historical-critical method being given full discretionary power to do with Scripture what a post-modern culture could accept. Central was the freedom, the assumed authority of the people of the community of faith, to come up with their interpretation of the authority and meaning of Scripture. The power to connect the Word of God to peoples' lives was handed over to post-modern presuppositions, not to God's Holy Spirit. Any resemblance of Scripture being the authoritative Word of God is purely coincidental. It is clearly *the tail wagging the dog!* Jodock exemplifies the epitome of what is happening in liberal denominations. He provides obvious clues in his view of the infallibility and inerrancy of Scripture. He maintains:

> Words like *infallible* and *inerrant* have been used correctly referring to inspired texts, but they are dangerously misleading in our own day. By calling too much attention to the scriptural words, they draw attention away from what the words are meant to point to . . . Scriptural infallibility lies in the Bible's failing in its proper task of pointing us in the right direction, toward revelation, toward the presence with us of the true God . . . . The terms *inerrant* and *infallible* are capable of misleading in yet another way. They obscure the need for ongoing reinterpretation.[13]

When God's Word is stripped of its inherent power and authority, and is judged to be less than what God has revealed it to be, it can be shaped like putty to resemble whatever a prevailing culture influences the liberal theologians to define as truth. As well, it opens the door for the "not so silent merger" of the world with the Christian Church. Jodock's presuppositions from where he believes biblical authority emanates, is most revealing.

All theories of biblical authority involve extra biblical appeals to values and assumptions held by the prevailing culture. As the values and assumptions change from one cultural epoch to another, new or revised understandings of biblical authority are needed. It is necessary to take the cultural context seriously in developing, adopting, and using any theory of biblical authority.[14]

If you, the reader, are scratching your head in bewilderment, wondering how such conclusions about the authority of Scripture could ever have emerged, you are not alone. They represent a liberal development of scriptural hermeneutics (the interpretation of Holy Scripture) which has descended upon the Christian Church since the Enlightenment of the 18th century.

Once more, it is cultural subjectivity over God's objective truth wherein authority is relative. The welcome mat for the world to enter the Christian Church with its relative subjectivity is in plain view. One of the tragic realities is that many of the laity in liberal "mainline" churches are unaware that God and His Word no longer hold top-billing. Deconstruction of the authority of God's inerrant and infallible Word is in full bloom. The Spiritual Arrest Religious Syndrome (SARS) has arrived.

Gene Edward Vieth provides substantiating evidence of this deconstruction of biblical authority when he pointed to the Barna Research Groups's finding that 49 percent of Protestant clergy reject core biblical beliefs. Vieth refers to George Barna's book, *Think Like Jesus*, where Barna shows what constitutes core biblical beliefs. They are: absolute truth is based on the Bible; biblical teaching is accurate; Jesus was without sin; Satan literally exists; God is omnipotent and omniscient; salvation is by grace alone; and Christians have personal responsibility to evangelize.

Among the interesting findings of Barna are the following: 71 percent of Southern Baptist pastors hold to a biblical world view while only 27 percent of Methodist pastors hold that view. In denominations that ordain women, only 15 percent subscribe to a biblical world view.

Vieth, quoting Barna, points to where all this deconstruction of authority emanates:

> Mr. Barna also found that pastors who attended a seminary are less likely to have a biblical world view (45 percent). This is doubtless due to the anti-Christian scholarship that dominates much of today's academic religious studies, such as the higher-critical approach to Scripture, which begins by assuming that the Bible is nothing more than fiction.[15]

David F. Wells provides a helpful clue to understanding biblical deconstruction by giving a meaningful evaluation concerning two opposing ways of thinking about the world. Behind his words is the issue of authority, because when people like you and me come to conclusions as a result of our thinking, our conclusions more than not stand as authority. Wells explains:

> There are, then, two opposing ways of thinking about the world that can be found in the West today. The one belongs to those who have narrowed their perception solely to what is natural; the other belongs to those whose understanding of the natural is framed by the supernatural. The one takes in no more that what the senses can glean; the other allows this accumulation of information to be informed by the reality of the transcendent. The one indiscriminately celebrates diversity; the other seeks to understand life's diversity in the light of its unity. The one can go no further than intuition; the other pierces through to truth. The one presumes that everything changes and that change is the only constant; the other measures the things that change by the standard of things that are changeless. The one looks only to the shifting contents of human consciousness, which differ from one individual to the next; the other holds the individual consciousness up for comparison to the larger realms of meaning in which are rooted those things that are common to all human nature. The one acknowledges no ultimate certainties; the other places the highest value on ultimate certainties. All of these differences arise

from the simple fact that the one perspective receives its meaning from God, and the other does not.[16]

Another modern day version of that last sentence by Wells comes from Peter J. Gomes who was named in the last chapter. Positioning himself squarely within the bounds of the historical-critical method, he looks for authority for God's Word outside the Word of God—in truth, somewhat nebulously defined as "someone, something, worthy of our loyalty, our ultimate concern, our trust." He takes on Martin Luther's teaching and the doctrine of orthodox Lutheranism where God's authority is firmly planted and fixed in God's inerrant Word, the source for all Christian doctrine. Luther used the Latin: *Sola Scriptura*, by Scripture alone, to be the determining factor for all Christian doctrinal authority because Holy Scripture *is* God's Holy Word, His love message in Jesus.

Gomes, on the other hand, presents a differing view, consistent with the historical-critical method.

> It was Martin Luther, however, whose reformation slogan, *Sola Scriptura,* "by scripture alone," gave rise to the greatest temptation yet, which was to make of the Bible a domesticated substitute for the authority of God.[17]

Gomes confuses the issue completely by intimating that the Bible is a "domesticated substitute,"

110

meaning that the Bible and God's authority flow from separate sources. This is another clever historical-critical manipulation which sees the Bible as coming from man apart from God's authority of inerrant and infallible inspiration. Then, if God wasn't in complete control of the Bible, and fallible human authors were, the Bible can be assigned to antiquated literature of past centuries and open to the same criticism of that type of literature. Then, "Pandora's Box" of evil consequences are ripe for the conjecturing of liberal theologians to be fed as *truth* to the unsuspecting laity of liberal denominations.

Holy Scripture is God's love message in Jesus and flows from His authority, not from man. It is God's Word which the Holy Spirit causes to come to faith in the lives of God's people and it can only do so because the Holy Spirit is God. *Sola Scriptura,* by Scripture alone, is not a temptation, but the authority made real by God's Holy Spirit and is the only foundation for the promulgation of Christian doctrine. Doctrine from any other source is heretical deception and confusion.

Waldo J. Werning sheds further light upon the inevitable consequence of doubting the authority of God's Word.

Attacks upon the authority and authenticity of the Scriptures as the infallible Word of God run counter to the Scriptures own unbroken testi-

111

mony to their complete integrity. It does no
honor to Jesus Christ to minimize the written
Word that He, the Incarnate Word, so constantly
taught. Only grievous harm will come to Christians and to Christian communities when doubt
is cast upon the unique authority and nature of
the Scriptures. [18]

I have been dealing with authority which
comes from God and authority which finds its
roots in man in the guise of academic freedom, a
well used tool of the *god of this world*. When the
Christian Church presents its love message in
Jesus, which is in accord with Holy Scripture, it
claims to speak and act with the absolute authority of God. This truth is not an accident of history, but the work of our God in history for the
salvation of all His beloved people who have faith
and life in Him. God conferred His authority upon
His Son, Jesus, and upon both the Old and New
Testaments. This authority is made known to us
through the Holy Spirit as the Holy Spirit works
in and through God's Word to work faith in the
believer. When the Christian Church is faithful
to God Who is revealed in Holy Scripture, the
Church is strong unto eternity.

A prime example of the tragic consequences of
a theologian who placed his faith in the subjectivity
of his theological conclusions is Paul Tillich. In
Chapter 2, it was presented that Tillich could not

and did not acknowledge Jesus as the Son of God, nor give any credence to the transcendence of God. Leonard F. Wheat gives one of the best summations of Tillich's theology:

> Here is Tillich's thought in a nutshell. He who frees himself from the tyranny of the false God, the God of theism, finds God in man. (Theism: belief in God—my insertion.) [19]

Tillich's death which ended in hopelessness stands as evidence of a theologian who lost the objective truth of God in Jesus Christ. His expansive theological search detached itself from the authority of the Scriptures and led him to deny the divinity of Jesus, whom Tillich considered to have brought about a new order of being through his humanity. Without Jesus as Son of God in his life, he tumbled into the depths of despair. That this was so is described by his wife, Hannah, as Paul Tillich lay on his hospital bed, terminally ill.

> He wanted to know what happens to his centered self after death; there would be no memory of his person as a person. I tried to tell him that his thought-images would be there, that his thoughts, having changed the substance of our cosmos, would enter the circle of the spiritual powers, which created the images of the world. He spoke about the Tibetan Book of the Dead. "Go after the clear light," I said, "the clear light will guide you, not any self-centered immortal-

113

ity." We talked about the Buddha powers which have the same spiritual unity—if you look through a many faceted crystal you seem to see many Buddha images, but if you forgo the crystal, there is one Buddha spirit and as much as you are the spirit you will be joined with it.[20]

When the vaporous conclusions of subjective truth are embraced, they have no answers to give in the face of physical death or the other dilemmas of man. Yet, in our post-modern world, the battle between the objectivity of God's truth as opposed to the subjectivity of truth as heralded by the *god of this world* will continue until God, Himself, puts an end to it with the Second Coming of His Son, as Scripture promises. In the meantime, the only way the world should ever enter the Christian Church is through confession of its sins and its need to be under the forgiveness and the Lordship of Jesus Christ, the Savior, Immanuel—God with us!

Deconstruction may be the way of the world, but the way of God is construction, true Christian spirituality—new lives for old! The Means of His Grace are His tools.

The people of Faith Lutheran Church, Kingston, Washington, will never forget a baptism which recently took place. Parents, who had joined our church through Confession of Faith, brought their twin three-year olds for Baptism into the faith and life of the Church. One child is severely crippled by cerebral palsy and had to be held over the baptismal font. As he was being baptized by Pastor Joel Wood, he dipped his one workable hand into the water and took a drink. Just think of that! He drank of the water of Baptism! That picture of truth is where all Christians are to be in Christ—spiritually drinking the waters of Baptism which along with the Lord's Supper and God's Word, builds up the Body of Christ, the Church. Yes, our God is in the construction business as He builds His servants in the fruit of the Spirit which God, through Paul, so eloquently describes in Galatians 5:22–26.

> But the fruit of the Spirit is love, joy, peace, patience, kindness, goodness, faithfulness, gentleness, self-control; against such things there is no law. Now those who belong to Christ Jesus have crucified the flesh with its passions and desires. If we live by the Spirit, let us also walk by the Spirit. Let us not become boastful, challenging one another, envying one another.

NOTES

1. Ravi Zacharias, *Can Man Live Without God*, (Dallas: Word Publishing, 1994), 21.
2. William James, *Pragmantism*, (New York: Longmans, Green and Company, 1910), 240–242.

115

3. Peter C. Hodgson, *Winds of the Spirit,* (Louisville: Warminster John Knox Press, 1994), 74.
4. Gordon D. Kaufman, *God - Mystery - Diversity,* (Minneapolis: Fortress Press, 1996), 22.
5. Charles S. McCoy, *When gods Change,* (Nashville: Abingdon Press, 1980), 67.
6. Ibid., 69.
7. Van A. Harvey, *The Historian and the Believer,* (Philadelphia: The Westminster Press, 1966), 16.
8. Ibid., 42.
9. Ibid., 104.
10. Ted Peters, *GOD - The World's Future,* (Minneapolis: Fortress Press, 1992), 25–26.
11. Darrell Jodock, *The Church's Bible,* (Minneapolis: Fortress Press, 1989), 5.
12. Ibid., 12.
13. Ibid., 102–103.
14. Ibid., 71.
15. Gene Edward Veith, "Stray Pastors," in *WORLD,* 7 February 2004, 25.
16. David F. Wells, *God In The Wasteland,* (Grand Rapids: William B. Eerdmans Publishing Company, 1992), 25, 26.
17. Peter J. Gomes, op.cit., 39.
18. Waldo J. Werning, *The Radical Nature of Christianity,* (Self-published, 1975), 56.
19. Leonard E. Wheat, *Paul Tillich's Dialectical Humanism: Unmasking the God above God,* (Baltimore: Johns Hopkins, 1970), 111.

20. Hannah Tillich, *From Time to Time*, (New York: Stein & Day, 1973), 222.

CHAPTER 4

Pluralism: The Grand Conglomeration!

And there is salvation in no one else; for there is no other name under heaven that has been given among men, by which we may be saved.

(Acts 4:12)

R.C. Sproul, one of many evangelical Christian theologians who views pluralism as the antithesis of Christianity, tells the following amusing, but realistic story.

Some time ago I spoke at a meeting of religious leaders and I told them, "If anybody comes to you and tries to sell you on the virtues of pluralism as a basis for church renewal, run for your life. Pluralism, as a philosophical idea, is the very antithesis of Christianity. No church can survive for long in that kind of chaos.

119

When I finished with my address, one of the members of the group stood up and began to speak in favor of pluralism. To avoid hypocrisy, as soon as he started to talk in favor of pluralism I ran from the podium and out the door. Needless to say, this was to everyone's consternation. I left hundreds of people looking for a speaker who had just vanished. Finally, I popped my head back in the door and said: "I just told everyone ten minutes ago to run for your life if anybody tries to persuade you about the virtues of pluralism, so I had to demonstrate it myself." I hope they got my point.[1]

Pluralism is one of the most recent "isms" upon the theological stage of new novelties of post-modern thought, a definite theological road block with drastic spiritual implications. If the history of theology has any consistency, other "isms" will not be far behind. Beside being new novelties of thought, they have one common thread of intent. That common thread is a relentless assault to do away with the God of Holy Scripture, His Son, and the power of the Holy Spirit. Pluralism wants to blend Christianity into a tasteless, non-authoritative, neutral conglomeration of religious possibilities which rank in equality with the other religions of the world.

In the quest for religious truth, Pluralism invites to the table all of the world's religions including Islam, Buddhism, and Hinduism. Pluralism puts them in tune with and on equal, authoritative footing with Christianity. This is pluralism on a world-wide scale. Narrowing pluralism so that it can fit within the parameters of a newly defined Christianity is the inclusion of liberation, process, feminist and whatever other theologies can be created by the human mind. All theologies must be accommodated and chiseled to fit within a post-modern day concept of "Christian" religious truth, a "truth" defined by man, not by God. Whatever name is given to this conglomeration of supposedly equal weight theologies, whether pluralism or religious confusion, it stands as a synthesis in diversity which attempts to find unity. Equality/neutrality reigns supreme.

In liberal churches where pluralism has become popular, the human ear will hear two words: *inclusiveness* and *diversity*. Inclusiveness, because any and all theories of theology are considered to have equal truth claims. Diversity, because it is considered a sin to say that faith in Jesus Christ as Lord and Savior is the "only way" of salvation. That would be exclusive theology, politically and theologically incorrect, the opposite of inclusiveness, the bedrock of pluralism.

The words *inclusiveness* and *diversity* are mainly confined to the category of immanence in that they pertain to this world. Pluralists do not discard transcendence completely, but use it in their theory of

121

pluralistic faith rising to whatever they define as radical transcendent truth in the *god* of all religious traditions, but not truth which is associated completely and fully with the Christian God of the Scriptures. While they use the name of God as a "symbol," it is not the God of Holy Scripture they refer to, but God as the "Real" or "Ultimate," terms used by John Hick, an English Presbyterian scholar and defender of pluralism.

Brad Stetson gives this assessment of Hick who had been moved by racism in the English city of Birmingham where he saw Muslims, Sikhs, Hindus, and other minorities maltreated by British citizens who Hick claimed were influenced by British imperialism and by their superiority over and above other races and nationalities. Stetson observes:

> So Hick's experiences in Birmingham, coupled with his observation of the evident piety of adherents of other faiths and his evolving philosophical/religious mind, led him to call for a "Copernican revolution" in theology and religious thinking. That is, just as Copernicus dispelled the Ptolemaic myth that the earth was the center of the universe, so, Hick holds, we must reject categorically all parochial conceptions of the centrality of our native faith (Hick, coming out of the Christian tradition, uses it as an example), and instead recognize the radical transcendence and

centrality of God alone in the universe of faiths.
He explains: "The needed Copernican revolution in theology involves . . . a shift from the
dogma that Christianity is at the centre to the
realization that it is God who is at the centre,
and that all the religions of mankind, including
our own, serve and revolve around him."[2]

Standing shoulder to shoulder with John Hick
is Gordon D. Kaufman of Harvard Divinity
School, a devotee of pluralism. He writes the following in regard to religious truth and pluralism:

> . . . religious truth is not so much a possession
> owned by a particular tradition as it is some-
> thing expected to emerge in the conversations
> among persons (dialogical, as in dialogue—my
> insertion) of differing faith-commitments—as
> they work together seriously in their collabora-
> tive effort to understand and assess their diverse
> frames of orientation. Instead of taking truth to
> be a property of particular words, symbols,
> propositions, texts, which can be learned and
> passed on (more or less exchanged) from one
> generation to the next, it is here regarded as
> a living reality that emerges from within and
> is a function of ongoing conversation among
> a number of different voices. In unpredict-
> able ways as the conversation proceeds, it is not
> expected, then, that some final, complete, or
> unchanging truth will ever be reached.[3]

The incompleteness of Kaufman mirrors the incompleteness of Brian K. Blount who was quoted in Chapter 2. Incompleteness is an unstable foundation for any theology. Question marks abound and doubt emerges. When one considers pluralism, it is most evident that pluralism is another engine of doubt which drives liberal theologians to promulgate it as "believable even though incomplete."

The doubt engine of pluralism chugs along the track of taking Christianity to the theological dump. Adding to the doubt factor is S. Mark Heim, professor of theology at Andover Newton Theological School in Newton Centre, Massachusetts. He argues for an accommodation by Christianity which recognizes the many diverse religious traditions and teachings of other faiths without compromising the uniqueness of the Christian faith or denying the validity of those other faiths.

> We need to learn that in relation to living religious traditions, the decisive witness to Christ is rightly expressed in relation to the neighbors' *actual* religious aim and practice. There is ample room to commend Christ in such terms. Such witness is consistent with the recognition that my neighbors (pluralistic, Buddhist, Muslim) appropriately also phrase their positive evaluations of my religious life in terms that are fundamentally theirs.[4]

While Heim's aim for witnessing Christ to neighbors of other religious traditions is commendable, his elevation of the validity of those traditions to the level of equality with Christianity is untenable. It is untenable on the basis of the revelation of God in Jesus Christ Who said in John 14: 6: "I am the way, and the truth, and the life; no one comes to the Father but through Me."

To even suggest that Christianity is not an exclusive faith bleeds heresy into the Christian faith. It denies God's way of salvation through faith in Jesus Christ as Lord and Savior. This faith is a gift of God's Holy Spirit as revealed in His Word, His love message in Jesus. This faith unto salvation has not been given by God to other religious traditions, although they may claim such. Salvation for the Muslim, Hindu, Buddhist, and members of other religious traditions is based on the merits, the good works, the spiritual achievements of the individual to gain their god's reward. Spirituality is reduced to works-righteousness, man the doer, man his own savior, so that the "good man" equals the epitome of spirituality.

In Christianity, salvation comes through Jesus Christ, His death upon Calvary's cross to pay for our sins, and His resurrection which defeats forever the power of sin and death to lay hold on those whose faith is in their Lord and Savior. In

Christianity, it is and always must be God's action, not man's merits or goodness which is the basis for salvation. Our spiritual response in faith and the spirituality which issues out of that faith comes from God's action through His Holy Spirit Who calls us to Him through God's Word. It is the transcendent action of God in Christ in the immanence of the world which has the power of salvation, not the immanent action of man in the immanence of the world. If some "Christian" theologians haven't learned by now that man cannot be his own savior, when will they learn?

Heim makes his position clear about salvation when he writes:

> Ours is not the only salvation: there are others. The "exclusive" witness of the various religious traditions are in this sense mutually confirming. Affirmation of a distinctive Christian path and end open the only space there could be truly to recognize other distinctive paths and ends. To say that a different religious tradition can serve as an ordinary or extraordinary means of attaining the religious aim *my* faith seeks, as my tradition can serve to realize the aim of the other faith, is to say something important.[5]

It sure does! It clearly says that salvation can be found apart from Jesus Christ. What is also astounding is the fact that this pronouncement comes from a Christian theologian, a good man to be sure, but one who must flatly deny Acts 4:12 which states: "And there is salvation in no one else; for there is no other name under heaven that has been given among men, by which they may be saved."

If the authority to reveal the truth of God is not in His Word, where is it? Acts 4:12 and John 14:6 are absolutes of God which cannot be denied by believing Christians. They speak of God's exclusive means of salvation through His Son, not through pluralism.

For a theology professor to write, and perhaps also teach, that there is salvation in other religious traditions apart from Christianity, imagine the spiritual impact upon future clergy who will fill the pulpits in the churches of our nation! Imagine, as well, the impact on the young and old who will come under the influence of their teaching! This is serious business and says "something important" about faculty members in liberal seminaries who have fallen in love with the theology of pluralism which is at the mercy of prevailing cultural trends and liberal theological winds of change. Could this be their intent and their way of welcoming the world into the church in a "not so silent merger?" If it is, it is heresy!

Kaufman joins Heim in reconstructing the meaning of salvation. Implicit in Kaufman's theological position is his concern for the survival of the human race, humanity, in the face of ecological disaster and the inhumanity of man to his fellow-man which results in war and the possible annihilation of humankind. He emphasizes the impotency of the past, the church, the Bible, and traditions to stand as authority for the salvation of man. Chugging along the track to the dump heap for Christianity, Kaufman maintains:

> The deterioration of this authority and normanativeness (as in an authoritative standard such as the Bible—my insertion) in Christian beliefs and institutions, however, signals a growing doubt regarding these claims about what is of ultimate importance to humanity, and a growing conviction that we ought to order our lives in terms of the actual problems that face us here and now in this world, rather than in terms of some alleged otherworldly destiny.[6]

The key to understanding Kaufman and other pluralist theologians lies in their biblical orientation according to the historical-critical method which presupposes a critical theology, one that is ringed with doubt as it questions the authenticity of God's revelation in Holy Scripture.

They then presume it is their right and duty to reconstruct biblical truth until it fits the dimensions and patterns of *enlightened* thought according to the modern or post-modern predicaments of man.

In this reconstruction, which is really deconstruction, it is not subtle alterations which are proposed, but sweeping changes which obliterate the very foundation of God's truth in Jesus Christ. The heart of Christian spirituality is torn to pieces. Once more Joe and Martha, sitting in the pews of their liberal churches, are gradually being led to a theology of the *enlightened* man. In this vein, Kaufman proposes the following radical agenda:

> We must be prepared radically to criticize and reconstruct traditional ideas about God, if God is to continue to serve as an appropriate object of devotion for our time, the one who truly mediates to us salvation (humanization).[7]

Please focus on the above quote and allow it to simmer for a while in thought. Do you see the audacity of the scholar to place his judgment upon whether or not "God is to continue" to really be God in that He can be controlled by a human theologian's whims and subjective conclusions? *Controlled?* yes, even to the point of redefining salvation through faith in Jesus Christ, so that salvation can be reconstructed to stand as *humanization?* This is clearly the theology of immanence. The transcendent holiness of God is desecrated. He is lowered to the status of the human, on equal footing with man, so as to be judged concerning His fitness to continue as God, or even claim the title of God.

129

Salvation from sin, the sin in all of us as portrayed in Adam and Eve's disobedience against God in Genesis 3, is of little concern in pluralism, for that would presuppose the need for a savior to deliver man from sin. Sin, for pluralism, is in the realm of being exclusive, of being ecologically unfaithful, or conjuring to make war and thereby threaten the annihilation of humankind. In pluralism, social sins are substituted for personal sin.

Theological scholars in liberal seminaries where pluralism is king, create and fashion a different theology which is in accord and harmony with their liberal, cultural thought patterns.

Basically, it is the motif of the historical-critical method which has become the entryway, the welcome gate, for the world in "a not so silent merger" as it elbows its way to power and influence in the Christian Church. Pluralism has followed this pied piper in its attempt to eliminate God as Father, Son, and Holy Spirit. It has no place for an exclusive holy God as the author of truth, nor the loving provider of man's eternal salvation through His Son.

For pluralistic theology to gain ascendency upon the theological stage, not only must it deconstruct theological truth as coming from God, but it must also take the divinity out of Jesus as being coequal with the Father and the Holy Spirit.

In that way it can level its theological onslaught against God in the person of His Son, a choice target of opportunity for pluralism.

Consider this pluralistic approach to Jesus as given by Kaufman:

> The absolutized picture of Jesus as uniquely and exclusively God's son has helped to generate other theological problems: it has, for example, fostered a highly individualistic understanding of both humanity and God, an understanding in many ways incompatible with today's ecological and systematic ways of thinking.[8]

I have chosen Kaufman as a prime example of the ecological and systematic thinking of pluralistic theologians, a calculated "left-turn" from the absolutes of Christianity. He walks to the cadence of a relativistic, post-modern culture. His radical ideas concerning what he perceives Christianity to be, bears no similarity to God's revelation in Holy Scripture, from which Christian doctrine is formulated and proclaimed as God's revealed, objective truth. Sadly, it must be stated and realized that Kaufman, as do other pluralists, has moved his theology from a Christ-centered theology to a polytheistic theology wherein many gods stand in equal supremacy with Jesus as one of the bunch. This theological stance of pluralism can never be considered to be Christian. It is mired in heresy up to its neck. Its identity is foreign to everything that Christianity proclaims as truth.

Another illustration of how pluralism is boldly embraced in liberal theological seminaries can be seen in Peter C. Hodgson, professor of theology at Vanderbilt Divinity School in Nashville, Tennessee. In writing about a theology of ecclesial community, he claims:

> Sure the Christian church, of all human institutions, ought to be such a community, a liberated communion of free people; yet it rarely is. Here resources from the Hindu tradition on which Gandhi drew might be tapped to help the church become what it is meant to be. In the process Hinduism and Christianity, precisely by realizing their own universal meanings more truly and radically, might be more alike.[9]

In relation to Buddhism, Hodgson envisions a marriage of grace with Christianity.

> Perhaps Buddhism can help the Christian church to be a community of grace in a graceless culture by showing more clearly what it means to have faith without attachment, to find fulfillment in utter emptiness, to become a communal self by giving up private selfhood. In the process Buddhists and Christians will move a little closer to each other. Spirit as it attracts is drawing us together without dissolving us into one.[10]

132

From all that has been presented so far concerning pluralism, it can be seen how easy it is for the world to enter the Christian Church by means of "a not so silent merger." The place of authority of Holy Scripture and Christian doctrine which flows from God's Word are tossed like leaves in the blowing winds of October and November. With no anchor in the authority of God, theological possibilities abound and run rampant. Evidence of this is seen in what is happening, not only in Christian institutions of higher learning, but also in Christian Churches in the world that receive from liberal theological musings these "tares,"—these non-productive weeds, as truth, ready for preaching and teaching.

James Barr, a confirmed devotee of the historical-critical method of biblical interpretation, provides additional evidence concerning how this method has influenced pluralism. In 1973, when Barr was Professor of Semantic Languages and Literature at the University of Manchester, England, he wrote these words which compromise God's authority:

> Theology is characteristically pluralistic and theologians, apart from those who sigh nostalgically for old times, accept this fact, not just as a fact but as a good thing. Within the older authority structures the authority of the Bible occupied a high place in the hierarchy: theoretically at least it was one of the very highest courts of

appeals for all sorts of authority, and it therefore had a defined place, very high in the hierarchical order. It was scarcely doubted that the appeal to scripture formed a major ground for discriminating between theologies, for preferring one and rejecting another. This is no longer in effect the case. The grounds for discriminating between one theology and another are multifarious (diverse—my insertion) but can certainly not be reduced to an ultimate appeal to scripture. Rather than scripture standing as an agreed authority, ready for use as criterion for any theology, each theology contains within itself (or may do so) an account of its own relation to the Bible. Within this newer context the idea of the 'authority' of the Bible has become anachronistic. (Anachronistic: an error in chronology: the science that deals with measuring time by regular divisions and that assigns to events their proper dates—my insertion.)[11]

When viewed from the vantage point of these words by James Barr, theology is freed, cut loose, by virtue of the discrimination of theologians to embrace any or all concepts because the authority of God's Word has been neutered. With the historical-critical method leading the way, pluralism has free reign to make a composite non-Christian theology of whatever appears as *supposed truths* within the world's religions or traditions. Once more we encounter man, standing as judge and jury over God's Word.

David Tracey, using Will Rogers humor, points to the absurdity of the pluralistic studies of today as never having met a religious position they didn't like.[12]

What you have read so far explains the subtle slide away from God's authority in His Word. Pluralism is but one force, one twisted and bare thread in the weakened fabric of deceptive theology, as it slips away in retreat from God's truth in Holy Scripture. A spiritual roadblock in the cause of "enlightened theological musings," it is! That it is popular in liberal theological seminaries is a sorrowful fact, another "ism" used by the *god of this world* in his attack upon God and the body of Jesus Christ, the Christian Church, to destroy its spirituality—its life in and through the Means of God's Grace.

It must also be noted that a sister "*ism*" which is in theological cadence with pluralism is *universalism*. This "*ism*" maintains that God will destroy or banish all sin so that mankind will receive salvation no matter what they believe or how sinfully they have lived in this life. They hold that after death a person will have the ability to make progressive progress toward achieving that which God wants them to be. God is viewed as a universal "sugar daddy" whose love cancels any type of eternal consequences for sin.

From their basic tenants, as stated above, universalists have no place for justification through faith in Jesus Christ alone, no recognition of the *god of this world*, no need for the Resurrection of Jesus, and no need for Christ's presence and absolution of sin in the Lord's Supper. All of this translates to no need for the forgiveness of sins, and on and on until one must conclude, there is no need for Jesus as Lord and Savior, or for His Church.

In universalism, the spiritual SARS virus is in full bloom. Christian spirituality becomes an unknown aspect of earthly life. Instead, a person has a "credit card of forgiving love" with no sin spending limits imposed and with the assurance that all accounts will be gracefully settled. While the *god of this world* is ignored, his handiwork is in full view—deception, confusion, and ultimately spiritual death with eternal consequences. Pluralism has many deadly cousins.

It is very easy to slip from one heresy to another. The tragic note is that these heresies are laid upon God's people as believable truth. John Hick, quoted earlier, and Paul Knitter, a pluralist who defined pluralism in ethical terms, were taken to task by Brad Stetson who quotes John Sanders in his criticism of Hick and Knitter regarding their concept of universalism in pluralistic theology. With great theological perception, Sanders analyzes the marriage of pluralism with universalism:

If the words "God will save" are to have any
meaning, they must have a particular content.
When Hick and Knitter claim that God will
save *all*, do they have a Christian understanding of God and salvation in mind? If so, then
they are not true pluralists: they are smug-
gling in a Christian conception and making
it definitive. If not, then, what exactly do they
mean? If they are genuinely including Hinduism or Buddhism, then they are radically
altering the Christian understanding of the
assertion that "God will save," since these
non-theistic Eastern religions posit a non-per-
sonal God who cannot *do* anything and a
nonindividualistic existence after death that
is quite different from the Christian conception . . . Pluralists such as Hick remove the
God of Christianity via the front door with
much fanfare only to smuggle him quietly in
the back door, and it is for this reason that
they are not successful in completing the revolution from a christocentric to a theocentric
theology.[12]

Yes, pluralism is a revolution in heresy. It stands
front and center. As the atom bomb was to Hiroshima
and Nagasaki in World War II in terms of total destruction, pluralism is to any unstable Christian
Church which has been built upon the shaky foundations of liberalism which casts aside the authority of God's Word in Holy Scripture.

I would be remiss if I did not include in this chapter two cousins of pluralism which have eased their way into our culture because of the mingling of diverse theological doctrines. They are *unionism* and *syncretism*. They have one common goal: the fusion of churches and faiths in community worship or national worship without regard for doctrinal differences. The result is a compromise of doctrine by those churches or faiths which participate. For example, The Lutheran Church- Missouri Synod is not in doctrinal fellowship with Protestant denominations where the historical-critical method of biblical interpretation is used. Islam is not compatible with Judaism or Christianity. Nor is Roman Catholicism in doctrinal agreement with Methodism. Yet because of pluralism, doctrinal boundaries have been cheaply handled in a false union of the coming together of different forms of doctrinal beliefs and practices. Thus, unionism and syncretism are doctrinal aberrations wherein only compromise and betrayal of doctrine can occur.

While destructive to those churches or faiths, pluralism has no power against evangelical Christianity where God is Father, Son, and Holy Spirit, our Triune God! It has no power against the bold and truthful preaching of God's authoritative truth in Holy Scripture! It has no power where God's Holy Spirit inspires the hearts of believing Christians to name Jesus Christ as their Lord and Savior! The ways of the world and one of its newest weapons, pluralism, have no means of entry for heretical theological penetration into the Church of Jesus Christ where His rule is supreme as Lord and Savior. They are impotent where His Means of Grace, The Word and the Sacraments, abound to abundant Christian spirituality!

NOTES

1. R. C. Sproul, *Lifeviews*, (Old Tappen, New Jersey: Fleming H. Revell Company, 1986), 120.
2. Brad Stetson, *Pluralism and Particularity in Religious Belief*, (Westport, Conn.: Prager, 1994), 6.
3. Gordon D. Kaufman, op.cit., 213.
4. S. Mark Heim, *Salvations*, (Maryknoll: Orbis Books, 1990), 229.
5. Ibid., 227.
6. Gordon D. Kaufman, op.cit., 25.
7. Ibid., 28.
8. Ibid., 119.
9. Peter C Hodgson, *Winds of the Spirit*, (Louisville: Warminster John Knox Press, 1994), 311.
10. Ibid., 312.
11. James Barr, *The Bible in the Modern World*, (New York: Harper Row Publishers, 1973, 29.

12. David Tracey, *Defending the Public Character of Theology*, in Christian Century 98 (1981), 355.
13. Brad Stetson, op.cit., 121.

CHAPTER 5

Man: From God or From the Apes?

*Then God said, "Let Us make man in Our image,
according to Our likeness; and let them rule over
the fish of the sea and over the birds of the sky and
over the cattle and over all the earth, and over every creeping thing that creeps on the earth. And
God created man in His own image, in the image of
God He created him; male and female He created
them.*

(Genesis 1: 26,27)

One of the greatest theological hoaxes
committed against man has been the elevation of evolution to a level of credibility wherein it can stand as an alternative or
superior truth to God's creation of man, which
the first chapter of Genesis describes. Any supposed truth that is an alternative, or superior to
that which God has revealed in His Holy Word

141

in Scripture becomes the basis for a theology without a rudder, another spiritual roadblock used by the *god of this world* to assault the Christian Church. It is also another arrow in his quiver of deconstructionism.

The theory of evolution abolishes God as Creator of the world, of nature, and of man who is created in the image of God. It stands today as one of the most devious plots of the enemy of God. Evolution seductively convinces some scientists that it has the answers to questions in biology, paleontology, and anthropology—questions that have plagued the scientific mind for centuries and still continue to do so.

Evolution has exploded upon the scientific and theological scene as *reasonable proof* that God could not have created the world and man in six days. It supports agnosticism which maintains that any ultimate reality, such as God and His claim for creation, is unknowable. The agnostic contends that God's revelation of Himself in Scripture is fantasy, His creation a pure myth. It is interesting to note that the word "agnostic" was invented by Thomas Henry Huxley (1825–1895) who subscribed to the theories of evolution as proposed by Charles Darwin and was his strongest advocate. Evolution found a willing ally in agnosticism. Agnosticism maintains that certain knowledge of the existence and nature of God and the supernatural world has not been attained. Atheism, on the other hand, is the complete denial of the existence of God.

One cannot dispute the theory that like attracts like. Those who embrace evolution as truth have turned away from God's revelation of creation. In essence they have turned away from the absolutes of God which are contained in His Holy Word. They have made of His Word in Scripture vaporous imaginings, compiled by ancient writers with varying intents, but most certainly not the direct, inspired Word of God.

The theory of evolution eased its way into the theological and scientific world in 1859, just prior to the Civil War, in a book written by Charles Darwin, *On The Origin Of Species*. It has created gigantic repercussions which have yet to cease. Evolution proposes the theory that all living organisms have been brought into being by a combination of chance and necessity, which Darwin termed as natural selection.

Darwin attempted to break down the distinction between man and animal. He viewed man as a more highly developed animal. He contended that man emerged by way of a ruthless struggle for existence. From this, the theory of the "survival of the fittest" developed, words first coined by Herbert Spencer who extended the theory of evolution to all areas of life, including ethics.

143

Darwin maintained that in this struggle, all living organisms were evolving and transformation was taking place in the development of new and distinct species that could survive in the world. Chance and change were the foundations upon which the theory of evolution was founded. God was not seen as creating the world *ex nihilo* (out of nothing) in six days, as the first chapter of Genesis declares. God wasn't even in the picture of natural selection. He had no hand in it at all.

That is the conclusion of one of evolution's strongest supporters, Richard Dawkins, Professor of the Public Understanding of Science at Oxford University in England. He jumped all over a thesis by William Paley, an Anglican clergyman and educator (1743–1805) who compared a watch and its skilled maker to creation and our God, who through intelligent design, created the world, where in creation everything fits together because God comprehended its construction and designed its use. Almost two centuries later, Dawkins came up with his own thesis, conditioned by Darwinianism, that creation came about by way of a "blind watch maker," certainly not God. He contends that creation came about by way of purposeless forces—random genetics and natural selection. In other words, God wasn't home when creation occurred. He wasn't involved. There was only a blind process by a "blind watch maker" wherein transformations occurred and are still occurring by chance and natural selection.[1]

An interesting program appeared on PBS television on 27 September 2001. Its topic was "Evolution: Religion: Science and Faith." There were four panelists: Francisco Ayala, Professor of Biological Sciences at University of California, Irvine, California; Mark Noll, Professor of Christian Thought at Wheaton College, Illinois; Arthur Peacocke, a physical biochemist and Anglican priest; and Robert Pollack, Professor of Biological Sciences and director for the Center for the Study of Science and Religion at Columbia University, New York City.

Ayala, who may well be Roman Catholic, stated his position in regard to evolution this way:

> Well-informed Catholics do not see conflict between their religious beliefs and the Darwinian theory of biological evolution. In 1996, Pope John Paul II stated that the conclusions reached by scientific disciplines cannot be in contradiction with divine Revelation, then proceeded to accept the scientific conclusion that evolution is a well-established theory . . . . (It should be noted that the Pope made this declaration on 22 October 1996 in his message to the Pontifical Academy of Science reaffirming the long-held position of the Roman Catholic Church on evolution: that evolution is not in conflict with Christianity. My insertion.)

> For more than a decade, I have taught the theory of evolution to freshmen. During the early part of the course students come to me, year after

145

year, to express their reservations based on their perceived contradiction between Christian beliefs and the theory of evolution. I treat these students with the great respect they deserve, but respond to them with two considerations very similar to the points made by John Paul II. One is that *the evolution of organisms is beyond reasonable doubt,* so that the theory of evolution is accepted in this respect with the same certainty that we attribute to Copernicus's heliocentric theory or the molecular composition of matter. The second consideration is that *science is a very successful way of* knowing, but not the only way. We acquire knowledge in many other ways, such as through *literature, the arts, philosophical reflection, and religious experience.* A scientific view of the world is hopelessly incomplete. Science seeks material explanations for material process, but it has nothing definitive to say about realities beyond its scope. Once science has had its say, there remains questions of value, purpose, and meaning that are forever beyond science's domain, but belong in the realm of philosophical reflection and religious experience.

Mark Noll explained his position on evolution this way:

Some evangelical Christians have trouble reconciling evolution and a traditional belief in *God as creator and sustainer of the world, but I do not.* Within the evangelical tribe, I belong to the Calvinist wing, where a long history exists of accepting that *God speaks to humans*

146

through "two books" (Scripture and nature), and since there is but one author of these two books, there is in principle no real conflict possible between what humans learn from solidly *grounded science and solidly grounded study of the Bible.* Of course, if "evolution" is taken to mean a grand philosophical Explanation of Everything based upon Pure Chance, then I don't believe it at all. But as a scientific proposal for how species develop through natural selection, I say let the scientists who know what they are doing use their expertise and whatever theories help to find out as much as they can. On the Bible side, *I do not think* it is necessary to read everything in early Genesis as if it were written by a fact-checker at *the New York Times.* But as a persuasive basis for believing 1) that God made the original world stuff, 2) that he providentially sustains all natural processes, and 3) that he used a special act of creation (perhaps out of nothing, perhaps from apelike ancestors) to make humans in his own image, *the Bible is not threatened by responsible scientific investigations.*

Arthur Peacocke had this to say:

As an theist—one who considers that the best explanation of the existence and lawfulness of the natural world is that it depends for its existence and inbuilt rationality on a self-existent Ultimate Reality (a Creator "God")— *I find the epic of evolution, from the "Hot Big Bang" to Homo sapiens, an illumination of how the Creator God is and has been creating.* Evolution enriches our insights into the nature and purposes of the divine creation—its fecundity, variety, its ability to manifest an increase in complexity to the point where the physical stuff of the world acquires the (holistic) capacity to be self-conscious, to think (in "mental" activity). I regard God as creating in, with, and through the natural as unveiled by the sciences: hence I espouse a *theistic naturalism.*"

While the quotations above are partial quotes taken from the PBS panel of evolution experts, it is plain to see that all three have adopted a Hegelian approach to the subject. That approach is synthesis, a compromise of absolutes so that differing positions can be brought together as a solution. Their positions are the commonly held positions of most of the clergy and laity of liberal denominations. While maintaining some allegiance to God and His Word in Scripture, they welcome evolutionist theories and give them equal weight. To do so is to hold God and His revelation in question while embracing the concept of "theistic evolution" as though God's revelation of creation must have an alternative explanation.

The fourth panelist, Robert Pollack as a devout Jew, took a different position:

Evolution is interesting to me because natural selection explains certain facts of life that touch on matters of meaning and purpose, and because the vision of the natural world these explanations produce is simply too terrifying and depressing to me to be borne *without the emotional buffer of my own religion.* This buffer is simple to describe: a Jewish understanding of our appearance by evolution through natural selection introduces an irrational certainty of meaning and purpose to a set of data that otherwise show no sign of supporting any meaning to our lives on Earth, beyond that of being numbers in a cosmic lottery with no paymaster.

I acknowledge there is a wholly consistent alternative description of the natural world and our place in it, which can lead one to exactly the actions I may wish to take or encourage others to take, all without any belief in God. Nothing is wrong with that position. It used to be my own, but as I have gotten older, I find I no longer can honestly hold to it. When I asked my teacher Rabbi Adin Steinsaltz how to respond to this criticism of my position by non-believing friends, he said, "If you know someone who says the Throne of God is empty, and lives with that, then you should cling to that person as a good, strong friend. But be careful; almost everyone who says that, has already placed something or someone else on that Throne, usually themselves."

I find myself accepting the God of my ancestors in part because it is my way of discovering meaning and purpose without denying or distorting

the data of science, and in part because otherwise I might put some person, some ideology,
some dream of completed science in God's place.[2]

As Professor Ayala taught his students at U.C.,
Irvine, that there is no conflict between religious
belief and Darwinian evolution, many liberal
scholars not only in colleges, universities, and
seminaries of America teach the same rationale.
It is "theistic evolution" as explained before
wherein evolution is held to be God's method of
creation. This position, without a doubt, compromises God's truth of creation, giving credence
to another spiritual minefield.

This compromise increasingly comes from the
lips of Christian laity today who wrongly con-
tend that evolution deals with material creation
while theology deals in the realm of morals and
spiritual formation. How the two can be separated from God, the Creator, amazes and confounds
me because if God is not involved in the former, He
has no place in the latter involvement. Christian
spirituality then stands captive to rational, subjective conjecturing. Without God being involved in
all of life, its creation, its spiritual life here on earth,
and eternal life with Him forever, He has no claim
whatsoever to be God, and that is the main contention of evolution. Just maybe this compromise is
symptomatic of the spiritual demise in denominations which have embraced the historical-critical

method of biblical interpretation where God's Word loses authority and credibility so that His perceived image becomes like play dough, able to be shaped by theologians and non-theologians according to the prevailing winds of a culture defined by man.

In the late 1970s my daughter, Mary Jo, was exposed to this kind of teaching in freshman anthropology at California Lutheran College in Thousand Oaks, California. When she, in disbelief at what she was being taught, asked the instructor if he believed in the evolution theory of Darwin that he was teaching, he replied: "Of course I do!" Parents, beware! Even when you think you are sending your child or children to a Christian college or university, liberal landmines of unbiblical truth abound, waiting to turn young students into "biblically doubting Toms and Janes." Their Christian spirituality can be easily questioned and altered.

It was in 1925 in the small town of Dayton, Tennessee, that the evolution issue in teaching aroused national attention. It was forbidden by Tennessee law to teach the theory of evolution in the classrooms of that state. A high school teacher by the name of Scopes challenged that law and the famous Scopes trial ensued. The attention of America was fixed on this trial as William Jennings Bryan, one of the greatest orators and Christian fundamentalists of the time, argued the case for the prosecution. The defense position for Scopes was taken by Clarence

Darrow, one of the leading defense lawyers in America. Although Bryan won the case, the popular thinking was already siding with the accused much like the jury sided with O.J. Simpson at his first trial for the murder of his wife. If a trial, like the Scopes trial, would occur today with evolution as the issue, the popular mindset of the 21st century would opt for acquittal. Untold numbers of teachers, instructors, and professors have already pitched their scholarly tents in the evolution campground.

In 1987 the Supreme Court ruled that the teaching of Bible-based "creation science" in public schools was unconstitutional. Fifteen years later, two House Republicans: Representatives John A. Boehner and Steve Chabot were pressing for the teaching of an alternative to evolution in Ohio public schools. It is called the "intelligent design theory" which maintains that the very complexity of life is evidence that the world was created by a guiding intelligence. As expected, objection was raised by W. Eric Meikle, outreach coordinator for the National Center for Science Education, a nonprofit organization that defends the teaching of evolution. Joining him was Senator Edward M. Kennedy, a Democrat of Massachusetts, chairman of the Senate's Health, Education, Labor and Pensions Committee, who stated:

> "I believe that public school classes should focus on teaching students how to understand and critically analyze genuine scientific theories.

152

Unlike biological evolution, intelligent design is not a genuine scientific theory, and therefore, has no place in the curriculum of our nation's public school science classes."[3]

No one can deny that Darwin's theory of evolution has taken over a major portion of public school science education. Nor can it be denied that liberal colleges, universities, and seminaries in America are under the spell of evolution in their slide away from God. Yet, the amazing truth about evolution is that it has never been scientifically proven. It is rather a fanciful idea or theory that scientists have run with for decades and still do, but as a scientific bucket, it has holes through which its seeming truth leaks. It cannot hold water!

A respected scientist who came to that conclusion is Colin Patterson, senior paleontologist at the British Museum of Natural History. After many years of scientific research into the theory of evolution, he wrote:

I had been working on this stuff (evolution) for more than twenty years, and there was not one thing I knew (that was true) about it. It's quite a shock to learn that one can be so misled for so long.[4]

When liberal theologians attempt to integrate evolution into Christianity, they have already ne-

153

gated the truth of God's revelation in Holy Scripture. It then becomes an attempt to correct, reinterpret, or deconstruct Scripture, mainly Genesis 1, a popular theological goal of liberal scholars to which unsuspecting church members in liberal congregations fall prey. One such scholar is Michael Muse, Professor of Philosophy at Florida State University. His recent book, *Can a Darwinian Be A Christian?* has evoked kudos from E. O. Wilson of Harvard University, Keith Ward, Professor of Divinity, Oxford University, Robert Pennock, University of Texas at Austin, and Edward T Oakes S.J., Regis University, Denver, Colorado. I bring these names to your attention as they mirror a common theological enthusiasm for Muse and his work to integrate, as in synthesis, Darwinism and Christianity. This is all within the domain of liberal biblical scholarship influenced by the historical-critical method.

Muse gives a good summary of both positions, but it is obvious that he holds the authority of Holy Scripture in question. One must do that in order to give credence to Darwinism. Muse opines:

> I conclude, both from the viewpoint of science and from the viewpoint of religion, that if one's understanding of Darwinism does not include a natural evolution of life from non-life, there is no reason to think that this now makes Christian belief impossible.[5]

He states how this can be accomplished:

154

Obviously, if you are a fundamentalist Christian, then the Darwinian reading of Genesis is going to give you major problems—insoluble problems, I suspect. But, as I have pointed out, biblical interpretation is a topic that Christians have been discussing and refining almost since their religion began. There are plenty of resources open to the Christian who would move towards science and away from a literal reading of the early book of Genesis.[6]

Of course Muse's thesis is going to give major problems to Christians committed to Holy Scripture as true Word of God. By embracing an unquestioned validity of science, he moves away and abandons the witness of Scripture. Using a favorite ploy of liberal 21st century scholars, he reverses the situation by asking the wrong question first. What if Muse had turned the question around? *Can a Christian Be A Darwinian?* What would you answer?

Yes, there are "plenty of resources open to Christians" and this has been the problem. The resources have been laid at the feet of the Christian Church as a gift from the *god of this world.* And liberal denominations have gobbled them up as *spiritual manna* from the minds and pens of scholars who presuppose that they know more than our God of all creation. Then, they feed these resources which are not of God to God's people who are influenced by their *Christian* mentors to accept what they are taught as truth to the peril of their spiritual lives.

155

In stark contrast to the synthesis proposed by Muse are Christians who believe that God's Word in Scripture is inerrant and infallible and who have no hesitation whatsoever in accepting what His Word declares regarding creation. In other words, God had a purpose and the word "purpose" causes grief within the hearts and minds of evolutionists because they view their theory as one that has no purpose, only chance and necessity. Christians believe God revealed His purpose according to intelligent design, a design which has become the open arena for the investigation of science. Christians have no argument with science as long as it doesn't elevate itself to the Throne of God as Robert Pollack has warned.

Each one of us is a beneficiary of science, science which comes from God. We have seen the multitude of blessings that have come and also some curses when science has been wrongly used. We cannot picture a world without responsible scientists. They are God's instruments of love for the physical health and the common good of His magnificent creation.

The main reason why evolution cannot hold water, be believable, is the truth of God's intelligent design which He has established in His creation. Dr. Alvin Barry gives the following lucid rationale:

> Proponents of Intelligent Design have made headway in recent years. Their findings have added muscle to the long-held Creationist

156

arguments on the Second Law of Thermodynamics, which, simply put, says that the way of all things, both living and non-living, is to go from a state of order to various states of increasing disordrer, not the other way around.

Other arguments being put forward are based on dubious dating-methods used by evolutionists, and on fossil record—the latter still showing no conclusive transitional stages in types or kinds (one would think every fossil would show a transitional stage). Together, these evidences, along with many others, form a convincing case for the idea of Creation and Intelligent Design.

Evolutionists appear unwilling to address the findings of biochemistry and other related fields. They are quick to say they are defending science, yet when confronted by an Intelligent Design paradigm that explains the data better than their own (such as on the human eye, a bird's wing or the process of blood-clotting), they offer no scientific defense at all. Instead, they lash out, ridiculing the Intelligent Design paradigm as nothing more than "religious."

Those who prefer the Creation and Intelligent Design explanation for life cannot be conveniently stereotyped as backward, ignorant, flat-earth fanatics. To the contrary, believers in special Creation and Intelligent Design are discerning rational people—tens of millions of them—who, upon weighing the evidence, have dismissed evolutionary theory as untenable. And these millions are being joined by growing numbers of biologists, geologists, paleontologists, physicists, medical doctors, mathematicians and other professionals in the pure and applied sciences.[7]

It is not surprising that as scientists dig deeper into the sciences mentioned above, they are enabled to see the consistent patterns of God's creation. One of the most respected biochemists in America, Michael Behe, a professor at Lehigh University in Bethlehem, Pennsylvania, in disputing Charles Darwin and his theory of evolution states:

> To a person who does not feel obligated to restrict his search to unintelligent causes, the straightforward conclusion is that many biochemical systems were designed. They were designed not by the law of nature, not by chance and necessity; rather, they were planned. Their designer knew what the systems would look like when they were completed, then took steps to bring the systems about. Life on earth at its most fundamental level, in its most critical components, is the product of intelligent activity.[8]

A most outspoken opponent of evolution upon the American church scene today is Dr. D. James Kennedy of Coral Ridge Ministries, Fort Lauderdale, Florida. He puts one of the final nails in the coffin of evolution when he refers to Dr. Francis Crick, the co-discoverer of DNA, and a recipient of the Nobel Prize for helping in that discovery. DNA is the master program of all genetic development. It is the program which maintains that double-helix molecule contains all the genetic information for making a plant, an animal, or a human being. Kennedy writes:

> DNA . . . is so fantastically complex that Crick decided to apply probability science analysis to the mystery of the origin of DNA. What are the odds, he asked, of the simplest DNA molecule arising by random chance? The god of evolution is a trinity of Matter, Chance, and Time, and evolutionists believe that, given enough time, anything is possible—even the chance formation of a complex molecule like DNA.

> So Crick applied the science of probability to the question of DNA. He assumed at the outset that it would be a simple matter to prove that, given 4.5 billion years of Earth history (by the evolutionist's estimate), the chance formation of a DNA molecule was virtually inevitable. After all, evolution was a fact in his mind, so it had to have been almost a foregone conclusion. But after he calculated all the variables that had to come together by random chance in order to form the first DNA molecule, he found that the odds were practically *one chance in infinity* of that happening! According to Crick's calculations, the DNA molecule could never have evolved natu-

rally within the entire 4.5 billion-year history of the world (once more, the estimate of evolutionists—my insertion)—and that's just one molecule. If a DNA molecule can't arise by chance in all that time, then certainly a single cell has no chance—much less an organism as complex as a human being.[9]

Kennedy quoted four respected scientists who upheld the unmasking of Darwin and his cohorts that evolution cannot hold water, that it leaks like a faulty bucket. Science journalist, Roger Lewin, the author of *Bones of Contention* is one of the four who must be heard and considered. Kennedy quotes him as follows:

The Darwinist approach has consistently been to find some supporting fossil evidence, claim it as 'proof' for 'evolution,' and then ignore all the difficulties. It is, in fact, a common fantasy, promulgated mostly by the scientific profession itself, that in the search for objective truth, data dictate conclusions. Data are just as often molded to fit preferred conclusions.[10]

Scientists can mold data just like liberal theologians can mold Jesus, in play dough fashion, to fit their liberal conclusions. Scientists and theologians committed to, or even giving the slightest degree of credence to Darwinian evolution stand on sandy foundations. The data of their conclusions are faulty, unsubstantiated data, but still they persist. So far they have been very successful in maintaining a deadly liberal beachhead in education in the schools, colleges, universities, and seminaries of America and in the minds of many church members. The question, however, still remains: "Can science claim it is creditable while using faulty evidence?"

The answer, I believe, is most simple. The alternative would be a recognition of God as the Creator of heaven and earth and of His Son, Jesus Christ, as Lord and Savior of sinful mankind. Then, their entire system, seconded and endorsed by the *god of this world* would collapse in ruin. It already is folding, but its demise will be stoutly resisted by liberal theologians and educators. The case for Intelligent Design is solid, but evolutionists will not give up.

Loren Eiseley in writing about Charles Darwin and God's design states: "Darwin did not destroy the argument from design. He destroyed only the watchmaker and the watch."[11]

Peter C. Hodgson of Vanderbilt Divinity School, mentioned before in his defense of pluralism, is a liberal theologian, an influential teacher of future pastors, who supports evolution. In spite of the shaky, sandy foundation of the randomness of chance, he persists in his defense of evolution. He compares randomness to computers as he states:

161

Unless we are to believe that the universe was rigidly programmed from the first moment of creation, then the most potentially fruitful source of innovation is random variation. Computers simulate creativity by generating a large number of possibilities of response, enabling the most appropriate ones to be selected. Thus randomness is the essential precondition of creativity; and *if* we wish to affirm that God acts creatively in the universe, then chance and random variation, far from being antithetical to this purpose, would be essential instruments of it. It is misleading to suggest that chance and randomness are themselves creative agents by means of which the potentialities of universes are being "run through" or explored. Chance rather is the space or instrument of creativity. Creativity is the work of God, of God's power of being.[12]

Let us take a closer look at this defense of evolution. The question begins with a conditional sentence which holds in question God's Intelligent Design of the universe which Genesis beautifully describes and which evolution cannot refute. It is most apparent that Hodgson does not hold the Genesis creation of the world as truth. Otherwise he would be in complete agreement. Instead, he joins many of those who are committed to the historical-critical method of biblical interpretation, which holds God's Word in Scripture captive to 18th century understanding of reason. Hodgson associates randomness as "the essential precondition of creativity." If that were so, then all of the ordered laws of biology, physics, paleontology, and geology would be merely a coincidence. While he mentions creativity as the work of God, God's power of being, he assigns God's power to randomness. His view of God's power is a limited, deconstructionist view. Hodgson marches in step with an evolutionary concept of theology which has been with us since the Enlightenment of the 18th century. It is a concept of liberalism which maintains that old biblical doctrines are in fact primitive, imperfect, and must be discarded or evolve into up-to-date, culture-relevant theologies which have no "taint" of their former weak, untenable biblical foundations.

Another limited view of God's power in creation is found today in process theology. Alfred North Whitehead and Charles Hartshorne were the early pioneers of this theology which wed itself to science as it emphasized the importance of the sciences in theological formation. The Divinity School of the University of Chicago has been one of the centers that have championed this philosophy as theology. In this innovative theology, God does not stand as the Creator of the world, who created the world *ex nihilo* (out of nothing) as Holy Scripture attests, but as a co-creator, a co-participator in the process of becoming. In this process, God is ever-changing, always evolving, not permanent nor fixed, because anything that is static or fixed is viewed as being evil. Therefore, because God is not viewed as evil,

He must also be in the process of becoming—a process that goes on and on *ad infinitum*.

Process theologians present a totally different concept of Jesus than that of Holy Scripture. The transcendent holiness of Jesus as true God is eliminated. They see Jesus, not as God, but as an ethical human being, who was more intimately connected and open to God's teachings than other humans, and as such, is a model or an example of how to love God and mankind. The influence of Ritschl who viewed Jesus as a hero who can lead mankind to discover the God of values is in full view in process theology. John R. Cobb, Jr. and David Roy Griffin point out that Jesus, more than any other human being,

> was himself open to creative transformation. Therefore, insofar as we genuinely receive Jesus as the revelation of the basic truth about reality, we are more open to the divine impulses in our experience and accordingly, are more apt to respond positively to (them).[13]

Jesus in creative transformation? Maybe in process theology, but not in God's revelation in Hebrews 13:8: "Jesus Christ is the same yesterday and today, *yes* and forever." The historical-critical method is in full view in process theology, a method which easily finds room for any and all liberal "theological" theories.

Evidence of the historical-critical method in process theology is plainly stated by David Basinger:

> . . . the Bible is not revelation and Word of God itself; instead it is an occasion for revelation and a vehicle for the Word of God to be heard once again. Rather than being a "transubstantiated" text, modern scholars affirm the Scriptures as another instance of the infinite being capable of the finite. We have the "treasure" of the human documents of Scripture, used by God as they are. The texts themselves are the swaddling cloths and manger for God's law and Gospel. The qualitative difference between Scripture and other literature is not its divine authorship but the role it has held in the Christian Church by mediating God's Word.[14]

Evolution and process theology are wed to each other in their denial of God as Creator and they will not give up.

In spite of all the evidence which points to Intelligent Design by God, evolutionists persist in their thinking which is not of God, but of man. An interesting story is related by D. James Kennedy concerning Sir Julian Huxley which shows how evolution was embraced by Huxley out of his rebellion against God and the morality of God which is revealed in Scripture.

165

Shortly before his death in 1975, Sir Julian Huxley gave a television interview that I happened to watch. Huxley was a widely respected scientist, the first director of UNESCO (United Nations Educational, Scientific, and Cultural Organization), and the world's leading evolutionist. He and his brother, novelist Aldous Huxley, were the grandsons of Thomas Henry Huxley, who was known as "Darwin's Bulldog" for his defense of Dawinian evolution. During the interview, the woman journalist asked Julian Huxley this question: "Why have so many scientists been so quick to adopt Darwin's theory of evolution."

Huxley's answer began with these words: "The reason we scientists all jumped at *The Origin of Species* was because"—

What do you think Huxley said next? And consider this: What would the average Darwin-indoctrinated high school or college student think Huxley said next?

Your answer might be—and the student's answer almost certainly would be—"The reason we scientists all jumped at *The Origin of Species* was because Charles Darwin had amassed such overwhelming scientific evidence and such compelling logical arguments that the conclusion was simply inescapable. The proof of Darwinianism forced us, in our scientific integrity, objectivity, and honesty, to accept evolution by natural selection as a self-evident fact."

After all, that is what we are constantly told in the media, and that is what our children are taught from kindergarten on up: Evolution is a fact. The evidence is irrefutable.

But let's go back to Julian Huxley's dangling sentence. Is that, in fact, what he said? No. He didn't talk about reason and logic. He didn't talk about evidence and objectivity. Here is his answer: "The reason we scientists all jumped at *The Origin of Species* was because the idea of God interfered with our sexual mores."

In other words, Huxley and his fellow evolutionists were biased toward evolution and bigoted against Christianity *because they wanted to live sexually promiscuous lives without having to account to God.* Evolution gave them a worldview in which they could erase God from the picture, view themselves as nothing more than rutting animals, and give free rein to their sexual appetites. This is hardly an objective, evidence-based motive for adopting a scientific worldview.[15]

It cannot be denied that evolution has destroyed and continues to destroy Christian spirituality in the doubts which it raises and its negation of God as Creator. Public schools, liberal colleges, universities, and seminaries have all championed evolution. Forceful Christian witness must come from congregations where God's inerrant and infallible Word is confessed as such. While even conservative congregations may feebly, at times, address the situation, it is like putting a finger in the dike while a mountainous wall of spiritual death rushes toward our youth to engulf them in the theories and ideologies of their school educators who have no place for God in their curriculums. If we don't see this as *undeclared war* on the spiritual life of our children, then we are spiritually blind.

The *god of this world* has invaded the Christian Church through imaginary evolution theories, but God's truth of Intelligent Design, as He revealed it, will prevail! God's creation continues to take place. He creates life in human birth and in spiritual birth, where new life in Jesus is created through God's Means of Grace, new life that is eternal. Earthly life and spiritual life are united in God's acts of Intelligent Design. See John 1: 1–5.

God's absolute truth as revealed in Holy Scripture can withstand the fantasies of liberal scientists and theologians. Dr. Gerald L. Schroeder, a noted physicist who taught at Massachusetts Institute of Technology and now at Weizmann Institute in Israel, after extensive research in both the sciences and biblical world, contends there is no divergence, but a convergence of scientific and biblical wisdom. Forcefully, he contends: "Our universe, tuned so accurately for the needs of intelligent life, indeed ticks to the beat of a very skillful Watchmaker."[16]

The *god of this world* is using blunt instruments against the God of Holy Scripture!

NOTES

1. See Richard Dawkins, *The Blind Watchmaker,* (New York: W.W. Norton and Company, 1996).
2. PBS Television: *Evolution: Religion: Science and Faith,* 27 September 2001.
3. Michael A. Fletcher, *Washington Post,* 29 May 2002, AO3.
4. Colin Patterson, *Harpers,* February 1985, 49,50.
5. Michael Muse, *Can a Darwinian Be A Christian?,* (Cambridge, United Kingdom: Cambridge University Press, 2000), 67.
6. Ibid., 217.
7. Alvin A. Barry, *Unchanging Truth in Changing Times,* (St. Louis: The Lutheran Church - Missouri Synod, 2001) Article: *Creation and Evolution.*
8. Michael Behe, *Darwin's Black Box: The Biochemical Challenge to Evolution,* (New York: The Free Press, 1996), 193.
9. D. James Kennedy, *Solving Bible Mysteries,* (Nashville: Thomas Nelson Publishers, 2000), 109.
10. Ibid., 108.
11. Loren Eiseley, *Darwin's Century,* (Garden City: Doubleday & Co., Anchor Books, 1961), 197.

12. Peter C. Hodgson, op. cit., 142.
13. John B. Cobb, Jr. and David Ray Griffin, *Process Theology: An Introductory Exposition*, (Philadelphia: The Westminster Press, 1976), 102–103
14. David Basinger, *Divine Power in Process Theology*, (Albany State University of New York Press, 1988), 7.
15. D. James Kennedy, op. cit., 103, 104.
16. Gerald L. Schroeder, *The Science of God*, (New York: The Free Press, 1997), 124.

CHAPTER 6

A United Christian Church in the World?

I do not ask in behalf of these alone, but for those who believe in Me through their word; that they may all be one; even, as Thou, Father, art in Me and I in Thee, that they also may be in Us; that the world may believe that Thou didst send Me. And the glory which Thou hast given Me I have given to them; that they may be one, just as We are one.

(John 17: 20, 21)

Some years ago, my friend, Don, was driving his daughter and her best friend to the movie theater in Hatboro, Pennsylvania. On the way they passed the church of his daughter's friend, St. John Bosco, a Roman Catholic Church, to which she pointed saying, "That's St. John's, my church." Shortly thereafter, they approached St. John's Lutheran Church where I was the pastor. Pam proudly pointed to her church and said: "There's St. Jack's Church where our family worships." To my friends, I have always been called "Jack," but never "Saint." Pam's father and I still chuckle when we recall my elevation to sainthood.

Isn't that the way most Christians look at the church, as "their church," the place where Christian worship, spiritual growth, fellowship, and witnessing emanates? For the laity, the church is localized in their community. What takes place on the national and world religious level, outside of their local church, evokes limited interest unless the roots of their Christian heritage are challenged from without or uprooted from within. When the words *ecumenical* or *ecumenism* are introduced in sermons, teachings, local church discussions, or newspaper reports, they appear to the laity to be remnants of a foreign language.

These words have been appearing in increased volume since 1948, following World War II when the World Council of Churches was organized in Amsterdam, Holland, with representation coming from the Eastern Orthodox Church and some Protestant Churches. Most of the dialogue revolving around these words has been in the confined theological arena of elite, liberal scholars and clergy. These words come from the Greek word *oikoumene* which means *world* as it points to the inhabited earth. Ecumenists use it to apply to a one world concept. Just as the United Nations was formed as a unifying body of nations following World War II, so the World Council of Churches was formed with the vision of unifying the Eastern Orthodox and Protestant churches of the world. The Roman Catholic Church takes part as an observer only.

The modern ecumenical movement began in 1910 when the World Missionary Conference was held in Edinburgh, Scotland. The intent of the conference was to help Christian missionaries in their work of spreading the Gospel message of Jesus. Differences in doctrine and methodology among the churches involved were proving to be barriers, causing confusion among those to whom the missionaries addressed the Gospel. Therefore, with good intent, the World Council of Churches was formed. It opened a can of worms, the like of which the Christian Church had not seen since the Reformation of the 16th century and beyond.

Centuries before, as a result of the Council of Nicaea II in 787, the Eastern Orthodox Church which is comprised of national churches of the eastern Mediterranean and eastern Europe, split from the Church of Rome. This split initially came because of controversy between Constantinople and Rome over the use of icons, images representing Christ and the saints. The Orthodox Church at the Council of Nicaea II maintained that icons were to be venerated by the faithful, but not worshiped. The Roman Papacy disagreed, so even before the Reformation there was schism in the Christian Church. The major fracture between Constantinople and Rome came over authority. Rome claimed that its bishop was the rightful successor of Peter and could define and promulgate dogma, teachings. Constantinople objected because they claimed all right-teaching bishops were successors of Peter and, through episcopal councils, had the authority for proclaiming and defining dogma. East is east and west is west and authority to promulgate and define dogma or doctrine still remains to this day the major hurdle to ecumenical unity.

The Reformation produced Protestantism, a theological revolt against the authority of Rome which was centered in the Pope. Catholicism and Protestantism have been in theological opposition and debate over Christian doctrine ever since. The third party to the debate is the Eastern Orthodox Church. The theological differences were not limited to debate and opposition among the three church bodies. Within Protestantism, theological differences in doctrine mushroomed among the various churches. That is why you will see in some towns and cities in America a Catholic church on one corner of the street, a Methodist church on the opposite corner, flanked by a Congregational or a Presbyterian church on the other corners, with a Greek Orthodox church around the corner. "Church rows" are not uncommon in America.

Getting back to the can of worms, what was it that the World Council of Churches was promoting? From any reading of its motives, it is most evident that the Council was more interested and concerned with social action, with a smoke screen of attempting to spread the Christian message in accord with social action. Their intent of promoting social justice and world peace was blended with emphasis upon tolerance of accommodation for varying doctrines concerning which there was no consensus. Tolerance, here, means there is no right nor wrong. When applied to Christian theology it means surrender, the surrender of doctrine, because tolerated diversity of doctrine becomes the "capitulated" absolute. Christian spirituality is ignored, bypassed, as that would entail a doctrinal stand for the absolutes of God which are contained in His Word in Holy Scripture. And that would be ecumenical sinfulness. The bonding element of unity in diversity, colored by accommodating tolerance, would melt faster than a snowball in Florida in July.

Tolerance is not an attribute of God. He is a God of absolutes as Holy Scripture attests. His authority is supreme. Within the ecumenical movement, however, the absolutes of God contained in Holy Scripture are pushed aside. Doctrinal differences among the member churches are soft-peddled and placed

175

in the background because they are viewed as possible divisive elements of strife and disagreement. This is the offensive can of worms. Without a shadow of doubt, the churches that comprise the World Council of Churches, some three hundred and thirty churches in more than one hundred countries and territories, are markedly influenced by doctrinal toleration and accommodation. A neutral and non-threatening theology of accommodation rules the roost in ecumenism and it is by design, not accident.

John Macquarrie aptly diagnoses the dangers inherent in ecumenism:

> . . . there are many dangers in ecumenism, and these are enhanced by the indiscriminate enthusiasm which it seems to engender. On the one hand, there is the danger of submerging legitimate differences, and thereby impoverishing the body which is enriched and strengthened by these differences. In spite of the protestations to the contrary, most schemes of union put forward seem to aim (perhaps inevitably) at the greatest measure of uniformity and compromise, based on the lowest common denominator of the various groups involved, or sometimes on the attempt to lump together in an incongruous mass different traditions of belief and practice. A nondescript church of this kind would probably turn out to be weaker than a group of

churches expressing the Christian faith in its authentic diversity.[1]

It is not that the World Council of Churches failed to consider the question of biblical authority as revealed in the Word of God. James Barr, a liberal English theologian, explains:

The World Council of Churches study on authority itself grew out of a previous study of the hermeneutical discussion (hermeneutics is the study of biblical interpretation— my insertion); that study seemed in its outcome to call for and lead naturally on to an exploration of biblical authority. More generally, the emphasis laid on the discussion of interpretative methods seemed to reduce the possibility of any simple reliance on the authority of the Bible. To put it at its simplest, if the Bible when interpreted in one way gave a quite different impression from the Bible when interpreted in another way, then the Bible in itself could hardly be taken as a decisive authority.[2]

The historical-critical method, as witnessed to by Barr, raises its head once more as the major reason for neutering the authority of God's Word. If scholars allied to The World Council of Churches are in opposition and in conflict with each other as to the question of biblical authority, then it can be surmised that biblical authority doesn't exist.

177

Barr adds this disturbing note to the theological discord created by the World Council of Churches in his 1973 observation:

> . . . in the recent World Council of Churches discussion the phrase 'Word of God' scarcely occurs at all, either in the preliminary study document or in the final report; . . .[3]

With the authority of the Word of God being ignored in the ecumenical movement and social action on the front burners of concern, it didn't take long before a theology known as liberation theology found a fertile home as the ecumenical movement zeroed in on this theology of world change. Issues of differences in biblical doctrine remained in the wine cellar, hopelessly fermenting, fearful that should the cork be popped the entire structure of ecumenism would lose its bubble and become tasteless. Therefore, it hooked onto liberation theology as its main theological horse to ride, in addition to its other concerns for world hunger, world peace, and the like.

Liberation theology exploded like a firecracker in the mid 20th century with a Marxist emphasis and is still high on the theological horizon. It attempts to couple theology, politics, and social action into one movement to liberate the poor and oppressed people of the world from domination, domination which liberationists claim is caused mainly by capitalism. Thomas C. Oden, Professor of Ethics and Theology at Drew University, Madison, New Jersey, makes the following observation about the World Council of Churches and its liberation theology which openly flows from its Geneva, Switzerland, headquarters:

> The WCC's (World Council of Churches—my insertion) offices were controlled for many years by leftist ideologies. By colluding with Marxist regimes, fixating on regulatory politics, fantasizing about various liberation theologies, fostering illusions about world anti-capitalistic revolutions, and advocating some forms of sexual liberation, the WCC has defined itself in ways that evangelicals (and good Orthodox and good Catholics) cannot in good conscience participate. Though many Marxist regimes have passed, the historical pro-Marxist flavor remains in much of the political and social interpretation that comes out of Geneva.[4]

The *Evangelical Dictionary of Theology* provides this insight:

> Liberation theologians agree with Marx's famous statement: "Hitherto philosophers have explained the world; our task is to change it." They argue that theologians are not meant to be theoreticians but practitioners engaged in the struggle to bring about society's transformation.[5]

The theology of liberation, however, does not flow only in one direction. It branches out into torrents of social protest as streams of action or "praxis" to confront oppression wherever oppression is perceived as an enemy of God. These many streams or torrents embodied in this praxis of rebellion against any and all types of oppression can be: African Liberation as seen in South Africa in the life and work of Nelson Mandella; Latin American Liberation, as seen in Gustavo Gutierrez of Peru, and from which many of the other streams obtained their steam; Black Liberation, as seen in the civil rights issues raised by Martin Luther King and others in the last half of the 20th and into the 21st centuries in America; Feminist Liberation; Gay Liberation; Palestinian Liberation; or any other movement against whatever is perceived as oppression.

It has exploded before our very eyes in America in the sexual realm of liberation where liberal clergy solemnize gay marriages and sanction homosexuality as a mere life-style, where fidelity in marriage is a non-issue, where liberal churches condone abortion as the woman's right of choice, where feminist liberation takes on the Fatherhood of God and attempts to reduce Him to Sophia, the image of Lady Wisdom. In "her" realm, poems of Jewish literature in Proverbs, Baruch, Sirach, and Wisdom portray divine wisdom personified as a woman.[6] Unseating God as

God Almighty with a "she almighty," freeing sex so that it has no bounds, condoning murder in abortion, and encouraging political as well as social revolution has been and are the "blessings" of the World Council of Churches, bequeathed in the Name of God. Can you detect any trace of Christian spirituality which flows from God's inerrant and infallible Word evidenced in these ideologies?

To see and understand how this could ever take place, Robert Benne, Professor of Religion at Roanoke College, Salem, Virginia gives a revealing clue. He describes a speech given by Robert McAfee Brown, a liberal advocate of liberation theology, at one of the meetings of the World Council of Churches in the mid 1970s:

> Brown has identified strongly with liberation theology, replete with its Marxist analysis of the relations of rich and poor, north and south, in the emerging modern world. At the World Council of Churches meeting in Africa in the mid-seventies, Brown refused to speak in English, the language of the capitalist oppressors of the Third World. He asserted that "the structures of our democratic society that benefit me here at home (the vote, the capitalist system, the police) often destroy others both at home and abroad." This systemic evil must be rejected and radically transformed toward socialism. The clues toward the direction we must move are in the liberation movements around

the world, such as those in Central and South America.[7]

Benne makes further comment concerning the rising tide of concern for social issues over religious or spiritual issues among "mainline" churches engaged in the ecumenical movement:

> Practically speaking, the central headquarters of the mainstream Protestant groups and their ecumenical agencies are absorbed in social ethics. A content analysis of their various communications would bear out an overwhelming commitment to ethical social concerns over specifically religious concerns.[8]

Benne follows with a quote from George A. Lindbeck regarding the recent trajectory or direction of the World Council of Churches.

> From the late 1960s on, the service of humanity, reconceived in liberationist and politically progressive terms, increasingly became the motor driving the ecumenical train. It now dominates the World Council agenda in the form of Justice, Peace, and the Integrity of Creation initiatives. However good these JPIC programs may be, they are more than questionable to the extent they become the goal and motive rather than the fruit and by-product of Christian life together. When it is work not worship that unites, human need rather than God's glory becomes central, and justification by service replaces justification by faith.[9]

What blatantly stands out in ecumenism of a liberal nature is the attempt to influence a sinful secular society through declarations of social injustice and peace which are as appealing as the liberal lifestyle it endorses. Liberal ecumenism has a faulty genesis or beginning. It emphasizes the disease of society in terms of poverty, political injustices, the selfish influence of foreign policy of imperialistic nations, sexual repression, and other social issues. All of these ills are mere symptoms of a much larger problem, human sin, which only God can address in both His Law and Gospel. By ignoring man's basic problem of sin, they attempt to bring correction through secular means such as discussions, statements of moral compromise, news releases, and other means of peaceful protest. This is like treating cancer topically with a salve.

Like a salve, it fails to penetrate where the disease emanates—in sinful human beings. Their remedy is not found in the clear teaching of Holy Scripture. Instead, they bring together, as in synthesis, various doctrines of the participating churches which have degrees of similarities of Christian truth which are not controversial. They claim that they agree on more doctrinal issues than they disagree, and thus establish a base for dealing with the world's ills. This alone, should raise a red flag of danger, especially as Barr noted that the phrase "Word of God" scarcely occurred at all in the preliminary study documents of the World Council of Churches.

How can there be unity in synthesis unless compromise becomes the way to unity? What is compromised? The answer is the authority of God in Holy Scripture. The secular freedom of redemption of the world takes precedence over the redemption of sinful man. Liberal ecumenists fail to understand that the redeemed of God through faith in Jesus Christ are God's agents for peace and for the abundant life here on earth, because the redeemed in Christ are empowered by God's Holy Spirit to do that which is the will of God as spelled out in His inerrant and infallible Word. God's love and compassion in human hearts has always provided blessings for the less fortunate. This is true Christian spirituality in action, the antithesis of liberal ecumenism.

What I am pointing to is authentic ecumenism which has unity in the authority of the God of Holy Scripture as opposed to a false ecumenism. False ecumenism is structured in a unity born of compromise as the *modus operandi* (a method of procedure) to combat and correct secular oppression and provide accommodation to be free from any restraints, even God's authority in His Word. It is an ecumenism built upon the instability of synthesis. When our Lord spoke the words which are written in John 17: 20,21, words with which this chapter began, He was pointing to the unity which comes through faith in Him, a blessed union of God and man—God's way. He was not intimating that unity can be achieved by synthesis.

Francis A. Schaeffer makes the point that Christian truth is founded upon the thesis-antithesis principle which always deals in absolutes, the absolutes of God which are the Word of God in both Law and Gospel. Thus, if God declares as His thesis that faith is a gift of His Holy Spirit through His Word, the antithesis would be that God does not work faith in man through His Word. Thesis and antithesis cannot stand together as comparable truth. They are opposites. Therefore, in establishing a synthesis where diverse positions are combined, the result must be a compromise of the former positions. So when the World Council of Churches attempts to find unity in diversity, actually, it gives credence to synthesis which negates the absolutes of God as truth. The foundation for the World Council of Churches rests on man's authority, not God's, even though it claims ties to the Christian Church.

George Wilhelm Hegel, the German philosopher of the late 18th and early 19th centuries, with his emphasis upon synthesis, continues to influence theology and the relationship of Christian denominations to each other. Francis A. Schaeffer commented on the synthesis that Hegel introduced which has brought relativism to the world's scene.

The result is that all possible particular positions
are indeed relativized. While it is an oversimpli-
fication of Hegel's complete position, this has led
to the idea that truth is to be sought in synthesis
rather than antithesis (that some things are true
and their opposite untrue), truth and moral
rightness will be found in the flow of history, a
synthesis of them . . . . Today not only in philosophy but in politics, government, and individual morality, our generation sees solutions in
terms of synthesis and not absolutes. When this
happens, truth, as people had always thought of
truth, has died.[10]

While the World Council of Churches has
been visible on the world scene, the National
Council of Churches of Christ in the USA has
been active in the American church arena. Comprised of 36 Protestant, Orthodox, and Anglican
communions which include 140,000 local congregations, and 50 million people in the United
States, their program emphasis, like the World
Council of Churches, is centered on peace and
justice.

At the 2003 Assembly of the Evangelical
Lutheran Church in America, ecumenism was highly
extolled. The Rev. Ishmeal Noko, general secretary
of the Lutheran World Federation, a partner of the
World Council of Churches and the National Council of Churches complemented the Assembly for
their emphasis on evangelism as an "opening up"
of ministry. Then, he quickly followed with the peace

and justice theme when he said: "You are opening up while the government of the U.S. is closing up. I have learned to make the distinction (between) the American people (and American churches) and the American government." Noko went on to say that Lutherans in America must commit to justice and a "prophetic voice" in the face of U.S. military power.[11] That the World Council of Churches and the National Council of Churches have a dim view of the United States of America is most evident. It is one of their dominant themes: "America the oppressor!"

The National Council of Churches has named three denominations as "nonconciliar churches," which means churches not in agreement with their theology of compromise and liberal agenda of postmodern relativism. They are: The Southern Baptist Convention, The Christian Reformed Church, and The Lutheran Church-Missouri Synod.[12] There are other "nonconciliar churches," but the NCC seems to have picked those three, thus limiting their recognition of opposition.

Thomas C. Reeves comments on a forty-five minute meeting that fifteen leaders of the National Council of Churches had with President Clinton in 1995.[13] The leaders praised his social policies and named him as "the guardian of the nation." They "laid hands" on Clinton and prayed that he would be strong in continuing welfare state spending against any action from congressional Republicans.

Reeves quotes a comment which came from syndi-
cated columnist and television commentator Cal
Thomas:

> Perhaps that's why so many mainline
> churches would be more properly labeled
> "sideline" churches. They, and others for
> whom politics and government have become
> the way of salvation, have squandered their
> moral power on a lesser and weaker king-
> dom that eventually will pass away and is
> incapable of changing people's hearts.[14]

What I have shown in this chapter is the false
presupposition of ecumenism which attempts to
make the salvation of the world of greater importance than the salvation of souls through
God's Means of Grace, His Word and Sacraments.
As such, liberal ecumenism ignores the basic essence of the Christian religion and its Christ-centered spirituality and is doomed to fail. Its hoped
for survival can be seen in the words of the Rev.
George Mastratonis of the Greek Orthodox Archdiocese of America, a member church of the National Council of Churches:

> By the end of the 15th century the movement
> (ecumenism—my insertion) began against the
> discrepancies of the current leaders of the West-
> ern Church, but it went far beyond the anticipa-
> tions of its leaders. Can we hope that at least by
> the close of the 20th century we will complete

the Hegelian trilogy of synthesis, i.e. the unity of all churches? For the Church of Christ was meant to be one.[15]

Like the words of a song: "Looking for love in all the wrong places," could this sentiment now apply to the World Council of Churches and The National Council of Churches? Certainly the words: "tolerance, compromise, unity in diversity via Hegelian synthesis" apply. False ecumenism will never bring peaceful reconciliation for the world through man's design and efforts. True ecumenism on the other hand holds fast to faith in the Lord Jesus Christ, a belief that comes through the Gospel, made alive by the Holy Spirit, wherein our gracious God has already effected reconciliation by Jesus Christ and not because of the mental and physical heat of the created.

NOTES

1. John Macquarrie, *Principles of Christian Theology*, 2nd ed., (New York: Charles Scribner's Sons, 1977), 403, 404

2. James Barr, op. cit., 8.

3. Ibid., 21.

4. Thomas C. Oden, "Whither Christian Unity?," in *Christianity Today, 5 Aug. 2002.*

5. Walter A. Elwell, ed., *Evangelical Dictionary of Theology,* (Grand Rapids: Baker Book House, 1984), 636.

6. Gail Ramshaw, *God beyond Gender,* (Minneapolis: Augsburg Fortress, 1995), 44.

7. Robert Benne, *The Paradoxical Vision: A Public Theology for the Twenty-first Century,* (Minneapolis: Fortress Press, 1995), 31.

8. Ibid., 100.

9. George A. Lindbeck, "Tilting in the Ecumenical Wars" in *Lutheran Forum* 26, no.4, (November 1992), 23.

10. Francis A. Schaeffer, *The God Who Is There,* (Downers Grove, Illinois: The InterVarsity Press, 1968), 14.

11. Evangelical Lutheran Church in America News Release of 14 August 2003.

12. See *www.cccusa.org*

13. Thomas C. Reeves, *The EMPTY CHURCH: The Suicide of Liberal Christianity,* (New York: The Free Press, 1996), 165.

14. *Milwaukee Journal Sentinel,* 10 December 1995.

15. Rev. John Reeves, "The Price of Ecumenism," from 1990–1996 Greek Orthodox Archdiocese of America, *www.goarch.org/en/ourfaith/articles/article7108.asp*

CHAPTER 7

A Public Theology?

I am the vine, you are the branches; he who abides in Me, and I in him, he bears much fruit; for apart from Me you can do nothing.

(John 15:5)

Variations on a theme by Jesus? You have read these variations in preceding chapters and perhaps you are wondering what next will come down the theological pike? It seems that the more books liberal theologians write, the more theories they posit as truth, the more they quote each other in endless backslapping, the more they agree and some times disagree with each other, the more the level of confusion and deception mounts for the people of God in Christian Churches. In confusion and deception, the world through its *god* has not only been knocking on the doors of Christian Churches

191

for entrance, it has been boldly merged in liberal fashion into their theology in a "not so silent merger." Not all Christian Churches have fallen for the confusion and deception, but enough of them have, to cause alarm.

One of the latest spin-offs of pluralism and ecumenicity is the call for a public theology. This call for a public theology is a trumpet call for a new basis of doing theology—the community of faith. It represents a major shift in authority, a common theme whenever dealing with theology. Instead of maintaining the foundational truth of God's Word as doctrinal authority, new corrective ideologies, masquerading as truth, are brought forward by liberal theologians as new gems which will make theology sparkle. In this theology, authority resides in the community of faith, an ecumenical smorgasbord with varying social objectives. Their aim: to bring justice to what they call an abusive, antiquated society ruled by conservative values, values appropriated from an archaic Scripture.

In Chapter 3, the subject of authority in terms of being objective or subjective was discussed. Darrell Jodock was pointed to as a theologian who wants the subjectivity of the community of faith to be the controlling authority over a revised Word of God in Scripture, a reinterpretation according to cultural needs. What Jodock and his theological associates fail to consider is the power of the Means of God's Grace to bring spiritual life to the people of God, His beloved Church.

A forceful example is in 1st Corinthians the 6th chapter where Paul points to the Christian community with all its sins and faults, and then reminds them that through the power of their Baptism these sins have been overcome. In the 11th verse he wrote:

> "And such were some of you; (meaning infested with the sins he listed in the first ten verses—my insertion) but you were washed, (meaning baptized—my insertion) but you were sanctified, but you were justified in the name of the Lord Jesus Christ, and in the Spirit of our God."

While Paul points here to the power of Baptism, The Lord's Supper cannot be overlooked, nor the Word of God which proclaims these New Testament Means of God's Grace, instituted by our Lord for abundant spirituality in the lives of His beloved who certainly live in community. They point to God's victory over sin which the "community of faith," as described by liberal theologians, has not accepted.

This is because public theology invents a new definition of sin. No longer is it personal sin, but the corporate social sin of an oppressive society. In that light, the cause of social illness is not recognized as coming from the sin of the individual person. Rather, Adam's placing of the blame on Eve for eating the forbidden fruit still continues *ad infinitum*, as mankind looks outward and not inward to access the blame. It is "others" who have caused the oppression. On the American scene today, the blame for much social illness has been placed upon white, Christian Europeans who built the original foundations of our nation. To say that our founding fathers and mothers of years gone by were without sin would be a lie. Yet, the nation they established had a responsible culture built upon Christian teachings. It wasn't a perfect nation, but one in which the God of Holy Scripture was in significant evidence. Another object of blame is seen in the "right-wing, bigoted Christians" of today who refuse to bow to the demands of tolerance for any and all theological or social theories which are proposed in the name of diversity and inclusiveness.

Since the beginning of the 20th century in America, conflicting social and theological ideologies, thought to be corrective measures, came to the fore in the form of opposition to the established culture. Robert Benne has aptly named them as *gender feminism, gay and lesbian liberation groups, multiculturalists,* and *ecological militants.*[1] A common thread in all of these is liberation theology which has created the stage for public theology. Feminists want freedom from what they perceive to be patriarchal oppression from men. Gays and lesbians want freedom from the heterosexism which the Bible condones in marriage. Multiculturalists want the end of oppression against minority cultures. Ecological militants want to end oppression against the earth and its environment. All of these movements have devotees among professors and students in liberal colleges and seminaries and their theological concerns seem to focus upon justice, the doing of justice, a common theme of public theology. Justification by faith as proclaimed in Galatians 2:16 and Ephesians 2:8 are soft peddled and ignored. Salvation takes on "in this world" subjectivity so that by confronting and addressing the oppressive and emergency needs of the culture, the community of faith claims true spirituality which can be labeled as "Christian."

Public theology is a popular subject among liberal theologians. They look for and investigate ways to inject their version of Christianity into a sin-sick society. Wanting to influence and thereby change what they perceive to be the downward trend of society and its culture, their means for doing so follows the historical-critical method. This method, as I have pointed out, attempts to correct and edify God's Word in Scripture. It is man editing and evaluating what God has decreed as His Word so that the result is a never-finished product, the supposed revelation of God as amended by man according to his theological presuppositions.

Ronald F. Thiemann, Dean and John Lord O'Brien Professor of Divinity from 1986 to 1998 at The Divinity School, Harvard University, Cambridge, Massachusetts, an advocate for public theology, gives a definition of public theology which, for the most part, would be in accord with the theology of his contemporary liberal theologians.

> The form of public theology I wish to defend in this volume takes its rise from the specific beliefs, rituals, and practices of the Christian community. Public theology is not a specialized discipline or a technical subspecies with a unique method of inquiry. Like all Christian theology, it is guided by the Anselmian credo "I believe in order that I may understand." Public theology is faith seeking to understand the relation between Christian convictions and the broader social and cultural context within which the Christian community lives.[2]

You will notice the authoritative place of the Christian community. In much of liberal theology, authority has been transferred from God's objective Word to the subjective community of faith, its specific beliefs, rituals, and practices. While reference is made to faith, it is a faith constructed by the community from its analysis and reinterpretation of Holy Scripture as it *struggles* with a contemporary culture. Faith then becomes a malleable product of man, capable of being altered or changed in the ongoing *struggle* of the community. The work of the Holy Spirit through God's inerrant and infallible Word is diminished or left out completely. Within contemporary liberal theology the word *struggle* appears time and time again as though the truth they seek is part of a birth labor they must endure to bring enlightenment and possible cultural salvation to society.

The Word of God is made to fit the cultural situation instead of the culture being changed by the power of God's Holy Spirit in and through God's inerrant and infallible Word. When God's Word is filtered through a theological consensus from the community it loses objectivity, as subjective and sinful man makes definitions of truth which compromise God's authority in Holy Scripture. It is synthesis all over again. Darrel Jodock, who advocates placing the community of faith as authority when dealing with Scripture, is in lock-step with Thiemann regarding the place of the community of faith and scriptural authority

No one who loves the Lord and His Word will ever dispute the blessings of responsible life in society for the well-being of all. It is joyous opportunity for service to mankind and to God. However, its genesis must always be seen as coming from God's Word and Sacraments to individuals through the power of the Holy Spirit. It is God-empowered, not community empowered. Please see the distinction I am making, because once God's objective truth in His Holy Word is in any way compromised, the door is open for the community of faith to endorse abortion as freedom of choice, sanction same-sex marriages and even perform them, and condone homosexuality and lesbianism as normal relationships.

Already we have seen elements of liberal churches in the name of the community of faith take such stands. There is no assurance that communities of faith will never turn out to be "loose cannons" upon the theological stage, bringing damage in the way of disobedience, instead of obedience to God's perfect revelation in His Son and in His Holy Word. The liberal media of press and television are continually bringing us stories of this disobedience which they seem to relish and condone. It makes good copy for a culture which is more inclined to read articles about filth than about wholesome life. Coupled with the cultural support from a liberal media and the influence of liberal clergy, in terms of the historical-critical method of biblical interpretation, it becomes most obvious that liberal denominations have joined forces with the *god of this world* in the abandonment of the absolutes of God in Holy Scripture.

These absolutes come in the form of Law and Gospel in Holy Scripture. For God's people, a balance between the two is essential. They cannot be separated, one from the other. The Law in Holy Scripture reveals God's absolutes for man's life. It plainly shows us our sin, our inability even by the sweat of our bodies and the determination of our minds, to meet the holiness that our God asks of us. The Law makes real to us our need for a savior. Our sin, our disobedience to our God, which is in Adam and Eve of the Genesis account, is your story and my story. No human being can run away from or escape the reality of original sin. All sin is self-centered, even in the demands and the cries of a new born baby.

God's good news, His Gospel in Jesus, on the other hand, proclaims what our God has done for sinners like you and me. In His death, Jesus destroyed the power of sin and death. To all who have been brought to faith in Him as Lord and Savior, by the power of the Holy Spirit, He has freely given salvation from sin and new life that is lived in and through Him. It is newness of life for those who are in Christ with the assurance of a life with Him that not even death can end. This is good news! This is Gospel which is God's love message in Jesus, revealed in the prophecy of the Old Testament and in the New Testament witness. It is imperative that this Gospel be seen in conjunction with the reality of the Law. Otherwise, we have a scripture that is not of God. All of God's revelation in His Word, Old and New Testaments, form the basis for Gospel.

Public theology, however, wants to concentrate upon Gospel to the exclusion of the Law which condemns sin. This is called "Gospel reductionism." Clearly and boldly, it is a theological attempt to elevate the Gospel, while at the same time, criticizing and undermining its scriptural foundation in God which contains both Law and Gospel. Since Holy Scripture contains both Law and Gospel, to concentrate upon Gospel and call it the exclusive norm for Christian doctrine is to deny the full picture of God's revelation in His Word. The same holds true for the Law. To preach and teach only the Law negates the Gospel of Jesus Christ. It is the authority of God in all of Holy Scripture that holds these two biblical doctrines in proper balance for the truth of Jesus Christ as Lord and Savior to be proclaimed.[3]

When public theology distorts the proper balance between Law and Gospel, new definitions are given to sin which are colored or shaded differently from the sin which is revealed in the Bible. Thiemann's view of sin is illustrative of the way public theology regards sin. He explains:

> We must exercise great care in interpreting the notion of sin in the New Testament. We have been influenced by centuries of interpretation

200

in which the concept of sin has become increasingly narrowed and personalized. We are apt to think of sin primarily in moral terms, as those acts of commission or omission by which we become guilty in the sight of God. The Gospel writers, however, have a much broader and more inclusive understanding of sin. For them a sinner is one who stands on the margins, one who is an outcast from the primary society, one who is vulnerable because of lack of health, or social standing, or economic status . . . . I realize that my suggestion that all these persons belong in the category "sinner" may be both surprising and controversial, but I believe a close reading of the Gospel narratives will confirm this interpretation. A sinner, in the Gospel texts, is one who has been rejected and marginalized, one who appears to be outside the protective care of God's covenant steadfast love.[4]

Public theology, as witnessed in these words, attempts to broaden the definition of sin. This is not uncommon among liberal theologians. Their base for defining sin many times lies in a changing culture. As culture changes, so does the definition. They tend to rely more upon psychology and sociology than theology which is grounded in the authority of the Word of God. Certainly, we can speak of a sinful society, a sinful world, but primarily sin resides in the individual, you and me. We cannot ignore what God caused the Psalmist to write in Psalm 51:4:

Against Thee, Thee only, I have sinned, And done what is evil in Thy sight, So that Thou art justified when Thou dost speak, And blameless when Thou dost judge.

While our sin can be directed against other humans, initially it is always against God that we sin. Scripture makes this truth most plain. Therefore, to see sinners as those who have been "rejected and marginalized" by society puts a different *spin* on sin. Public theology ignores the individuality of sin, the personal accountability of each one of us while highlighting the "rejected and marginalized" of society as the object of the Gospel. All of us, every human born to earth, stand in the light and truth of Law and Gospel, not simply as a community of faith, but as individuals who have been created by God and who are redeemed from sin and death by faith in Jesus Christ as our Lord and Savior. This is most certainly a gift of God.

True Christian theology and spirituality must always be seen in terms of the way in which our God deals with His people. It is in terms of the individual that God addresses His revelation in His inerrant and infallible Word and in His Living Word, Jesus Christ. Without it, theology is an ecclesiastical flag blowing in the wind, susceptible to the changing wind currents of the culture, such as gay rights, abortion, infanticide, euthanasia, and whatever other cultural winds blow across the theological tundra of social issues.

When social movements are in accord with God's Word, meaningful life for society can be realized and lived in responsible love to God's glory and the good of His beloved people. The full power of God's Grace is unleashed. It is Christian spirituality in action. However, the authority of the community of faith, an authority which is prone to reinterpret God's Word according to the prevailing culture, is not a theology that can be blessed by God. The authority is of God, not of the community!

NOTES

1. Robert Benne, op. cit., 35–37,
2. Ronald F. Thiemann, *Constructing a Public Theology*, (Louisville: Westminster/John Knox Press, 1991), 21.
3. See C.F.W. Walther, *God's No and God's Yes*, (St. Louis: Concordia Publishing House, 1973) for a more complete study regarding the proper distinction between Law and Gospel.
4. Ronald F. Thiemann, op. cit., 105, 106.

CHAPTER 8

God's Truth At the Scholars' Mercy

*See to it that no one takes you captive through phi-
losophy and empty deceptions, according to the traditions of men, according to the elementary
principles of the world, rather than according to
Christ.*

(Colossians 2:8)

Sixteen years after the Pilgrims landed in
Massachusetts, Harvard University was
founded at Cambridge. The year was
1636. The university was founded with one purpose in mind: to train a literate clergy.[1] The word
"Veritas" still upon the Harvard University seal
in Latin means divine truth. The motto at its
founding was officially: "For Christ and the
Church."[2] On the wall by the old iron gate at the
main entrance to the campus this inscription can
be seen:

After God had carried us safe to New England and we had builded our houses, provided necessaries for our livelihood, reared convenient places for God's worship and settled the civil government, one of the next things we longed for and looked after was to advance learning and perpetuate it to posterity, dreading to leave an illiterate ministry to the churches when our present ministers lie in the dust.[3]

The intent and purpose of America's first university was directed toward Jesus Christ and His Church, that future clergy trained in Christian faith, would carry on the truth of Christianity in their ministry. Commitment to Christian spirituality, life in Christ, was their objective.

In 1701, Yale College, later named Yale University was founded in Saybrook, Connecticut, and later moved to New Haven. The goal of Yale College, as defined by the founders, stated:

Every student shall consider the main end of his study to wit to know God in Jesus Christ and answerably to lead a Godly, sober life [4]

The educational intention of the college was spelled out in the Yale Charter of 1745:

Which has received the favorable benefactions of many liberal (generous) and piously disposed persons, and under the blessing of

206

Almighty God has trained up many worthy persons for the service of God in the state as well as in the church.[5]

The original purpose of the first universities in Europe and America was to faithfully serve God and man. The bedrock of their curriculums was God's Word in Holy Scripture. This was an undisputed reality. Like Harvard and Yale, the first 123 colleges and universities founded in America, sprung from Christian roots with the main purpose to train men of God to be pastors and teachers to serve God's people in both church and state. The spiritual side of life held top priority in the early years of America's history.

Then, something happened not only to Christian founded colleges and universities but to the theological seminaries as well. It was the 18th century Enlightenment impact of man's reason as the dominating force for scholarship, whether in sociology, anthropology, psychology, or theology. Instead of education having its base, its foundation, in the authority of God's Word, the enlightened scholars of reason using the authority of academic freedom rose to academic power; and education for education's sake became popularized, while Christian truth in academic disciplines was questioned and discarded. An example of this "enlightened" academic thinking comes from Philip Rieff, Professor of Sociology at the University of Pennsylvania. In the course of an

interview with *Insight* magazine, Professor Rieff
made the following quite clear:

> Students who arrive at universities rooted in
> a religious faith embedded by family, or who
> have a moral code they have adopted at their
> own choosing, are taught that the aim of edu-
> cation is to undermine these givens and show
> how inadequate they are.[6]

One scholar, who believes this radical change
in education had a jump start as World War II
was coming to an end, is George Marsden, Professor of History at the University of Notre Dame.
Marsden points to the Harvard Report of 1945,
General Education in a Free Society, written by some
of the best known scholars in America. In accentuating "General Education," they firmly rejected
religious based education, great books education,
education organized around contemporary problems, and education which flowed from the scientific method. In regard to the religious
implications of "General Education," Marsden
maintains:

> The Harvard reporters thus summarized the
> religious implications of one of the major
> curricular trends of the past half century. In
> effect they were recommending a liberal Prot-
> estantism with the explicit Christianity re-
> moved. They were affirming, as liberal
> Protestantism had done, the religious values
> of the best in Western culture itself. If the cul-

ture defined the highest ideals, then the specifically religious dimensions were expendable. Though the Harvard Report tended to emphasize the humanities rather than empirical social sciences, from a religious perspective the committee's position was similar to John Dewey's. If religion was valued primarily for its civilizing moral ideals, then one could identify those moral ideals and determine how to promote them without directly resorting to Christianity.[7]

David F. Wells sheds additional light on this predicament, this change in the base for education in colleges and universities as well as in seminaries. He writes:

The revolution in the university, the consequences of which are a fact of academic life today, occurred mainly in the period from 1870 to 1910, as Richard Hofstadter has noted. The Civil War eliminated all but 20% of the colleges that had existed in the first half of the century and in its wake a complete revamping of the system occurred. The major universities moved to emancipate themselves from denominational control and from the hold which religious interests had exercised over them. Increasingly, the model of the German university came to be accepted as normative for America. And in this model only two conditions were seen to be necessary for a university education: scholarship and freedom.[8]

Scholarship under the guise of academic freedom, the new absolutes for liberal higher education, provided the arena for reason to have its day in academia. This is not to say that reason must be excluded from education. Without it there can be no discipline of thought. It is when reason becomes the sole controlling factor for education that it runs amuck. Reason confines itself to the practical, the empirical, that which can only be ascertained as empirical truth, by experience or observation. This method has long been used in the colleges and universities of our nation and in Europe. Its foundation was established long ago by Descartes who attempted to find out what was reasonable in the realm of man's thinking and believing. If it could be employed in other disciplines, why not theology? In so doing, not only was God taken out of the educational disciplines named above, but the God of an inerrant and infallible Scripture also was taken out of theology.

There is no way that God and His revelation in Jesus can fit into the mold of academic freedom ruled by pure human reason and maintain its authority. This would mean that His Word in Scripture, His transcendent power in creation, and the sending of His Son as Lord and Savior would be at the mercy of human scholars. This is exactly what has taken place in liberal theology. It became the blueprint for the historical-critical method of biblical interpretation, which was explained in Chapter 2. Its impact on authority was explained in Chapter 3. Yet, this is what has sadly happened in the majority of the colleges and universities of America, as well as in liberal seminaries. What Rieff said in 1992, I experienced in 1951 when I entered the Lutheran Theological Seminary at Philadelphia. A professor told our class: "We are going to do away with your Sunday School faith and build you into a mature faith." Little did I know at that time what lay ahead. I later discovered it was the historical-critical method, a favorite weapon of the *god of this world*. I soon found that with God's authority questioned and discarded, He stood as an impotent target of liberal musing in theology and the other disciplines. The story of how I left The Lutheran Church in America which became The Evangelical Lutheran Church in America is described in my first book, *Blessing & Honor/Honor & Blessing*. Suffice it to say that our God is in the moving business by the power of His Holy Spirit.

In no way am I ruling out scholarly research into God's revelation in Holy Scripture. Such research is essential, but it must be research with the presupposition that the inerrant and infallible Word of God is being studied, a revelation from God to His beloved people. The Holy Spirit works faith in God's people through His Word. There are no academic means or standards by which faith can be measured or infused. Faith is a gift of God, not a commodity that can be purchased or manufactured apart from the Holy Spirit's working. Therefore, when theologians or scholars from other disciplines attempt to fit God and His revelation solely into the limits of empirical or scientific inquiry, they are attempting the impossible. God is greater than the working of man's mind. (See 1st Corinthians 1: 20–25.)

When theologians and other educators attempt to out-think God according to their empirical means based on observation and experimentation, while supported by academic freedom, theologies and theories crop up which are not in accord with God's revelation. Today, they are in great abundance. They stand left of center in the liberal fast-lane which has become the avenue of choice to lead college, university, and seminary students away from God.

The two conditions mentioned by Wells necessary for a university education, scholarship and freedom, has copiously flowed into liberal seminaries as well. What *brews* in liberal colleges and universities, *stews* in liberal seminaries as they feed off each other. Liberal education in a university or seminary setting always finds authority within its own pursuits of scholarship and freedom. Any revelation from God is viewed as intrusive interference.

Thus, on the campus of any liberal seminary today you will hear students discussing issues of pluralism, the many spectrums of liberation theology, ecumenism, feminist theology, evolution, and the like. These are the topics that are championed in their classrooms, topics that center around a liberal social agenda as though salvation from God is only realized here on earth with *enlightened* scholars leading the way.

Instead of preparing pastors to be trained in the truth of God's Word for eternity which certainly impacts upon Christian spirituality, life in Christ, they are caught up in "religious" training that has taken a left-hand turn in the direction of sociology and psychology in order to equip the laity for life in an ever-changing culture. Regarding that theological alteration, the Rev. David A. Gustafson, pastor of Peace Lutheran Church, Poplar, Wisconsin, wrote about The Evangelical Lutheran Church in America's failure to deal with seminary curricula:

> Over the years, requirement in the core disciplines of Bible, church history, and theology were reduced as sociological and psychological courses were added, either in the form of requirements or as electives. This can only result in seminary graduates having less knowledge of the Scriptures and the tradition (or confused) consciousness of what it

213

means to be a pastor. If the church does not deal with this matter, Lutheran identity will be threatened, and the ELCA will experience the theological erosion that is so characteristic of American Protestantism. [9]

This is not merely one denomination's educational emphasis. It extends to the curricula of liberal seminaries which influence their denominations. Thomas C. Reeves explains:

Seminaries are frequently the scenes of "pathbreaking" statements, publications, courses, and bizarre events designed to reveal the "latest breakthroughs" by their faculty (as though like scientists, they are continually bombarded by new information) and win denominational support for an assortment of liberal causes. Graduates often emerge with little faith in the integrity of Scripture, a minimal grasp of church history and orthodox theology, and armloads of politically correct positions on social and political issues. [10]

The Washington Times of 21 April 1994 revealed some interesting comments from liberal theologians and some Harvard University Divinity School students. Patricia Harris Thompsett, dean of the Episcopal Divinity School in Cambridge, Massachusetts, stated that the emphasis of the divinity school is feminist liberation theology. Thompsett said: "Certainly we do attract students who are left of center."[11] Barbara G. Wheeler, president of Auburn Theological Seminary in New York city, gave her interpretation of trends in theological education: "Gender studies, race studies, and deconstructionism are present to some extent at all the theological schools." [12] From one student at Harvard University Divinity School came this quote:

> Pluralism is the God at Harvard. The basic presumption is that Western religion is not good, and Christianity is the worst. The new slur, like being 'homophobic,' is being 'Christo-centric.'[13]

The description of a course which candidates for a Master's degree at Episcopal Divinity School, Cambridge, Massachusetts, are required to take, sheds light on their liberal theological emphasis.

> FTP 1010 Foundations for Theological Praxis (Praxis means action—my insertion.) "Foundations for Theological Praxis" is EDS's way of introducing all incoming Master's degree students to the understandings and commitments underlying the school's purpose statement "to form leaders of hope, courage, and vision" who "serve and advance God's mission of justice, compassion, and reconciliation." Reflecting on vocation both as personal and social call to transformation, participants in the course primarily focus on rac-

ism as one of the major manifestations of op-
pressions facing U.S. society and the church today and its connections to other forms of
injustice. In reflection and action students are
encouraged to engage their own context(s) addressing the ways their own social location
shapes their theological praxis in the struggle
for justice in the church and beyond.

The purpose of this course is to enable students to do theological reflection on religious
vocation from a liberative perspective; that
is, vocation both as the call to personal transformation and to action as God's agents of
change and transformation within human
society. This perspective on vocation is re-
flected in the School's commitment to the
education of religious leaders dedicated to the
eradication of all forms of oppression, and
equipped to live out their vocation in a climate of religious and cultural pluralism.[14]

Barbara G. Wheeler, mentioned above, gives
added definition to liberal theology which has
left God's Word in the dust as it deconstructs
the authority of that Word. Deconstuctionist art,
as explained in Chapter 3, and deconstruction
theology emerge from the same mold of incompleteness and imaginings, by-products of post-
modern relativism. Wheeler, in a speech at the
Covenant Network in Atlanta on 5 November
1999, quoted in brief portions due to the length
of the speech, reveals the way a liberal seminary

president thinks and influences students under her care.

> I have a practical problem. I joined the Presbyterian Church as an adult, in significant measure because I admired this denomination's theology of the church and its processes for making decisions. Today I find myself in strong disagreement with the Church about an important matter. How shall I conduct myself now that I think my denomination has taken the wrong side of an important issue?

> The particular matter about which I disagree with the Presbyterian Church is this. The denomination has declared that homosexual acts are invariably sinful. I think that homosexual acts are morally equivalent to heterosexual ones. In some circumstances, both may be deeply sinful. Under other conditions, both may be used in God's service.

> ... Through the whole history of God's dealings with us, God has exercised God's freedom to demolish categories we invent for our own convenience. I am convinced that God is doing this today, demolishing the categories we invent for our peace of mind, not God's glory. I want to testify here is that I did not learn about this deconstructive activity of God from a liberal political handbook. I learned it from the scripture that deconstructs me, freeing me, as Paul says, to delight in the law of God.[15]

If that kind of reasoning flows from God's Word, then I know there has been a "not so silent merger" of the world and its *god* with liberal seminaries which influence liberal denominations. This is one more example of how the historical-critical method of biblical interpretation attacks the very foundation of life in Christ, Christian spirituality, by bending and twisting God's Word to fit a liberal agenda.

Liberal theological absurdity continues. If you want to see how words bounce around in liberal theological seminaries, much like ping pong balls, consider these words of another Harvard Divinity School student:

> I learned word games. *Capitalism, patriarchy, Christianity, patriotism, America, tradition, Republican, hierarchy*—these bad words. *Feelings, liberation, oppression, victimization, conversations, dialogue, caucus,* and *empowerment* were good words.[16]

The liberal attack on Christianity and on America, sponsored by liberal seminaries, knows no boundaries. Every established entity, even our own country, is at the mercy of their liberal garbage. Whatever threatens their agenda must be attacked. Liberal theologians are among America's most vocal critics, even though they have been blessed by freedom at the cost of young Americans who died in the Revolutionary War, the Civil War, World Wars I and II, Korea, Vietnam, Desert

Storm, Operation Iraqi Freedom, and the continuing war on terrorism.

In State sponsored universities the separation of state and church is "religiously" observed. Courses on comparative religions are taught in a general way without getting too deep into specific doctrinal issues. Otherwise, secular educational neutrality concerning religion under the protective umbrella of diversity would be seriously compromised.

Abby Nye, a sophomore at a university in Indianapolis, Indiana, wrote an article for WORLD magazine which explained how to survive "orientation" at a secular university. She wrote:

> The first shocker was Freshman Orientation, which you should know right now is a terrible misnomer. The correct term would be Freshman Indoctrination. Many schools basically hold students hostage for three or four days and attempt to reprogram their brains on matters of moral relativism, tolerance, gay/lec blan/transgendered rights, postmodernism, and New Age spirituality. Orientation skits sent messages like, "it's okay to have premarital sex, just use a condom," "underage drinking is accepted (and expected), but if you have sex when you're drunk you have the right to press charges for rape," "homosexuality is normal, get

used to it." And that was all before the first day of class. [17]

Not even colleges and universities founded by Protestant denominations have escaped the secular-power emphasis of liberalism which has consumed state sponsored universities. Where liberalism has ruled supreme in denominations through their seminaries, it has also rushed headlong into their colleges and universities. As previously noted, it began in America prior to World War I with the dominance of secular thought which flowed from European universities and their *enlightened* faculties stressing scholarship and freedom. The attractiveness of the reason of man over revelation from God was too tempting for liberal educators to ignore. Diversity honored in tolerance has become their mantra. Intolerance of tolerance is the real evil.

St. Lawrence University in Canton, New York, is a typical example of how diversity has become embedded in the curriculum of liberal institutions of higher learning. A course is offered in their Cultural Encounter Program (note the emphasis on "culture") entitled: "Fundamentalism as Cultural Encounter." Heralded by *www.diversityweb.org,* is the following course description:

RELIGIOUS STUDIES 248N: FUNDAMENTAL-ISM AS CULTURAL ENCOUNTER

The word "fundamentalism" was coined in the United States in the early 20th century to describe a certain type of Christianity that was opposed to "modernism" in religion. It was opposed in particular, to Darwinian theories of evolution and favored literal reading of the Bible. In the 1950s the term became applied more broadly to apparently similar tendencies in other religious traditions, particularly Islam. Today it is used widely and often uncritically to identify movements among Hindus, Muslims, and Jews as well as Christians. It is often thought to overlap with religious nationalism or with religious enthusiasm generally. This seminar will test a recent hypothesis which suggests that fundamentalism is a particular, generic kind of religiousness that represents a "revolt against the modern age." This will involve two interrelated tasks: (1) exploring the usefulness of the concept "fundamentalism" as a comparative category and (2) becoming familiar with the dynamics of cultural and social change in a variety of settings, but not limited to, modern India, the Islamic world, and North America.

From the above quotation, it is plain to see that "fundamentalism" points to orthodox Christianity which is normed by God's Word in Holy Scripture. It represents a "revolt against the modern age." This is indicative of liberal education which has to take that position because its presuppositions are anchored in the dissolution of any and all kinds of absolutes. If absolutes stand, the absolutes of God, then diversity crumbles and dies. At the forefront of this movement with its cry for "diversity" is The Association of American Colleges and Universities (AAC&U), headquartered in Washington D.C. The major target on their horizon is Christian spirituality.

Diversity Web is sponsored by the AAC&U and it has the following as its "Welcome."

> Welcome to Diversity Web, the most comprehensive compendium of campus practices and resources about diversity in higher education that you can find anywhere. This site is designed to serve campus practitioners seeking to place diversity at the center of the academy's educational and social mission.

Lest you think that the AAC&U is a fly-by-night organization, please note that in October 2001, their Board of Directors approved a

> Presidents' Campaign for the Advancement of Liberal Learning (Presidents' CALL) . . . to educate the public—both within and outside of higher education—about the value of liberal education for all college students in the twenty-first century whatever their chosen field or vocation.[18]

222

By 31 October 2002, more than five hundred college and university presidents signed the CALL for the advancement of liberal education through diversity. If this isn't a threat to the Christian spirituality of our youth in such institutions of higher learning, I don't know what is! A spiritual war has been declared upon our youth. Christian pastors, you have a mission field that has become a theological, spiritual minefield! The spiritual lives of our youth are at stake. And this threat is not only among college and university youth as it has also descended into the entire public school educational system. The spiritual SARS virus abounds in liberal education.

Marshall Allen, in an article entitled "Speaking for Your Faith," details his experience as a Christian student in a hostile university setting where the world's real evil is portrayed as organized religion and Christianity. In the article, he refers to an e-mail sent to him by Amy Wells, a student at the University of Wisconsin. Amy considered her

> "Asian American Literature" class a form of sexual harassment. There she was instructed to read graphic depictions of homosexual relationships and references to bestiality and pedophilia. The class had to watch movies too—including films that depicted homosexual sex and children being molested. The class made her "sad, anxious and pessimistic," Wells said. At the end of

the class, the students applauded the professor. "When the class applauded this teacher I felt shocked, alienated and depressed. It made me see how weird we Christians really are."

Allen does more than describe assaults against Christianity. He presents a workable challenge to Christian students engulfed in educational diversity. He further writes:

It is also important to befriend students from diverse backgrounds. It's tempting for Christians to band together on a secular campus, circling their wagons in a hostile environment. But genuine friendships are a great way to communicate our faith to others, because they don't just have to hear us talk about faith—they can experience our Christian life through us. Friendships also allow us to share the Christian point of view on destructive philosophies espoused in the classroom. Sharing our faith is important because so many of our friends are genuinely seeking spiritual truth. If we withhold it from them, we're not being true to ourselves or to them. [19]

Allen also points out the futility of challenging professors in the classroom where they will not relinquish their positions of authority. He contends it is more meaningful to confront them outside the classroom. They may not change their positions, but they have heard the Christian witness. Allen's point is that God is not finished with them.

Here in America, prior to and shortly after World War II, parents who sent their children to church related colleges and universities believed their children would receive an education that was grounded and supported in biblical truth. This was also true of the many veteran service men and women who were able to attend college under the G.I. Bill. Some chose to attend church related institutions of higher learning. Many had come from the horrors of war and were looking for spiritual truth in a world gone mad. A great number of veterans chose church related colleges and universities expecting a Christian education.

After that war, this expectation dimmed. Many of these Christian colleges and universities gradually fell under the control of secular administrators and professors who challenged the truth of God's revelation in Holy Scripture, following so it seems, the influence of the Harvard Report of 1945. Doubt as to Holy Scripture's authority was raised. It was cast into the category of "out of date" literature, not relevant for changing times. The historical-critical method, the main contributor in this attack upon Scripture, helped to alter the foundation for the teaching of the other academic disciplines. God and His perfect revelation of the Lordship of Jesus for all of life was minimized to the degree that Christianity and the other academic disciplines were like oil and water. They did not mix. The secularization of Christian colleges and universities raises the question of their survivability as Christian institutions. How do they differ from other colleges and universities which were never founded upon Christian principles?

Reeves points to the scholarship of Robert Lynn Wood concerning the survival of Protestant colleges. Influenced by Wood, he writes:

> Colleges and universities founded by mainline churches have in large part become secular, largely secular, or obscure. In 1990, the presidents of 69 Presbyterian colleges and universities issued a manifesto that discussed "the demise of Protestant hegemony (predominant influence—my insertion), the decline of mainline churches and the importance of denominationalism" and concluded that "The Presbyterian Church could be close to the point where its involvement in higher education might be lost forever.[20]

Marsden gives a pertinent example when he points to Duke University, with supposed ties to The United Methodist Church, a "mainline" denomination. On a 1924 plaque at the center of West Campus are these words of mission statement: "The aims of Duke University are to assert faith in the eternal union of knowledge and religion

226

set forth in the teachings and character of Jesus Christ, the Son of God." However, in 1988, Duke University stated its goals as follows:

> Duke University shall endeavor to accomplish these missions: to educate students for meaningful, ethical and productive lives, to discover and interpret significant new knowledge; to promote the spirit of free inquiry on moral and intellectual issues; to foster the exchange of ideas and information within and across traditional disciplinary boundaries; to enrich the lives of the residents of our region by producing a variety of educational, medical, cultural and recreational services; and to support diversity and mutual tolerance throughout the university.

Included in that statement was the following caveat: "Duke cherishes its historic ties with the United Methodist Church and the religious faith of its founders, while remaining non-sectarian."[21] Marsden observes: "This delicately stated formulation suggests that, so far as the university's purposes are concerned, Christianity (not mentioned by name) is a thing of the past; yet at the same time the church connection is to be revered."[22] Duke University is typical of liberal church related colleges that have abandoned Christianity in their academic pursuits.

Robert McAfee Brown reflects upon the transition of higher education from its base in Christian truth to its new underpinnings: pluralistic culture.

227

We can thus no longer speak of a Christian culture, or even a Protestant culture; we must speak of a pluralistic culture.

What does this mean for education? It means, quite simply, that the term "university" is becoming more and more a misnomer. There was a time, indeed, when a university was just that, a "universitas," a place where there was sung "one song," where there was a single overarching frame of reference in the light of which the pursuit and the transmission of knowledge was effected. But this can no longer be presupposed in the modern university in the modern pluralistic culture. The university has become a "multiversity," in which a variety of songs are sung, in which a variety of pursuits are conducted in a variety of ways, and in which a single overarching frame of reference is no longer discernable.[23]

One beautiful fall day in the early 1970s I found the impact of Brown's words embedded in my alma mater. Barbe and I had returned to Allentown, Pennsylvania, to visit some dear friends and to watch the Muhlenberg "Mules" play Franklin and Marshall College in football. I asked Wally, our host, if we might leave for the game an hour early so we could stroll around the campus.

The first place we visited was the magnificent Gothic Chapel that had been part of my spiritual growth. As I entered the nave from the narthex, some blue lights to my left grabbed my attention. They were votive candles brightly burning below an effeminate mosaic picture of Jesus. It was a depiction of my Savior that was weird and foreign to me. I walked toward this display at the back corner of the chapel and there I read these words: "The Androgynous Jesus." I knew what the word "androgynous" meant. It signifies a person who has the characteristics of both male and female. I was horrified that in this chapel where God's Word had been proclaimed as truth, stood this feminist assertion which attempted to reconstruct or deconstruct God's truth about His Son, Who was not His "daughter." This, I must believe, was not a student prank or insistence, but a theological expression that came from within the college and its chaplain who at that time was an "enlightened" woman. "Multiversity" had found a home.

In 1947 when I entered Muhlenberg College, its seal had the Latin words "Trinitati Sanctissimae," Trinity Most Holy, at the top of the seal. The interior section was ringed with a banner containing the Latin words "Crux et Patria Calamus." These Latin words are translated as "Cross and Native Land or County" followed by the word for "a reed pen," a writing instrument. At the heart of the seal was the Bible, with the Latin word "Biblia" as the base with the cross and an America eagle perched upon the Bible, holding the banner in its mouth. While the seal remains unchanged, the theology practiced there has been altered to fit modern theological thought, as have most liberal Christian colleges and universities. In Chapter 3, Darrell Jodock, a former faculty member of Muhlenberg College was quoted in regard to the authority and reinterpretation of Holy Scripture for Christians today. The college still has a relationship with the Evangelical Lutheran Church in America, a church that has fully embraced the historical-critical method.

In 1999 I wrote to the Alumni Office at Muhlenberg College inquiring about the number of pre-theological students who were enrolled in present year group classes. On 10 February 1999 I received word that in the Classes of 1999 and 2000 which totaled 1074 students, only 9 students were pre-theological students, less than 1% in both classes. In my Class of 1951 with 222 students, we had 18 pre-theological students, almost 8%. The decline, I believe, can be attributed to the influence of the historical-critical method of biblical interpretation, a theological virus that has infected many liberal Christian colleges in the last half century.

Peter Bredlau, chaplain at the college, writes the following about diversity at Muhlenberg:

> Some suggest that there are no Lutherans at Muhlenberg! The numbers aren't what they used to be, but times and connections have changed.

Muhlenberg College is growing where it is planted and the Northeastern soil is diverse—radically, ethnically, economically, and religiously. That diversity should be a cause for celebration! When students leave Muhlenberg College, they enter a world that includes people from a wide variety of faith traditions. Preparing students to learn, to live and to work with difference, is one of our primary calls. We do it well. More than 1/3 of our students have a Roman Catholic background, between 1/5 and 1/4 of our students consider themselves Protestant Christian, Jewish, or our fastest growing group—unaffiliated. A smaller number of students are Muslim, Hindu, Buddhist, or other faith traditions. Because of the beauty of difference, our students, faculty and staff are immersed in a living laboratory that raises questions about religious diversity every day.[24]

Certainly America is a nation of diversity, but when a Christian college mirrors the world and celebrates its diversity, the doors are wide open for the world to become the controlling influence, through the schemes of its *god*. This is more than an unintended consequence. It is liberal theological seduction which has allegiance with the authority of an *ever changing* world rather than with the true authority of a *never changing* God, authority in His Holy Word to bless, lead and educate.

That this consequence was more than unintended is seen in what occurred at the 1998 graduation ceremonies at Muhlenberg College. The Episcopal Bishop of Newark, New Jersey, John Shelby Spong, was welcomed to the campus and awarded the degree of Doctor of Humane Letters, an honorary degree. Spong is an ultra liberal theologian, a popular writer whom the media spotlights because of his abandonment of biblical Christianity in a heretical way. Spong is well known to champion the cause for homosexuality and lesbianism, as he denies the validity and truth of Scripture. As a gay rights advocate he maintaines that St. Paul was nothing more than a repressed and frustrated homosexual.[25]

In 1994 Spong wrote:

If the resurrection of Jesus cannot be believed except by assenting to the fantastic descriptions included in the Gospels, then Christianity is doomed. For that view of resurrection is not believable, and if that is all there is, then Christianity, which depends upon the truth and authenticity of Jesus' resurrection, also is not believable.[26]

Spong's liberal, anti-Christian, pro-gay positions were well known in the theological world of academia. Yet, here in a supposedly Christian church related college was the honoring of one who dishonors the revelation of God in His Holy Word. The *god of this world* certainly had a hand in this action by way of the liberal presuppositions of those who

232

define the tone and tenor of education at Muhlenberg College. A portion of the citation given to Spong states:

> As Bishop of the Episcopal Diocese of Newark, your dedication to the church and your leadership in spreading the good word of Christianity have provided many with renewed devotion to their beliefs.

> In your 22 years of ministry, you have been a faithful servant, an enlightened author and an inspirational messenger of the church's teachings. An esteemed theologian and respected leader, you have provided spiritual guidance and have encouraged intelligent questioning and dialogue about the need for change within the Christian community. Your forthright approach has earned you both praise and criticism; yet, you have achieved success in fostering open communication among those who recognize the importance of Christianity in today's dynamic world.

> It is for this, your selfless commitment to God, the Episcopal Church and your congregations as well as your courage in expressing your convictions that we salute you.[27]

Had Spong been invited to a dialog on campus with those who would have disagreed with his liberal views, that would have been a different matter. To confer on him an honorary degree is a statement of complete agreement with his anti-Christian, heretical views. This is another example of "the not so silent merger" of the world with the church. It points to a new direction being taken in liberal higher education. What this does to Christian students and their spirituality as they come under this influence of a *different* religiosity, which by no standard whatsoever can be called "Christian," is devastating to their spiritual lives.

Calvin College in Grand Rapids, Michigan is one of the most highly regarded liberal arts colleges in America. It, too, has fallen under the spell of biblical abandonment. Founded in 1876 in a one room schoolhouse by the Christian Reformed Church for the training of its pastors, Lynn Vincent reports how its biblical foundations have been lost:

> ... Calvin's commitment to traditional Reformed teaching seems to be fraying at the edges: On theology-rooted issues such as origins (evolution—my insertion), feminist theology, and homosexuality, the school's policy and curricula have drifted from Scripture .... Pro-homosexuality material has crept into Calvin's curriculum. The school offers a gender-studies minor, with a video library that includes *Pink Triangles*, a documentary that criticizes 'homophobic attitudes and the enforcement of rigid sex roles in our culture.' Meanwhile, the minor's program's official website links to such groups as the Gay, Les-

bian, Straight Educational Network, the group that brought us 'Fistgate,' the infamous state-funded workshop in Massachusetts that included gay-sex how-to presentations for high-school students.[28]

Diversity may be acceptable for a nation, but deadly when it becomes the motivation and platform for education in Christian colleges and universities as it seeks to erase, remove, biblical foundations. It is not only an open betrayal of our Lord God, but a subtle, devastating spiritual betrayal to students who believe they are entering a Christian college or university for a Christian related education. It is incumbent upon Christian parents to investigate the Christian college, university, or seminary where their child or children want to enroll for higher education. All the years of precious Christian training spent in love can be seriously challenged and damaged.

Please note that I am not maintaining that all the disciplines of higher education should be constructed to resemble theological seminaries. What I am pointing to is the positive affirmation of God and His Word in the life of students in church related institutions of higher learning. If Christian colleges and universities are to be what they were established to be, their academic spine must be strong in witnessing to Jesus as Lord. Education, if it is to be Christ related, must strengthen and undergird the spiritual side of life to equip young lives to live productive, spiritual lives in a secular culture. Mind and body are also intertwined with the spirit as it is the entire spectrum of a person's life which must be the loving objective of Christian education.

The *god of this world* will always look for the weakest link of Christian education to make another one of his beachheads. He has found it and is skillfully using it today in liberal Christian colleges and universities that follow their pied pipers of liberal denominational influence. These institutions then graduate and send out into secular society the beloved of God who have been morally and spiritually ill-equipped to handle the pressures and temptations of life in a secular culture. They become casualties of that culture to the great delight of the *god of this world*. That this has also occurred in state sponsored universities is a foregone conclusion, no less a tragedy. That it has occurred in liberal church related colleges and universities is spiritual betrayal with untold tragic consequences.

From my two tours in Vietnam as a Navy chaplain, one with the Navy and the other, a year long tour with the 11th Marine Regiment in combat, I know something about casualties. The casualties of war can be counted, a number assigned, but in terms of the *lost* and *wounded* in the liberal churches of America, it is a number known only to God. How God's tears must flow! He gave to all His beloved

236

His precious Word which is His love message in Jesus. If the shepherds who were called to lead and teach the sheep in Christian colleges and churches, fail to do so, placing reason before revelation via academic freedom, standing as judges over God's Word, they and their educational mentors will be held accountable by God. Our Lord makes this plain in the Gospels of Matthew, Mark, and Luke. Luke 17:1, 2 clearly states:

> And He said to His disciples, "It is inevitable that stumbling blocks should come, but woe to him through whom they come!
>
> It would be better for him if a millstone were hung around his neck and he were thrown into the sea, than that he should cause one of these little ones to stumble."

Not too many lay people know the etymology or the source of the noun "seminary." It comes from Middle English roots and means a seed bed or a nursery. Have you ever thought of seminaries in those terms? That is what they are and for all intents and purposes, colleges and universities are also "seed beds." What do seeds produce? They produce fruit, products either fit for the market or for the garbage heap. We know most plainly that good spiritual seeds produce good spiritual fruit as our Lord explains in the Parable of the Sower in Luke's 8th chapter. There, God's Word is compared to seed in good ground, the ground prepared by God, not by man. In verse 15 of that chapter, Jesus explains: "And the *seed* in the good ground, these are the ones who have heard the word in an honest and good heart, and hold fast, and bear fruit with perseverance."

What about seed that is sown in ground dominated by religious liberalism? An honest appraisal was given by Dr. David Carlson in an interview with Thomas Reeves.

> Dr. David Carlson, a one-time resistance leader in the Evangelical Lutheran Church in America, thinks that the widespread ignorance of Scripture, theology, and history contributes greatly to liberal dominance. Appeals to anything beyond current events often get nowhere with church members, he says, for people no longer know what you are talking about. "We've lost the Scriptural and doctrinal underpinnings."[29]

The theological and spiritual pipeline from seminary to the congregation flows in a direct line. It always has and always will. While the proof of the pudding is in the eating, the proof of the spiritual condition of congregations will be in the theology taught and preached. Either the spiritual lives of God's people will be nourished by God's Means of Grace, or variations on a theme in concert with the prevailing culture will be offered instead. Carlson underscores the second theological diet to the spiritual detriment of God's beloved. This is

238

nothing more than theological tomfoolery because the spiritual plays second fiddle to cultural variations on a theme by the *god of this world.*

Lest you think that theological tomfoolery is consigned to liberal Protestant seminaries, consider what Michael S. Rose writes concerning what has been occurring in recent years in liberal Roman Catholic seminaries. His words echo rebellion against the doctrine of his church as liberal theological faculties attempt to change the Roman Catholic Church in America in protest against the orthodoxy of Roman Catholic doctrine they consider to be outdated.

> All too often seminary faculty members use textbooks written by noted dissenters from Catholic teaching—for example, theologians Richard McBrien, Edward Schillebeeckx, Hans Kung, and Charles Curran—and they parrot the dogmas of Catholic dissent: that the Bible is not to be taken seriously because it is "culture bound"; one religion is as good as the next; the pope is not infallible; the magisterium is authoritatively abusive; the Real Presence of Christ in the Eucharist is just old pre-Vatican II myth; Christ was not really divine; God is feminine; Mass is simply a meal in which we should eat bread that "looks like real bread"; women should be ordained priests in the name of equality; homosexuality is normal; and contraception is morally acceptable.[30]

Sound familiar? The *god of this world* doesn't play favorites, unless they are in his employ. While orthodox Protestants may disagree with aspects of Roman Catholic dogma, as did the Reformers of the 16th century, the pattern of assault is the same: any authority attributed to God, His Word, and His Body, the Church, must be changed or altered, according to the prevailing liberal ecclesiastical and societal currents.

As this chapter began, it was noted that education in the early American seminaries, colleges, and universities had a scriptural foundation that honored our God. The absolutes of God in His Word were upheld without question. The spiritual side of life influenced all of life.

David F. Wells comments upon the then and now.

The norms, values, and principles that were once seen to be enduring absolutes, along with the knowledge of God in which they were grounded, now seem quite uncertain and perishable, anything but the markers that once provided safe moral passage through life. The world that God was believed to have created then was easy to understand; the world we have created out of our technological and marketing genius is dark and confusing—although the thing about it is quite certain: if God could be blamed for that world (and he was), he cannot be blamed for this one, since everyone from the most muddle-headed secularists to the most intractable Marxists insist that he has had nothing to do with it. We have created it and we must stand judged by our creation. [31]

A troubling feature is that God's people in liberal churches, for the most part, are unaware of the genesis of the confusing darkness. They are led to believe that the Bible is not trustworthy, that pluralism is the only way for theology to go, that homosexuality and lesbianism are normal, that pro-choice for the right of abortion is the right choice, and justice is the Christian Church's main concern, to name a few of the conclusions of liberal Christianity, a Christianity that bears little if any semblance to the Christianity proclaimed and normed in Holy Scripture. They are taught by their denominational leaders and pastors that abnormal is normal. All the above are liberal theological aberrations embedded in liberal education from which God and His Word have been excluded.

Over a century ago in 1887, Dr. Archibald Alexander Hodge, son of Dr. Charles Hodge, both respected Presbyterian evangelical theologians at Princeton Seminary before liberalism took root in that institution, made a prediction which is now in full bloom in the secular education of the 21st century. He looked into the future of national higher education, an education separated from the roots of Christianity, the roots that had established our colleges, universities, and seminaries in our early American history. This was his prediction:

> I am as sure as I am of Christ's reign that a comprehensive and centralized system of national education, separated from religion, as is now commonly proposed, will prove the most appalling engineer for the propagation of anti-Christian and atheistic unbelief, and of anti-social nihilistic ethics, individual, social and political, which this sin-rent world has ever seen.[32]

Only the socially and theologically blind will dispute Dr. Hodge's forecast. It has come true. On the political front, as predicted above, many liberal educators in our colleges and universities have great disdain and even open hostility toward America and its leaders. Patriotism to them is a dirty word. One blatant example came as our nation joined in a coalition of nations to topple the horrific regime in Iraq. A Columbia University professor, Nicholas De Genova, told an anti-war rally that he would like to see "a million Mogadishus"—pointing to the tragedy where eighteen American soldiers were killed in 1993 in Somalia.[33] At Princeton University is an ethics professor by the name of Peter Singer who advocates infanticide, the killing of the handicapped, animal-human sex, and is an evolution supporter of Darwin.[34] And parents keep sending their impressionable youth to institutions of higher learning where such treasonable garbage is dumped as truth upon their inquiring minds and hearts.

As documented in this work, the theological, the spiritual life of America has also been negatively impacted by liberal education that has no anchor in Christian truth as revealed by God in His Word. A spiritual holocaust has come upon us. Human reason has been elevated above God's revelation as truth for a post-modern society.

There can be no doubt that America lives in a *liberally educated* and *Satan oriented* culture to the detriment of its children, the prime target of the *god of this world*. Though post-modern youth have been raised in Christian homes, the relativistic world tempts, the liberal church deceives, and liberal education corrupts until many of God's beloved children have no moorings, no spiritual foundation in the authority of God's Word. They flail about ready to take on any fad of a decadent culture until in appearance, language, attitude, and behavior they mirror a world void of God's authority, a world of their own belly button authority. God becomes merely a word before "dam."

The wonderful exceptions are families where the exclusive authority of God's Word is honored for all of life. Then, parents are selective, not inclusive. They see themselves as the prime theological teachers of their children, as Martin Luther maintained,

243

who are supported and spiritually nourished in churches where God's Word is held as truth and by institutions of higher learning where education is conditioned by Christian spirituality anchored in the Means of God's Grace.

This is not an impossible dream. I have seen the reality of this Christian witness explode in the lives of youth to God's glory. God's Holy Word is true! Its spiritual power, as a gift from God, cannot be denied. It is real life in Jesus as Lord through the working of God's Holy Spirit in both Word and Sacraments. Redeemed lives know this power and are always overjoyed when others in the world come to new life in Jesus as Lord and Savior. This truth must be at the heart of education in all Christian colleges, universities, and seminaries, but is it? From what you have read in this chapter, you make the decision. As Bill O'Reilly states on his Fox News program: "We report; you decide."

A new chapter in education will be written by our God. It will embrace theology, centered in God's inerrant and infallible Word. All academic disciplines which He has enabled to be established will praise Him. Those who stubbornly try to maintain their liberal status will fall on their swords of unbridled reason and rebellion. God's truth will prevail! It will not remain at the mercy of liberal scholars—nor will His beloved! In God's perfect timing, it will be so!

NOTES

1. Tim La Haye, *Faith of Our Founding Fathers*, (Brentwood, Tennessee: Wolgemuth and Hyatt, Inc.,1987), 32.
2. Stephen K. McDowell and Mark A.Beliles, *America's Providential History*, (Charlottesville: Providence Press, 1988), 91.
3. Tim La Haye, op.cit.,75.
4. William C. Ringenberg, *The Christian College: A History of Protestant Higher Education in America*, (Grand Rapids: William B. Eerdmans Publishing Company, 1984), 38.
5. Quoted in Richard Hofstader and William Smith, eds., *American Higher Education: A Documentary History*, (Chicago: University of Chicago Press, 1961), 49.
6. *Insight*, 23 March 1992, 36.
7. George M. Marsden, *The Soul Of The American University*, (New York Oxford: Oxford University Press, 1994), 388, 389.
8. David F. Wells, "Word and World," in *Evangelical Affirmations*, Kenneth S. Kantzer and Carl F. Henry, eds. (Grand Rapids: Zondervan Publishing House, 1990), 167, 168.
9. David A. Gustafson, "The ElCA: Its Past, Present, and Future," LOGIA, vol.V, no. 2, (Plymouth, Minnesota: Eastertide, 1996), see 41–44.
10. Thomas C. Reeves, *The EMPTY CHURCH: The Suicide of Liberal Christianity*,

(New York: The Free Press, 1996), 16.

11. *Washington Times,* 21 April, 1994.

12. Ibid.

13. Ibid.

14. The web. *www.episdivschool.org.* 2001.

15. The web. *www.auburnsem.org.* 2001.

16. *Washington Times,* op.cit.

17. Abby Nye, 'Have no fear of them,' WORLD, 23 August 2003, 21.

18. See *www.aacu-edu.org*

19. Marshall Allen, "Speaking for Your Faith," in 27 Feb. 2003 edition of www.boundless. org.

20. Thomas C. Reeves, op.cit., 16.

21. *Crossing Boundaries: Interdisciplinary Planning for the Nineties*: Duke University Self-Study (1998), 3–4.

22. Marsden, op.cit. 421.

23. Robert McAfee Brown, in *Theology and Education in the Scope of Theology,* ed. Daniel T. Jenkins. (Cleveland and New York: The World Publishing Company, 1965), 229, 230.

24. Peter Bredlau, "Keeping the faith," in *Muhlenberg,* vol.12, no. 1, 2001, 32.

25. John Shelby Spong, *Rescuing the Bible from Fundamentalism: A Bishop Rethinks the Meaning of Scripture,* (San Francisco: Harper-Collins,1991) see 116–119.

26. John Shelby Spong, *Resurrection: Myth or Reality?* (San Francisco: HarperCollins, 1994, 238.

27. May 17 1998 citation from Muhlenberg College, Allentown, PA, of honorary Degree of Doctor of Humane Letters awarded John Shelby Spong.
28. Lynn Vincent, "Shifting sand?" in WORLD, 10 May 2003.
29. Thomas C. Reeves, op.cit., 16
30. Michael S. Rose, *Goodbye, Good Men,* (Washington, D. C.: Regnery Publishing, Inc., 2002). 90.
31. David F. Wells, *No Place For Truth, op.cit.,* 44.
32. Archibald Alexander Hodge, *Popular Lectures on Theological Themes,* (Philadelphia: Presbyterian Board of Publications, 1887), 283.
33. The Associated Press Release, March 29, 2003 12:00 A.M.
34. Ronald Bailey, "The Pursuit of Happiness" in Reason magazine, December 2000.

CHAPTER 9

Homosexuality

For they exchanged the truth of God for a lie, and worshiped and served the creature rather than the Creator, who is blessed forever. Amen. For this reason God gave them over to degrading passions; for their women exchanged the natural function for that which is unnatural, and in the same way also the men abandoned the natural function of the woman and burned in their desire towards one another, with man committing indecent acts and receiving in the their persons the due penalty of their error.

(Romans 1:25–27)

In the last hundred years, America has survived two dastardly attacks. 7 December 1941, Pearl Harbor, and 11 September 2001, New York, Pennsylvania, and Virginia are dates and places emblazoned upon our history. While these attacks cannot be erased from the minds and hearts of

249

Americans, another attack upon the American family and our culture has been going on for many years and could prove to be more devastating. Once confined to the background of our culture, it has suddenly exploded. It is the homosexual revolution, a revolution about sex, the family, and the culture of America. The Christian Church feels its impact because many liberal theologians and denominations attempt to incorporate this movement within Christian theology, calling it "Sexual Liberation Theology." They err mightily, because what they champion is not Christian theology, but a liberal ideology (a systematic body of concepts especially about human life or culture). Human ideology and Christian theology can never be seen as equals.

In Christian theology, sex within the bonds of marriage is spiritually and physically beautiful and fulfilling. It is God's plan not only for procreation, but for order within the society and culture of sinful human beings, people like you and me. If God had deemed it otherwise, He would have revealed His will for the human race to experience unbridled sex, passion and lust unlimited. He did not do so. Instead, He established sex as a responsible gift of mutual serving love within marriage, between a man and a woman, to be lived in fidelity for family unity and procreation, and as a foundation for a strong church and nation. Within His Law and Gospel in the Old and New Testaments are His proclamations regarding sexual behavior. God was emphatically establishing the foundation of sexual sanity for His beloved whom He has called to serve Him and other human beings of His creation. Within this context, sex is natural, safe, and fulfilling.

St. Paul, in his Epistle to the Romans, makes most clear God's eternal will of salvation. In doing so, he realistically portrays the stubborn sinfulness of man apart from the Lordship of Jesus Christ. He does not hide the corruptness of mankind as ". . . they exchanged the truth of God for a lie, and worshiped and served the creature rather than the Creator . . ." Here Paul points to the work of the *god of this world* who has as his main mission to turn mankind away from the Creator so that the created will worship the passions and lusts of their bellybuttons upon which their hearts and minds can easily be focused. Paul, inspired by God, goes on to make a specific charge against a most unnatural and sinful sex practice: that of lesbian homosexuality, women in sex relationships with other women, and gay homosexuality, men in sex relationships with other men.

Because homosexuality is a term that includes both male and female homosexuality, I will use "lesbianism" to refer to a lifestyle that exalts sexual relationships between women and "gay" to refer to a lifestyle that endorses sexual relationships between men. We dare not exclude a third sexual preference or lifestyle which is that of the bisexual, persons who participate in both heterosexual and homosexual relationships.

Since I am targeting how the *god of this world* has invaded the Christian Church in our post-modern culture and attempts to destroy Christian spirituality, I will focus upon the unnatural and sinful sex of this era that has been condoned by some liberal theologians. They, in turn, have had great influence upon the leaders and clergy of liberal denominations which have been caught up in liberation theology where homosexuality has found a welcoming home. Their sermons have not fallen on deaf ears or cold hearts, because many people of God in liberal denominations are looking for spiritual direction for their lives and are being fed non-biblical, ideological musings of a revolutionary nature that are really counter-culture and non-Christian. Unsuspectingly, many Christians follow in lock-step, because they trust their shepherds. Also, many have fled, knowing that what is being preached and taught is not in harmony with God's Word which was taught to them in their youth. It is the post-modern day youth who are most susceptible to revolution-ary, controversial ideas. The world through its liberal media and sex-oriented television, has been a willing co-conspirator of immoral sex, pre-senting it as an adventure for their newly realized libidos.

The liberal courts in the American judicial system may prove to be the greatest enemies of God-ordained marriage, as they can be influenced to side with homosexual activists who claim that the government, and not God, has the sole prerogative to make definitions concerning sex and marriage. Zealous support to do so comes from liberal "mainline" denominations whose leaders have become enamored with liberation theology as the main driving force for social justice. Just as they have turned from the authority of God's Word, so they entreat liberal courts to turn from their appointed task of interpretation of the law to legislation by means of the law.

In Chapter 6, I pointed to liberation theology where it defines oppression as sin against the poor and against racial intolerance and any form of domination. Another praxis or stream of action coming from a form of liberation theology in liberal seminaries today is sexual liberation theology, freedom from any form of sexual oppression. It is bold defiance of God's Word in Scripture. This "theology" unabashedly affirms lesbian and gay lifestyles. It is presented as reconstructed truth once the authority of God's Word has been deconstructed by the historical- critical method. Even the deceptive use of the word "gay" misrepresents the truth.

Sexual liberation theology made its debut upon the theological stage in the 1960s and early 1970s. It maintains one core drive: sexual freedom with no constraints from an antiquated Scripture. Whatever may have been the orthodox, biblical, ethical consensus of societies in the past, those who espouse this radical theology believe the time has come to break from biblical ethical values, calling them oppressive. Their reasoning revolves around the theme that many of life's problems are sexual problems. Thus, sexual repression of any kind is a biblical culprit which has to be met and squashed by complete sexual liberation.

The influence of an American secular society of tolerance for any and all theories of diversity and liberation from absolutes at any cost, became the potting soil for secularized sex "theology." Here, once more, is the world in a "not so silent merger" entering into the church. Christians in liberal churches began hearing about a new slant of permissiveness. After all, if the Bible as God's Word is pushed aside as non-authoritative truth from God, the field of man-made ideology is wide open for the most bold and daring theories to be tried on for size. The source for such musings is found in human commentaries, not in the inerrant and infallible Word of God in Scripture. Leviticus 18:22 and 20:13, Deuteronomy 23:18, and Romans 1 are ignored.

Liberals in love with freedom from the authority of Scripture can now assume their own authority to ride the waves of societal transition and hook onto the prevailing culture of neutral authority. Decadent sociological currents have always attempted to weaken orthodox Christianity, and the sad recounting of much of the history of the Christian Church has been the compromises and surrenders to the prevailing decadence of Western culture which was spawned in the shallows of *reasonable neutrality*—a by-product of The Enlightenment of the 18th century. Reasonable neutrality buries any kind of authority in the grave of diversity.

While lesbianism and gay homosexuality spring from a common root—same sex activity and expression—their main objective is to have their lifestyles sanctioned as being equal with the heterosexual standard for sex that God revealed in His Word. They maintain that their *liberated sex* is merely another alternative lifestyle, not sin. To object to their way of sexual expression is considered intolerance, the *real* sin, as these objections stem from questionable biblical or ultra-conservative societal grounds. This is regarded as sexual domination and they cry out for liberation from this *sin*.

Dissenters to their sexual lifestyles are labeled as "homophobic," an irrational fear of homosexuality or homosexuals. Many nominal Christians buckle under and surrender to accepting homosexual lifestyles as normal, rather than being tagged with that label. Then, add an implied hatred toward persons of that lifestyle which is portrayed as non-Christian, and one can easily see the guilt trip that is laid on those who truly hate the sin of homosexuality. True Christianity never hates the sinner, only the sin. Christians are openly admonished by liberals to display tolerance which is acknowledgment of the right of homosexuals to live sexual lives as they please with a "normal-natural" tag attached. This compromising atmosphere of tolerance permeates the American culture which has turned its back on the authority of God. A society ruled by tolerance wherein there is no "right" or "wrong," will inevitably call sin "normal-natural." Hence, lesbian and gay lifestyles become normal-natural expressions which are to be accepted. After all, isn't that the American way?

From where and whence did this change of tolerance for homosexuality originate? In cultures that have been influenced and blessed by Christianity, homosexuality was always considered to be abnormal. Then in 1973, the American Psychiatric Association, under great pressure and lobbying from homosexual groups, redefined homosexuality as pathological (caused by disease) *only* for those who sought psychiatric treatment for it. In 1975 the American Psychological Association followed suit. No longer was it held to be abnormal by the great majority in the psychiatric community. If no longer abnormal, it couldn't be a sin, but merely a disease *only* for those who sought healing.

The upshot of labeling abnormal sexual behavior as normal caused a flip-flop upon the American religious and ethical scene. Homophobia now appeared as sin, the culprit enemy which must be attacked and destroyed if homosexuality was to survive as an accepted sexual lifestyle. In many of the public schools in our land, this lifestyle is being taught as normal behavior, while those who oppose it are labeled as intolerant bigots, infected with homophobia, the new found sin of the 20th and 21st centuries. This stance of calling abnormal normal has invaded liberal denominations which have lost the biblical understanding of sin. God's Word in 1st Corinthians 6: 9, 10 need not apply for them because God's authority has been culturally neutered.

> Or do you not know that the unrighteous shall not inherit the kingdom of God? Do not be deceived, neither fornicators, nor idolaters, nor adulterers, nor effeminate, nor homosexuals, Nor thieves, nor the covetous, nor drunkards, nor revilers, nor swindlers, shall inherit the kingdom of God.

One way for gay proponents to make their point and establish their position, is to make Jesus appear as gay. Terrence McNally attempted to do so. In his play *Corpus Christi,* which in Latin means "The body of Christ," Jesus appears as Joshua, a gay man of sorrows. The Manhattan Theater Club in New York city recently scheduled the play only after the protest by the Catholic League for Religious and Civil

257

Rights was overturned by counter-protests from the "arts community." James Nuechterlein describes how the arts community rescued a "turkey" which was supposed to be played to full houses, but fell on its sword as the response of the audiences was what Nueshterlein termed as "tepid." Nuechterlein continues:

> The story of the play follows, in rough outline, the pattern of the original. Joshua/Jesus is born in a cheap motel in Corpus Christi, Texas, to a bewildered Joseph and a well-meaning but feckless Mary. (Mary's wispy vulnerability raises faint echoes of Blanch DuBois in *A Streetcar Named Desire*.) Joshua senses from the outset that he is different (he tries to like football and girls, but fails at both) and that he is fated to a tragic end (he has ominous visions, and the hammering of nails in a cross echoes intermittently offstage throughout the play).
>
> After unhappy early experiences—lots of nasty encounters with priests and nuns, a sexually humiliating senior prom—Joshua leaves Corpus Christi. He gathers a group of gay disciples, and they gambol about the countryside performing miracles and doing good (interspersed with frequent bouts of boozing and sex). In the end Joshua returns to Corpus Christi, where he is betrayed by Judas (who first seduced him on prom night) to the "fag haters in priests' robes" and crucified in the presence of all who

tormented him in his youth. He dies as "King of the Queers."[1]

Philip L. Culbertson states his case as a gay activist who wants the Christian community to be receptive to his views of sexual liberation.

> . . . adult intimate friendship offers men riches other than the riches of marriage. It offers us the chance to express the values of unconditional love, of beauty, tenderness, and loyalty, and as marriage remains so transient, offers us a different possibility of permanence. The Christian community cannot be healthy until women and men are liberated from the gender-role expectations which imprison them. Christ the Liberator has called the church to be a faithful community in service to the oppressed, affirming equality and justice for all people as mature beings in God's image, and modeling God's all encompassing love for the human community. Men's fear of intimate male friendship is one of the most critical forms of oppression under which they live. As men struggle toward a profeminist, less-abusive masculinity, uncowed by the abuses of other men, our first step must be reclaiming our right to be intimate friends with other men.[2]

Gay activists will use many arguments to defend their cause. Not only do they stand on the platform of liberation theology as their way to dispute God's revelation of His will in Scripture for sexual behavior, but also offer "off the wall" speculations about homophobia resulting from men's fear of losing control of women. James B. Nelson, who is Professor Emeritus of Christian Ethics, United Theological Seminary of the Twin Cities, New Brighton, Minnesota, uses this kind of reasoning:

> The dynamics of homophobia are numerous and multi-faceted. But one thing seems sure: homophobia in straight-identified males (where it is typically strongest) is directly connected to the fear of losing the institution of compulsory heterosexuality and men's control of women. The threat, in short, is the loss not only of male power, but also—and importantly—of men's erotic pleasure.[3]

Nelson who represents the United Church of Christ, one of the first "mainline" denominations to affirm lesbian, gay, and bisexual relationships, and ordain them for ministry, calls for a critical and erotic transformation in theology and in culture. He maintains:

> The notion of a God who demands our submission further reinforces the eroticization of dominance and control in men. Thus, it is not that we are bereft of the erotic. More accurately, male eroticism has been largely shaped around the pleasures of dominance and control.

We need erotic transformations both in our bodies and in our notions of the sacred. It is difficult for me to see how one will come apart from the other. Part of the transformative work is theoretical . . . Our alliance with pioneering feminists and with creative gay and lesbian liberationists in recovering and re-imagining alternative images of the divine is critically important. But theory and praxis must go together. So, an inescapable part of the transformative process is hard political work for the sexual justice that will change religious and societal structures to nurture the hunger for life, not suppress it. The process may yet allow men's hands and men's bodies to incarnate the hands and body of God. And that will be erotic pleasure for us all.[4]

You will recall in Chapter 2 how G. B. Caird described the New Testament scholar of today as using "sympathetic imagination" to project himself or herself back to the days when the New Testament was written, so that imagination might become "the chief source and the norm for all theological thought." By the same token, Nelson introduces "re-imagining alternative images of the divine." It appears that liberal theologians have found the source of authority in imagination, rather than God's revelation of Himself and His will in Scripture.

It is important to realize that here, and in all other areas of liberal theology, we are dealing with two different playing fields. The first, the biblical, has been abandoned as untenable, archaic myth, not relevant for today's game of life. The game has been moved to a different playing field where ideological commentaries from human liberal theologians redefine the game; where tolerant diversity, speculations of creation, authority in imagination, and sexual permissiveness attempt to establish new rules for today's game of life. The tragic reality is that life is not a game. It has temporal responsibilities and eternal implications which biblical Christianity clearly teaches. Physical and spiritual life are inseparable.

In homosexual lifestyles there is concentration upon the here and now, the immanent. Very little is said or written about the eternal implications of that lifestyle. They surely must realize that what they proclaim as truth in liberationist fashion is centered upon this world: liberation from white supremacy, capitalist exploitation, homophobic presuppositions, anti-Semitism, cultural imperialism, and male-gender superiority, to name a few of their enemies. This constitutes their definition of sin. Heterosexism (sex between male and female) also falls into this category. From the above conglomeration of social ills, it seems most apparent that liberationists want a liberal form of socialism to prevail in order to eliminate domination and oppression while touting same sex activity as heaven on earth.

Nelson, in 1977, called for a different source of authority for the homosexual surge in society, a time when it was beginning to impact upon the mainline denominations. He called for authority from the world so that the church might reexamine its theology and practice in order to get in step with the world and its secular scholars who had already written off God's authority. He asserts:

> The church is called to do its ongoing theological and ethical work as responsibly as possible. Fresh insights from feminist theologians, gay Christians, and those secular scholars who frequently manifest God's "common grace" in the world reminds us of the numerous ways in which our particular sexual conditions color our perceptions of God's nature and presence among us. If the Protestant Principle turns us against absolutizing historically relative theological judgments, so also our openness to continuing revelation should convince us, with some of our ancestors-in-faith, that "the Lord has yet more light and truth to break forth."[5]

The words "continuing revelation" must be separated from God's revelation in Holy Scripture. That God's revelation in His Word through the power of the Holy Spirit continues day in and day out and will do so until Jesus comes again, is not disputed by orthodox theologians. It is when God's revelation depends upon the authority of man, that obvious exception must be taken. Can you imagine, there is that word again, that Christian theology should be based upon a multiplicity of daily, continuing revelations coming from liberal theologians? One would have to wet his or her finger and put it into the wind to see supposed theological direction(s) that wouldn't be of God, but of sinful humans. Hence, it would be non-theology, or "manology," or "womanology," or "biology" (whoops, that word is already in use) or whatever name you would dare to give it. Would "ideology" fit? How about "heresy?" Taking place once more is the "not so silent merger" of the world in the church.

Nelson also maintained that anti-homosexual bias has come from the church "in shaping, supporting, and transmitting negative attitudes toward homosexuality."[6] Amazing. Could the Church of Jesus Christ do any other? It cannot embrace or endorse sin. The true Christian Church whose theology is normed by Holy Scripture will always have a bias against sin, but at the same time, love the sinner! The Christian Church, as Christ's body, exists solely for the redemption of sinners, like you and me. It is as sinners that we are inside or outside the Christian Church. Sin escapes no one. Yet, the theology of the Christian Church does not originate in sinners who are attempting to establish new ideologies, but in God's revelation of Himself in His Son and in His Holy Word. The emergence of a theology from any other source must be considered heresy with its inherent spiritual minefields which threaten Christian spirituality.

To think that lesbians, gays, and bisexuals are not within Christian denominations would be saying that the Christian Church is free of sinners. No way! As a pastor and chaplain, I have seen their pain and have heard their confessions. When they come as sinners and seek God's redemptive forgiveness through faith in Jesus, they are the same as heterosexuals who seek God's forgiveness for their sins through faith in His Son. There is no difference. The difference comes when they exploit their sinfulness and attempt to change Christianity to liberated sexuality, which the Holy Scriptures condemn. Then trouble arises *big time*. We see this conflict in Christian denominations which have drifted to the left theologically, condoning lifestyles contradictory to Scripture. They leave in a quandary their Scripture-honoring members, those members who believe in Jesus Christ as Savior and who believe in the morality that issues forth from God's Word. To say these beloved people of God are confused and deceived, is an understatement.

To believe the clergy of Christian Churches are free from homosexuality is a myth. Clerical robes are not the "guard-all" from sin.

265

Within Judaism, Roman Catholicism, and Protestantism, some rabbis, priests, and ministers have
fallen prey to homosexual lifestyles which have been
exploited on innocent youth. Denominations have
different means of handling this situation. It can
mean expulsion from the clergy roles, reassignment
with the help of biblical counseling after repentance,
or even celebration and acceptance by those liberal
denominations which endorse homosexuality as
normal. However, the failure to take appropriate
and decisive action in these matters by responsible church leaders has proven disastrous for
abused youth, and for the credibility of the
church. An increasing number of Catholic bishops, including Bernard Cardinal Law of the Roman Catholic Diocese in Boston, have paid the
price for delayed action in defrocking gay priests
who molested children. Litigation has mounted in
ever increasing volume. On the Protestant side, individual clergy found guilty of such crimes, for the
most part, face the law rather than their supervising
ecclesiastical body.

Gay lifestyles of priests within the Roman
Catholic Church have been exceptionally troubling to Rome. James B. Wolf points to a survey
of 101 gay priests. Those who were ordained before 1960 remember their seminary as having 51
percent gay. Those who were ordained after 1961
say their seminaries were 70 percent gay.[7] Sur-
veys will always produce varying results. Much

depends upon the person being interviewed. In my duties some years ago as Force Chaplain, Fleet Marine Force, Pacific, and later as Fleet Chaplain, U.S. Atlantic Fleet, I encountered disciplinary action against a few Roman Catholic chaplains, but nothing like the above figures purport or imply. I must add that there were also Protestant chaplains caught in gay and lesbian activity. Every denomination has had to face the reality of gay and lesbian lifestyles among some of their clergy. The *god of this world* has not declared a "no fire zone" when dealing with clergy.[8]

Mary Walsh comments upon the revealing work of Michael S. Rose in *Goodbye, Good Men,* which uncovers how the world has merged its ideology with liberal seminaries within Roman Catholicism. Rose shows the results: orthodox priests eliminated on the road to ordination while homosexuality is accepted as a normal lifestyle in liberal seminaries rooting for sexual liberation which would include ordination of women.

> *Goodbye, Good Men* arrived at precisely the right moment to explain the current "Lavender Mafia" crisis in the church. It's not as if God ignored the prayers of his faithful for priestly vocations. The dearth of vocations is the direct result of 30 years of yahoo theology, aversion to prayer and sacraments, adjusted morality and instruction in dissent in a gay subculture. The good bishops have a Herculean task ahead of

them. Oremus. (Oremus in Latin means: "Let us pray."—my insertion).[9]

Barbara Olson writes about homosexuals in the military and how President William Jefferson Clinton responded to this problem, a problem which can wreck havoc on the morale of those in the Armed Forces. Olson reports the Clinton compromise:

> Within days of being sworn in as president, Clinton also issued an order about homosexuals in the military, changing existing policy to what became "don't ask, don't tell." That order responded to pressure from Clinton's homosexual supporters, who had raised $3.5 million for him. In the words of Clinton's openly homosexual advisor David Mixner, "Clinton became the Abraham Lincoln of our movement."[10]

As a Navy chaplain serving in ships that have confined quarters for the crew, as well as a chaplain in combat in Vietnam, I can testify that homosexuality can compromise mission operation effectiveness. I need not draw word pictures to substantiate my position. Those who have been and are in the military understand and I am confident that they support my position. I firmly believe that gays and lesbians have no place in the military. I have too much evidence which I can not disclose because of my respect for the

sanctity of the confessional position I hold as a clergyman. Some homosexuals as well as liberal clergy
and laity may vehemently disagree with my position of no gays in the military, but I am certain that
I am most qualified to make that statement.

Howard Phillips sheds light on ignoring the
problem of homosexuality in the military. He
states:

> . . . the practical problems, as well as the
> moral ones are enormous. It would be only a
> matter of time before exclusion of HIV-carri-
> ers would be regarded as discriminatory.
> Under the Americans with Disabilities Act, such
> is now the case for private businesses.

> Military service would become particularly
> appealing to AIDS-infected homosexuals,
> who, though possibly unable to secure pri-
> vate insurance, could quite readily stick their
> medical bills to the defense budget and the
> American taxpayer.

> Everyone involved in the armed forces would
> be placed at greater risk for contracting not
> only AIDS, but other diseases which are the
> by-products of sexual degeneracy.

> Battlefield transfusions could be more danger-
> ous than enemy bullets. A good night's sleep in
> a barracks room permeated with sodomites
> would become combat zones, and fox-holes

could become death chambers without a single
enemy shot being fired.[11]

An interesting development in the Russian
military recruitment policy no longer allows gays
in the Russian armed forces. This became effective on 1 July 2003. While homosexuality in the
military was not described as a medical matter,
it was classified as "an untraditional sexual orientation." It was classified in the category of a
personality disorder and therefore not in com-
pliance with medical examination rules for ser-
vicemen.[12]

Tucked away and out of sight is the AIDS epidemic that has been on the rise worldwide. Very
little mention is made by the media, except to report the fact that a famous actor, musician, athlete,
or politician has died of that disease. Women have
also died of this dread disease which they acquired,
in many cases, from heterosexual relations either
inside or outside of marriage. The plight of infants
and children who are born with this disease of unbridled sexual behavior tears at our hearts. They are
the real victims.

Apart from praying for the victims of AIDS,
liberal denominations have not been proactive
in attempting to combat the spread of this disease. Advocating the use of condoms has been
proven to be" unsafe sex." Distributing them, as

did the National Episcopal AIDS Coalition at the 1994 General Convention of the Episcopal Church, is a tepid corrective response, to say the least. Is this an admission that to take a positive stand against unsafe sex would be a compromise of liberation theology, so that not even the awful ravages of this disease need be addressed, as that would put a check on the homosexual lifestyle which demands release from any type of oppression or restraint? Could it also be that AIDS condemns their liberated approach to sex and proves it to be deception unto death? Their silence is deafening!

Thomas C. Oden believes that the AIDS epidemic is snapping people to reality regarding the hedonistic sexual revolution. He maintains:

> The party is over for the hedonic sexual revolution of the period from the sexy sixties to the gay nineties. The party crasher is sexually transmitted diseases. We are now having to learn to live with the consequences of sexual, interpersonal, and familial wreckage to which narcissistic self-indulgence has led us. [13]

His optimism, sadly, is writhing in the dust of the homosexual strategies being played out not only in the media, but in the "mainline" churches in this new millennium. Thomas C. Reeves in reporting about the 1994 General Convention of the Episcopal Church writes:

At the same conclave, Bishop Jane Dixon wore a large button that read "SEXUALITY, NOT SPIRITUALITY." There seems to be a mainline obsession with sex, a topic of often intense debate at meetings and conventions of all sorts. This again reflects the mainline's absorption of contemporary liberal mores. As William Murchison put it, "a healthy and vigorous sex life is the great modern desideratum (something deemed as essential—my insertion)—the Holy Grail of a self-regarding society.[14]

In an article, *Episcopalians: The Leftward Center*, Murchison reveals what has happened to his church as the issue of homosexuality has descended upon it. Reporting on the triennial General Convention in Philadelphia in July of 1977, he claims that "the church came close to scraping bottom." He continues:

In recent years, Episcopalians have seen it all: bishops proudly ordaining active homosexuals and an official church court declaring (with more than a tinge of satisfaction) that no discernable doctrine prohibits such a practice; general apathy toward moral issues such as abortion that engage other Christians; disrespect for scriptural authority; sluggishness in evangelizing; the trial and conviction of the national church treasurer on charges of embezzling $2.1 million to support herself and her Episcopal priest-husband; bishops implicated in adultery; seminary approval of homosexual living arrangements for students; a major East Coast diocese riven by the style and agenda of its radical bishop (probably Bishop John Shelby Spong.—my insertion). Unsurprisingly, membership in America's formerly most prestigious church has fallen by a third since 1965.[15]

It must be noted, however, that the bishops of the Anglican Communion in August of 1998, at their Lambeth Conference in England, declared homosexuality incompatible with Scripture by a vote of 526 in favor and 70 against, with 45 abstentions. This conference is held every ten years. Even with the declaration of the bishops, the homosexual issue is far from settled in the Episcopal Church, and for that matter, in most "mainline" American denominations.

In concert with that vote, the Archbishop of Canterbury Rowan Williams, in July 2003, convinced the Rev. Jeffrey Johns, an openly gay homosexual priest, to withdraw his acceptance of appointment as bishop of Reading in the Oxford diocese. Johns complied because he didn't want to fracture the Anglican Communion.[16]

That could not be said of the Rev. V. Gene Robinson, an openly gay homosexual with his male lover at his side at the August 2003 triennial convention of the Episcopal Church, USA, (ECUSA) held in Minneapolis. Knowing that confirmation of his election as bishop of New Hampshire could bring schism to his church, Robinson nevertheless pushed forward for confirmation. After some allegations of misconduct had been cleared as non-substantial, the Episcopal bishops by a vote of 62 for and 43 against approved Robinson as bishop-elect of New Hampshire.[17] Robinson had already been passed as acceptable by the Committee on the Consecration of Bishops and the House of Deputies, a legislative body composed of clergy and lay people. On 2 November 2003, dozens of ECUSA bishops joined Presiding Bishop Frank Griswold in the consecration of the Rev. Robinson as Bishop of New Hampshire.

Laity in conservative denominations in America were nonplused, perplexed as to how this could ever happen because the action to confirm and consecrate a homosexual as a bishop, let alone even to ordain a homosexual by a supposedly Christian denomination, is contrary to the directives of Holy Scripture. This question was answered on national television via the 5 August 2003, Fox News Channel show, "The O'Reilly Factor." Bill O'Reilly interviewed the Rev. Ed Bacon, Rector of All Saints Episcopal Church, Pasadena, California, a friend of Robinson's for over thirty years. Father Ed Bacon made it quite clear that "The Anglican Communion does not have Scripture as its ultimate authority. We always have the Holy Spirit working in community as the ultimate authority."

The situation is crystal clear. The majority of bishops and laity in the Episcopal Church, USA, are of the mind that Holy Scripture does not have authority. A supposed antiquated Scripture which the historical-critical method trashes must now be replaced by a community trying to fathom the Holy Spirit. Before the emergence of that method, the Holy Spirit was held by Christian churches to work through the authority of God's Word. Contradiction? Of course it is! Then, the Holy Spirit of God is at the beck and call of the community of faith as Chapter 7 describes. The authority shift is devastating to Christian spirituality which is founded in God's Word in Holy Scripture. Holy Scripture is consigned to the trash bin. Sadly, the dissenting bishops and laity who hold to the authority of Holy Scripture were quietly put in their place.

However, the conservative branch of bishops in the Episcopal Church, USA. along with dissenting laity, met in Dallas, Texas in early October 2003 and called upon the archbishop of Canterbury and 37 other leading bishops in the Anglican Communion, of which the Episcopal Church, USA, is a branch to create an undefined "new alignment for Anglicanism in North America." They also vowed to withhold financial support to the ECUSA.[18]

In mid-October 2003, the archbishop of Canterbury and the 37 primates of the Anglican Communion met in London, England, to consider the consecration of an openly avowed homosexual bishop. They issued a warning that the scheduled consecration of Robinson on 2 November 2003 will "tear the fabric" of their world-wide association of churches. This gave additional impetus to the network of dissenting American bishops and congregations in the ECUSA to believe they have support to move forward with a realignment of the Episcopal Church apart from the ECUSA. The Rev. Peter Moore, an evangelical and head of the Episcopal School for Ministry in Pennsylvania, believes a split will occur in the ECUSA even if Robinson stands down or is made to stand down, now not possible. He based his reasoning on the fact that the ECUSA allows bishops to decide whether or not to permit same-sex blessings in their dioceses and Moore doesn't expect this policy to change.[19] Other "mainline" churches may also face schism.

The Evangelical Lutheran Church in America (ELCA), in full communion with The Episcopal Church, USA, The Presbyterian Church,USA, The United Church of Christ, Reformed Church in America, and The Moravian Church in America, also has been experiencing major rumblings within its membership over the homosexuality issue. An 11 August 2001 news release from the ELCA indicates their indecisiveness on the issue. A Pro-Gay and Anti-Gay protest outside an ELCA Assembly in Indianapolis triggered the following:

"On numerous occasions, the Evangelical Lutheran Church in America (ELCA) has called for listening and conversation among its members on issues related to gay and lesbian people in the church. In the ELCA, there is no consensus or common understanding on many issues related to homosexuality," said the Rev. Joseph M. Wagner, executive director of ELCA Division for Ministry, in a statement released Aug.11 on behalf of the church. Wagner is also convener of the ELCA Interunit Work Group on Homosexuality. "Last year, the ELCA Church Council asked each synod to discuss these issues at their annual assemblies by 2003; it also asked that ELCA rostered lay and clergy leaders engage in similar discussion by 2003. The ELCA is committed to ongoing conversation on homosexuality and the church in a spirit of trust and openness."

When any denomination calls for a "listening and conversation among its members" in order to "set the course" (a good Navy order given to the helmsman to steer the desired course), you can be assured that they are waffling as to what direction to take. They waffle because they may have lost their compass, the infallible and inerrant Word of God in Holy Scripture. As evidenced in the news release: ". . . there is no consensus or common understanding on many issues related to homosexuality." The winds of this world are powerful, seductive forces and when any denomination rides the wind, instead of bucking the wind which impedes God's revealed will, you can be assured of the influence of the *god of this world*. He will always "set the course" that leads to spiritual destruction which he has established in deconstructionist theology, man at the helm, and God as a passenger. The *Spiritual Arrest Religious Syndrome* (SARS) continues to infect and multiply.

WORLD magazine reported the following, exposing where the ELCA may be headed:

> In April, the ELCA Task Force on Human Sexuality met in Chicago for its second conference. The denomination commissioned the task force "to guide" the ELCA's decision making on gay clergy and the blessing of same-sex relationships. But its expert panels may actually be a series of stacked decks. For example, task force science panelists included a pair of Lutheran clinical psychologists who offered as fact the opinion of the gay-friendly American Psychological Association: "(Sexual) orientation is not a choice, it cannot be changed, (and) efforts to attempt to modify it may even be harmful." Another science panelist cited the discredited Kinsey Report as support for legitimizing homosexuality.

> Roanoke College religion professor Robert Benne, a biblical conservative and task force panelist, told WORLD the ELCA task force "certainly is weighed toward those who are open to revising basic teaching on homo-

sexual relations." In addition, he said the presence of open homosexuals at every discussion "makes it difficult for folks who are uncertain or just plain nice to voice objections or even reservations about the revisionist agenda. Most church people like to be polite and accepting, so they often accept that agenda out of the desire to 'keep the peace in love.'"[20]

The Rev. Mark Hanson, Presiding Bishop, in an ELCA statement of 5 August 2003, did not condemn the action of the bishops of the Episcopal Church, USA, to approve the Rev. V. Gene Robinson as the bishop-elect of New Hampshire, an action not in accord with Holy Scripture. Instead, the 2003 Assembly placed the entire human sexuality issue on the back burner for further study to be completed and acted on by the 2005 ELCA Assembly in Orlando, Florida.

This was not the case with the Lutheran Youth Organization (LYO) at its July 20–23, 2003 Triennial Convention in Atlanta, Georgia. The 15 to 18 year olds adopted a resolution supporting the blessing of "same-sex unions" and the ordination of "non-celibate individuals" of "all sexual orientations" in "committed relationships."[21] Did the influence for such a resolution come from their pastor mentors or from their school educators, many of whom view homosexuality as a lifestyle and not a sin? These youth will be heard from at the 2005 Assembly.

The Rev. Herbert W. Chilstrom, a former presiding bishop of the ELCA, called for a policy change in the ELCA in regard to expectations for ordained pastors. At a 15 August special "Festival Worship" service held during the 2003 Assembly, Chilstrom firmly endorsed ordaining people in committed homosexual relationships and blessing same-sex relationships.[22]

In 2001, presiding bishop Hansen initiated a process called "Faithful Yet Changing." With the force of change heading in the direction of partner communion churches: The United Church of Christ, The Episcopal Church,USA, and the Presbyterian Church (USA); the ELCA's future portends spiritual chaos for its members if professor Robert Benne is correct, if Chilstrom's endorsement has legs, and if the LYO's resolution further infects the spirituality of the ELCA.

In Chapter 3, Gordon Kaufman was quoted: "Theology can no longer look simply to authoritative or normative decisions or situations in the past for its principle guidance." In essence, he was saying: "God's authority in His Word no longer matters. Let's look ahead and see what we can come up with." That is exactly what the Episcopal Church,USA, is doing as Father Bacon reveals in his statement: "We always have the Holy Spirit working in community as the ultimate authority." This was plainly affirmed by their House of Bishops. Once more it must be stated that the Holy Spirit always works through the Word of God, not the community of sinners as we all are. When authority rests in the created, watch out! You are seeing such God-less authority at work in supposedly "Christian" denominations.

When Bishop Hanson accentuates "Faithful Yet Changing" as the theme for the ELCA, in what direction is he pointing? Must God and His Word change? Our unchanging God is now at the mercy of changing theologies rooted and grounded in the historical-critical method, sacredly held in the ELCA and the Episcopal Church, USA, and other "mainline" denominations. The spirituality of the people in such "mainline" denominations are at their mercy. It is grand spiritual deception and confusion! Spiritual SARS is in full bloom!

The Presbyterian Church (USA) has not escaped the force of the winds of pressure to recognize and endorse homosexuality as an acceptable lifestyle. Beverly Wildung Harrison, a feminist proponent, reports a failed attempt:

> . . . the General Assembly Committee on Human Sexuality of the Presbyterian Church U.S.A. in 1991 called on its denomination to ordain without regard to sexual orientation (with a specific provision that celibacy not be made a condition for homosexual ministers) and to work actively for the repeal of all

laws discriminating against homosexuals (including laws criminalizing "private acts between consenting adults"). The Presbyterian Church U.S.A. as a whole, however, rejected this resolution.[23]

At the 215th General Assembly of the Presbyterian Church (USA), held at the end of May 2003 in Denver, the ordination of homosexuals was again a hot item. While the move to grant ordination was once more defeated, the matter was referred to the Task Force on Peace, Unity and the Purity of the Church. They will consider the issue and report their findings in 2006. The Rev. John Berkley of Bellevue, Washington, an official with the conservative Presbyterians for Renewal said: ". . . sending the report back to committee was a way for liberals to keep it from dying."[24]

The General Assembly elected the Rev. Susan Andrews of Bethesda, Maryland, to be the first female parish pastor to hold the position of moderator for any General Assembly. Andrews showed her liberal colors when she said it was her "fondest dream" that the church lift its ban in ordaining noncelibate gays and lesbians in her lifetime. But she said she did not think this was the year to attempt it.[25]

That this issue is eating away at the membership of the Presbyterian Church (USA) cannot be denied. The Associated Press story of 23 May 2003, concerning the 215th General Assembly included the following:

> The 2.5 million-member Presbyterian church is losing roughly 35,000 members a year, and the Rev. Parker Williamson, who heads the conservative Presbyterian Lay Committee, believes frustration with church leaders who won't enforce the ban is part of the reason.

Duke Divinity School in Durham, North Carolina, related to The United Methodist Church, greeted its nearly 500 student body upon their return from spring break 2003 with the promulgation of a new ethics code for the seminary which didn't go over well with many students. WORLD magazine gave this report:

> The "conduct covenant" covers the usual bases: no stealing, cheating, or plagiarizing. It calls on students to live in Christian community and to be accountable to one another, open to judgment, to show respect and honor friendships. It also calls on them to be welcoming, hospitable, and "chaste."
>
> Gays and lesbians on campus had a problem with that word. Did it mean gays and lesbians would violate the code if they had sex?
>
> Not to worry. Ethics professor Amy Laura Hall said the faculty unanimously agreed that chas-

tity could include sexual relations among homosexuals.[26]

The General Conference of The United Methodist Church met in Pittsburgh, Pennsylvania,
from 27 April to 7 May, 2004, and affirmed the
stand of the denomination against the ordination and placement of practicing homosexuals as
ministers by a 674 to 262 vote. However, it was
only by a 579 to 376 vote that language was accepted which more clearly articulated their stand
on the issue. They affirmed: "The United Methodist Church does not condone the practice of
homosexuality and considers this practice incompatible with Christian teaching." At the same
time, they made clear that God's grace is "available to all, and we will seek to live together in
Christian community."[27] The difference in the
voting numbers may be a harbinger of declining
margins where "mainline" denominations take
their stand on homosexuality.

Another issue which surfaces is the relationship
of Duke Divinity School to The United Methodist
Church in light of the action by its General Conference. Can a positive relationship be maintained
when there are differing definitions about the acceptability of homosexuality being compatible/in-
compatible with Christian teaching?

With some congregations in the Episcopal
Church, USA, now blessing same-sex unions and

questioning biblical authority, a group of 37 parishes known as Anglican Mission have separated from the national church and will ordain four new bishops. The bishops who will consecrate the new bishops are from the Anglican Church in Malaysia. They were the bishops who consecrated Bishops John Rodgers and Charles Murphy, the originally consecrated bishops of Anglican Mission.[28]

This troubling issue in a growing number of "mainline" denominations is once more proof positive of their inability to be decisive about homosexuality and other theological issues which are based upon the authority of God's Word in Scripture. The historical-critical method of biblical interpretation, which they endorse, reveals their shifting-sand foundations as they embrace non-biblical conclusions, such as unbridled liberation theology, and flow with the winds of the world. The *god of this world* claps his hands in glee as he is a *god* of spiritual death and not of salvation. This is a reality which gay and lesbian theorists never seem to comprehend because their attention is focused on liberated, erotic sex, here and now. The foundation for "liberated sex theology" has been laid, and in the years to come, the "fruit" will buckle the vine.

The arguments made from the lesbian side for liberation, in order to be considered Christian, relevant to the spiritual needs of the modern world, follow the same direction as the prevailing liberal cultural wind. When their direction is placed beside the pure teaching of Holy Scripture one can readily and plainly see the divergences. They just don't jive. Yet, lesbian liberationist theologians proceed on the assumption that they have the truth and that those who disagree with them oppress them because of homophobia. They are labeled "patriarchal" (the supremacy of the father in society and religion), "andocentric" (men as the center of dignity and power), and "misogynist" (hatred of women by men).

One of the most blatant theological proposals by a lesbian liberationist theologian comes from Carter Heyward, ordained as an Episcopal priest in 1974 and currently professor of theology at the Episcopal Divinity School in Cambridge, Massachusetts. She lays as her theological foundation for liberation, *erotic power.* She argues:

> From a theological perspective, coming out as lesbians—icons of erotic power—is not only a significant psychological process. It is also a spiritual journey, a movement of profoundly moral meaning and value, in which we struggle, more and more publicly, to embrace our sisters, our friends and ourselves as bearers of sacred power . . . the erotic is our most fully embodied experience of the love of God. It is the source of our capacity for transcendence, or the "crossing over"

among ourselves. The erotic is the divine Spirit's yearning, through us, toward mutually empowering relation which becomes our most fully embodied experience of God as love.[29]

To characterize lesbianism as a "spiritual journey" is quite an imaginative stretch as is extolling erotic power as the means of experiencing God's love. Heyward has a target in mind for that erotic power. It is the destruction of responsible society which is built upon heterosexual love, the love of a man for a woman and love of a woman for a man in marriage. As such, the family unit, one of the orders of God's creation, would be destroyed. Regarding this, Heyward contends: "Heterosexism is a social structure pervasive in our culture and worthy only of being undone."[30]

Liberation theology has also steadily attacked both the State and the Church, the other two orders of God's creation: the State in the liberal imposition of influence upon law wherein the guilty are coddled and left free to again wreck havoc on society, and the Church as this work here depicts.

To further show how far-out Heyward's theology is in relation to God's revelation of His Son in Holy Scripture, she concentrates on Jesus as a body and merely limits His power to "body power." Here, the historical-critical method is in full force. She negates the truth that the Son was with the Father and the Holy Spirit at creation. To acknowledge the truth that Jesus is the Son of God, *coequal* with the Father and the Holy Spirit, having creation and redemption power, would dash feminist theology upon the rocks. However, in spite of the witness of Scripture, Heyward maintains:

> Jesus' power in relation, that which he knew as his *Abba*, was manifest in and through Jesus' flesh and blood, as he chose to touch, address, and relate to others. It was in relation that Jesus had power. And it was in and through his body that he experienced his power in relation: his *Abba*, our God, our sister, and lover, friend and brother, that which compels us to pick up our beds and walk.[31]

One last quote from Heyward shows the feminist evaluation of Jesus in regard to faith. Her position concerning faith is not at all untypical of the position of liberal feminist theologians who cringe at the thought of Jesus as God's Son, a patriarchal and androcentric God figure. Thus, Heyward can easily compromise the essence of faith which is believing in Jesus as the Son of God. Her theology brings her to this conclusion:

> Faith is believing not in Jesus, but rather in the power that goes forth from him: the power of God, which is, by its nature (the nature of God) shared—never a "possession" of Jesus, you, me, the United States, the Christian church, or the Ayatollah Khomeini.[32]

Among the greatest supporters of this move away from God and His authority in Holy Scripture have been the liberal press and television. They view the subject as attractive, eye-catching news and programming. ABC, a Disney Company owned television network, introduced *Ellen*, a show about lesbianism, mocking Christianity in the situation comedy *Nothing Sacred.* Other networks have picked up on this controversial theme because it attracts viewers; and viewers watch commercials; and commercials mean profit for the sponsors.

Under pressure from the gay community, Disney instituted a "Gay Day" at their theme parks and I suspect they are still feeling the reverberations that have come from Christian denominations who have boycotted the Disneyland Resort in California and the Walt Disney World Resort in Florida. At first, when these "Gay Days" appeared without notice, many families with young children were unaware. They found themselves and their children subjected to this social and theological intrusion and vowed never to return. They love their children too much to expose them to sights of fondling and kissing among those of the same sex. Nor do Christian parents accept endorsement of an unnatural lifestyle by any commercial enterprise not only for their children, but also for themselves.

Instances of the impact of homosexuality upon the American scene are described by James Dobson and Gary L. Bauer, but mainly ignored or glossed over by a tolerant society which has been brainwashed by liberal press and television to regard homosexuality as an acceptable lifestyle, a lifestyle sanctioned by public education. Dobson and Bauer point to the following:

> College students who oppose the gay rights agenda on their campuses are expelled for discrimination. Gay politicians celebrate their homosexuality and are routinely re-elected. Even a homosexual Congressman who allegedly seduced several male pages was returned to office, and Massachusetts Congressman Barney Frank, who admitted paying for sex with a male prostitute, merely received a slap on his wrist by fellow Congressmen.[33]

An issue of great interest for the media in the last few years has been the ban on homosexual scout leaders by the Boy Scouts of America. This ban was upheld in a decision by the United States Supreme Court in June 2000. With approximately 60% of Boy Scout troops sponsored by local church congregations, it became particularly objectionable for some congregations related to liberal denominations to continue sponsorship because of their open acceptance of the gay lifestyle. Sponsorship was withdrawn and many Boy Scout troops were left out in the cold. Among denominations leading the charge is the United Church of Christ.[34] While they, like other councils of many Protestant denominations issue resolutions, it remains for the local congregation to act independently. As a result, some United Church of Christ congregations, like the one in Taunton, Massachusetts, voted not to renew its charter with its Boy Scout Troop. "Tension was pretty high," said the Rev. Beverly Duncan, pastor. "Yet, I feel pretty good about the church having done that."[35]

Taking the same stance as the United Church of Christ in issuing policy statements, not binding ecclesiastical law, the governing members of the United Methodist Board of Church and Society issued the following statement during their 7–19 October 1999 meeting:

> "While the General Board of Church and Society would like to enthusiastically affirm and encourage this continuing partnership of the church and scouting, we cannot due to the Boy Scouts of America's discrimination against gays," the board stated. "This discrimination conflicts with our (church's) social principles."[36]

It should be noted that the United Methodist Church sponsors 11,738 troop units in which 421,579 boys from the ages of 7 to 20 participate. On the national scene, the Boy Scouts of America serve more than 5 million young people.

The General Convention of the Episcopal Church, meeting in Denver in July of 2000, passed a resolution on "Homosexuality: Boy Scouts of America Policy of Homosexuals." Among the four points of the resolution, the second states: "Encourage the Boy Scouts of America to allow membership to youth and adult leaders irrespective of their sexual orientation."[37]

This Boy Scout issue still boils over in liberal denominations where homosexuality is regarded as a lifestyle, not a sin. While the governing bodies of these denominations are ready to issue *quick-draw* resolutions and statements, individual congregations within liberal denominations struggle and some times resist because their leadership still holds homosexuality as sin. It would be a most interesting and volatile survey to determine how many congregations have stood up to the liberality of their denominations and have embraced Scripture as true Word of God. The Boy Scout issue would indeed be an interesting litmus test.

Additional pressure from the liberal world has descended upon the Boy Scouts of America when The United Way, Chase Manhattan Bank, and Textron withdrew millions of dollars in contributions. More corporations may follow suit so they can be in step with a culture which they project will provide profit. Thankfully, there are Christian congregations who have adopted scout troops that were exiled. My son's congregation at Grace Lutheran Church in Rialto, California, is such a congregation. The troop is thriving and has assisted in many church maintenance projects.

To destroy Boy Scouting is another ploy of liberal theologians who condition their denominations to follow their lead. Because Boy Scouting gets in the way of their agenda, it must be attacked. These theologians are leading not only their liberally influenced denominations, but our great country into spiritual destruction as they challenge authority, whether from the state or from God, Himself. Their present targets are both nation and God, especially His Word, His love message in Jesus. And you know the ultimate target—yes, the family.

The biggest myth within the gay and lesbian community is their insistence that homosexuality is genetic, already established in a person at birth. James Dobson, who has a doctorate in child development and is a child psychologist, appeared on the 4 February 2002 television show, "Hannity and Colmes," on the Fox News Channel. Alan Colmes asks Dobson:

You know it's rather controversial about whether or not it is chosen—people to be gay! Or whether it is genetically dictated, and I don't think we've settled that yet, have we?

James Dobson replies:

We've settled it, Alan, and almost no one, and I mean no one in scientific circles, is now saying that homosexuality is genetic. There was a big flap about ten years ago when it was thought that maybe there was a gay gene. They looked for it and it's simply not there. Even homosexual activists now are saying that there is no gay gene. I mean you just look at identical twins. If it were strictly genetic, you would always have homosexuality in both pairs, you know, both sides of that, and it's not true. It's about 50%. So there are a lot of other reasons to know that it is not genetic. It is frequently related to the temperament with which a child is born, but then goes on from there to environmental factors.

Marlin Maddoux writes regarding homosexuality as genetic:

The truth is that none of the biological and statistical studies suggesting a genetic cause for gayness have been replicable and most have indulged in false logic.

In one study, Dr. Simon LeVay, a homosexual biologist, claimed to have found a tiny differ-

ence in the brains of homosexual and heterosexual cadavers. Further investigation, however,
revealed that the sample size, only 43 men, was
far too small to be reliable. Also, the men whose
brains were sampled had all died of AIDS, which
could have altered the brain structure. Finally,
LeVay couldn't verify that the "heterosexual"
samples were in fact heterosexuals—the fact that
they had died of AIDS actually suggested they
were homosexual. In other words, Dr. LeVay was
probably comparing homosexual with homosexual brains! This, of course, would prove nothing about the differences between gay and
straight men.

In another study, it was found that if one set
of twins was homosexual, that his or her twin
had a better chance of being homosexual as
well. A biological link? That's what the media concluded. Yet the same finding would
also be true if the causes were related to family influences, not a more iron-clad genetic
blueprint. The truth is that extensive psychological research and counseling have already
uncovered the problem causes of homosexuality, none of which are genetic.[38]

Maddoux, in the same article, pointed to thousands of homosexuals who have been cured of that
lifestyle. His conclusion is that homosexuality is
learned behavior, and as such, can be "unlearned."
His proof are the lives of thousands who have
changed.

Don Feder gives further evidence that homosexuality is a learned behavior. He quotes "Dear Abby" who wrote about Dr. Joseph Nicolosi, a clinical psychologist who treated over 250 homosexuals in fifteen years of practice. Nicolosi believes homosexuality is "a treatable developmental disorder" which can also be classified as a learned behavior. Nicolosi contends the condition comes primarily from a son's failure to identify with his father because of absence, emotional detachment, weakness or brutality. The response of the son is withdrawal. To counter this, Nicolosi enables clients to understand the origins of their erotic feelings and includes building nonsexual intimacy and trust among men.[39]

With the explosion of homosexuality on the American scene as never seen before, one must certainly ask: "Is this a new sexual fad, something new for sexual experimentation?" The human libido, cut free from the constraints of the Law and Gospel of Holy Scripture, has written a filthy and despicable testimony in increasing volume on the centuries following the Enlightenment of the 18th century. Not that it was absent before that time as sin has many avenues of abominable expression. Human history overflows with examples of sinful sexual decadence, but you will note one missing factor: the authority of God's Word in the lives of His created beloved. The *god of this world* still deceives, confuses, and is the author of spiritual death.

Evolving from homosexuality, as could have been predicted years ago, is same-sex marriage, a hot-potato of liberal "mainline" denominations, as previously evidenced. In 1995, Sweden legally recognized gay and lesbian marriage. The Netherlands in 2001 adopted same-sex marriage and offers the same benefits that are given heterosexual marriage partners. Belgium followed suit in 2003. Even though in 2002 and 2003, courts in three Canadian provinces held that the opposite-sex definition of marriage was contrary to Canada's Charter of Rights, the Justice Minister in Ottawa, Martin Cauchon, urged all provinces in July 2003 to apply a draft bill to allow same-sex marriages even though the bill has not been vetted by the Supreme Court of Canada or approved by Parliament.[40]

On 5 June 2003, when a Swedish national vote was held, Swedish legislators voted to allow same-sex couples to adopt children. The Salt Lake Tribune in a 6 June 2003 news release further commented upon this action by the Swedish legislature:

> . . . a decision that gay activists hailed as a step toward getting the full benefits of marriage. Under the bill, gays registered in a legal partnership, allowed in Sweden since 1995, can be considered joint adoptive parents of children adopted in the country or abroad. One of the partners also will be able to adopt the child of another.

The measures, approved Wednesday after several hours of heated debate, make the nation of about 9 million people one of the few countries to give homosexuals the right to enter legal partnerships and adopt children.

Even rarer was the inclusion of adoptions of children abroad, although it could have little practical effect since most countries forbid adoption by homosexuals.

That last sentence of the above quote should not stand as the final judgment upon same-sex adoptions. The pendulum of liberal social pressure is swinging toward spiritual anarchy in the social and theological pursuits, not only of governmental agencies, but those of the liberal Christian churches as well. Christian spirituality through the Means of God's Grace, then becomes a non-issue, something to be buried in the grave of the archaic past.

In April 2000, Vermont became the first state in the nation to establish civil unions which for all practical purposes are the equivalent of same-sex marriage. Hawaii's Supreme Court decision allowing gay "marriage" denies traditional marriage by defining marriage in terms of legally protected economic benefits. Other nations, and some states here in America, are now being confronted with these many theological, social, and economic repercussions. The major issues, however, involve procreation and nurture of children through the family, as well as family unity which has held our American culture together. The main objection for Christians is that same-sex marriage is an abomination to God. God ordained marriage for a man and a woman to be joined together as one flesh. Genesis 2: 22–24 is most explicit:

> And the Lord God fashioned into a woman the rib which He had taken from the man. And the man said: "This is now bone of my bones, And flesh of my flesh; She shall be called Woman, Because she was taken out of Man." For this cause a man shall leave his father and his mother, and shall cleave to his wife; and they shall become one flesh.

This Godly concept of marriage has been redefined by liberals in the "mainline" churches of America, by those in places of influence in education, and by a media bent on Christian bashing to the point where they are aiming their hedonistic logic at Christians, trying to convince them of a new definition of marriage. The word "commitment" takes center stage as they claim marriage is merely a commitment between two people, no matter what their sex may be. The implications for such a definition to take national root and become accepted by tolerant folk, whether Christian or non-churched, will tear the family unit apart.

In February 2002, the American Academy of Pediatrics (AAP) insisted that new laws be passed allowing same-sex couples to adopt children. Their reasoning followed the liberal lines that all is well if the children are physically cared for. They had nothing to say about the spiritual care of such children.[41] If by now you are not convinced or aware not only of the liberal neutrality toward God and His directives as perceived in national and state government and liberal church agendas, you may possibly have missed the, subtle, liberal coup d'état of spiritual affirmations in Holy Scripture.

The American Family Association (AFA) made this reply:

"This was not a decision based upon science, but instead reflects a growing tendency on the part of medical and mental health organizations to adopt the role of political advocacy groups," said AFA President Don Wildmon.

The AAP said in a press release that "there is a considerable body of professional literature that suggests children with parents who are homosexual" grow up no differently than those with heterosexual parents. As a result of its report, the AAP called for "legal and legislative efforts that provide for the possibility of adoption of . . . children by the second parent or coparent in same-sex relationships."

"I'm not sure what 'professional literature' the AAP looked at," Wildmon said, "but as recently as last summer researchers were calling into question this whole idea that kids raised by homosexuals turn out exactly like those raised by a mom and dad."

Wildmon referred to a report issued last July by University of Southern California sociology professors Judith Stacey and Timothy Biblarz, published in the American Sociological Review. While careful to say they believed that homosexuals suffered discrimination, Stacey and Biblarz also said political considerations had led researchers to downplay the fact that the sexual orientation of parents who were "gay" or lesbian did make a difference for children raised in such homes.

In reexamining these tainted studies, Stacey and Biblarz found that the research actually indicated that: young people raised in lesbian homes were much more likely to have had same-sex experiences; young girls raised by lesbian "mothers" were more likely to be sexually adventurous; and boys raised by lesbians were less likely to behave in typically masculine ways.[42]

Governor Rick Perry of Texas on 27 May 2003 signed a "Defense of Marriage Act" which stated that same-sex or civil unions will not be recognized in Texas. The Houston Chronicle included the following quotes:

"It's about politics. It's about scapegoating gays and lesbians," said Randall Ellis, executive director of the Lesbian Gay Rights Lobby of Texas.

Existing statues specify that, in Texas, this state's laws apply even to marriages performed in other states, Ellis said.

. . . But supporters said the act was needed to protect Texans from the legal decisions of judges in other states where same-sex unions could be recognized.

"What this does, it protects your state from having a different definition forced on you from another state," said Kelly Shackelford, president of the Plano-based Free Market Foundation, a group that describes itself as dedicated to strengthening families.

. . . "Like the vast majority of Texans, I believe that marriage represents a sacred union between a man and a woman. With passage of the Defense of Marriage Act, Texas now joins more than 30 states in reinforcing that basic belief," Perry said in a prepared statement afterward.

Texas becomes the 37th state to enact such a law, Shackelford said.[43]

On 28 April 2003, Jeffrey Satinover, M.D. gave the following testimony before a Massachusetts State Senate Committee:

302

> What is known, from decades of research on family structure, studying literally thousands of children, is that every departure from the traditional, stable, mother-father family has severe detrimental effects upon children; and these effects persist not only into adulthood but into the next generation as well. In short, the central problem with the mother-mother or father-father families is that they deliberately institute, and intend to keep in place indefinitely, a family structure known to be deficient.

Many weak arguments are made by liberal theologians to substantiate the cause of same- sex marriage, all emerging from sexual ideology and not from God's Word. One such argument comes from James B. Nelson, who claims "there is some emerging evidence that the union of gay or lesbian Christians were celebrated earlier than heterosexual marriages."[44] "Emerging evidence" reeks of reconstructed history, for if the evidence was in the history of mankind, it would have surfaced long ago.

Further complicating the homosexual issue was the 6–3 decision by The United States Supreme Court on 26 June 2003 which struck down Texas' sodomy law thus giving sodomy a guaranteed right for all.[45] This reversed the Supreme Court's 1986 ruling in Bowers v. Hardwick which stated: "The Constitution does not confer a fundamental right upon homosexuals to engage in sodomy." Liberal courts and liberal churches are morally and spiritually changing America. They are confusing civil rights with God's institution of marriage. They champion sin while ignoring God's design for the family which leads to procreation and societal equilibrium.

Interestingly enough, on 30 July 2003, President George Bush disclosed that government lawyers are exploring measures to legally define marriage as a union between a man and a woman. Bush said: "I believe in the sanctity of marriage. I believe a marriage is between a man and a woman, and I think we ought to codify that one way or another."[46]

Amid the legal posturing, the State of Massachusetts began legalizing same-sex marriages on 17 May 2004. Governor Mitt Romney's last ditch efforts failed to reverse a court order which gave a green light to same-sex marriages.[47] The battle between traditional and same-sex marriage recognition will eventually have to be settled by the adoption or the defeat of a federal constitutional amendment banning same-sex marriage.

Now from the legal, back to the historical which also has theological implications. Liberal theologians and denominations, beside junking the authority of God in Scripture in their mad scramble to be liberally relevant in and to a postmodern culture, ignore the irrefutable evidence of history. *Every civilization or culture that has embraced homosexuality has fallen in ruin.* Not one has been proven to be able to survive its depravity. Liberals have tried to rewrite history to their benefit, but when it comes to rewriting and reshaping morality, history has proven them to be total failures. The basic truth is that our God will not bless what He cannot honor, nor honor what He cannot bless. The truth of history cannot be ignored.

Sexual liberation concentrates on the erotic in this world. It has nothing to say in support of Christian spirituality normed in and through Holy Scripture. As such, it has nothing to say about salvation from sin and death. It is an ideology of man that has been seductively introduced into Christian theology by liberal theologians. When stripped of its pretenses it is nothing more than sexual hedonism (a doctrine that sexual pleasure or happiness is the sole or chief good in life).

It is bankrupt theology because God, as Father, Son, and Holy Spirit has no place in it, other than to be mentioned for His attribute of love. In reality, gay and lesbian activists and theologians are running away from God because they do not want to live by His absolute rules for marriage and responsible sex which He offers as gifts in His Holy Word, the Scriptures. When denominations side with homosexuality and same-sex marriage, do they understand that what they are doing is legitimizing sexual sin as normal Christian behavior? Christian spirituality in the holy bonds of matrimony is then placed upon the sacrificial altar of the *god of this world* to be consumed by the fires of human reason—fires lighted by liberal clergy and theologians in denominations where the authority of God's inerrant and infallible Word has been desecrated as unfit for a post-modern, ever-changing, relativistic culture.

In the face of all heretical reasoning posing as up-to-date Christian theology, stands God, the Creator, Redeemer, and Sanctifier of His beloved. God is still God no matter how liberal theologians may attempt to alter or even negate His Lordship as Father, Son, and Holy Spirit. He is not a "She," nor is He susceptible to change by a changing society and culture. Hebrews 13:8 declares: "Jesus Christ is the same yesterday and today, yes and forever." He is Alpha and Omega! His decrees in Holy Scripture regarding sex and marriage will never be overcome as will any of His truths in His Holy Word in Scripture, lovingly shared and inspired by His Holy Spirit to all His beloved.

NOTES

1. James Nuechterlein, *The Gayest Story Ever Told,* in First Things, December 1998: 8, 9.
2. Philip L. Culbertson, *Men and Christian Friendship,* in Men's Bodies, Men's Gods, B.

Krondorfer, ed., (New York: New York University Press, 1996), 174.

3. James B. Nelson, Epilogue, in *Men's Bodies, Men's God's*, B. Krondorfer, ed. (New York: New York University Press, 1996), 317.

4. Ibid., 317, 318.

5. James B. Nelson, *Homosexuality and the Church*, in Christianity and Crisis, 4 April 1977.

6. Ibid.

7. James G. Wolf, ed., *Gay Priests*, (New York: Harper & Row Publishers, 1989), 60.

8. See *Goodby, Good Men*, Michael S. Rose, (Washington D.C.: Regnery Publishing, Inc., 2002). Rose reveals a seminary underworld where homosexuality is widespread and where seminarians who support the teaching of the Roman Catholic Church are persecuted.

9. Mary Walsh, "Clean Out the Seminaries' Closets," in *Human Events, 24 June 2002*, 16.

10. Barbara Olson, *The Final Days*, (Washington D.C.: Regnery Publishing, Inc., 2001), 78, 79.

11. Howard Phillips, *"The Bottom Line,"* in *Gays in the Military*, ed., George Grant (Franklin Tennessee: Legacy Communications, 1993), 76, 77.

12. Rossiikaya Gazeta, 13 March 2003, as translated and reported in *The Salt Lake Union Tribune* of that date.

13. Thomas C. Oden, *Requiem: A Lament in Three Movements* (Nashville, Abingdon Press, 1996), 116.
14. Thomas C. Reeves, op.cit., 21.
15. William Murchison, First Things 77 (November 1997), 16, 17.
16. Edward E. Plowman in WORLD, 19 July 2003, 24.
17. David Skidmore, *Episcopal News Service*, 6 August 2003.
18. Richard N. Ostling, The Bremerton Sun, "Conservatives begin rally," 8 October 2003.
19. Rachel Zoll, "Episcopal Church schism," The Seattle Times, 18 October 2003
20. Lynn Vincent. "Go forth and sin" in WORLD, 2 August 2003, 23.
21. ELCA News article of 12 August 2003.
22. ELCA News article of 18 August 2003.
23. Beverly Wildung Harrison, *Theology of Pro-Choice,* in *Women and Religion,* Elizabeth A. Clark and Herbert Richardson, eds., (Harper San Francisco, 1996), 294.
24. Eric Gorski, *Denver Post,* Religion Section, 25 May 2003.
25. Ibid.
26. *World,* "Defining ethics down," 19 April 2003, 79.
27. *World,* "4 More Years," 22 May 2004, 26.
28. Kevin Eckstrom, Religious News Service, 21 June 2001;

29. Carter Heyward, *Coming Out and Relational Empowerment* in *Women and Religion,* Elizabeth A. Clark and Herbert Richardson, eds. (Harper, San Francisco, 1996), 304, 305.
30. Carter Heyward, *Our Passion for Justice,* (New York: The Pilgrim Press, 1984), 89.
31. Ibid., 173.
32. Ibid., 119.
33. James Dobson and Gary L. Bauer, *Children At Risk*, (Dallas: Word Publishing 1990), 107.
34. United Church News, April 2001.
35. Ibid.
36. Ibid.
37. 73rd General Convention of the Episcopal Church, Denver, Colorado, July 2000.
38. Marlin Maddoux, *"The Seven Myths of Gay Pride,"* in *Gays in the Military,* (Franklin, Tennessee: Lacey Communications, 1993), 30, 31.
39. Don Feder, *Who's Afraid Of The Religious Right?* (Ottawa, Illinois: Jameson Books, Inc., 1996), 86.
40. See *http://law-library.rutgers.edu/SSM.html* for a comprehensive review.
41. American Academy of Pediatrics (AAP) news release, 4 February 2002.
42. American Family news release, 4 February 2002.
43. Associated Press, *Houston Chronicle*, 27 May 2003.

44. James B. Nelson, *Body Theology*, (Louisville: Westminster/John Knox Press, 1992), 64.
45. See http://manifestonews.org/Morgue/2003/JuneJuly/News/Nation/News01.html
46. USA Today, 30 July 2003.
47. Pam Belluck and Katie Zezima, *The New York Times,* as quoted in *The Seattle Times,* 16 May 2004, 1.

CHAPTER 10

Abortion

*For Thou didst form my inward parts; Thou didst
weave me in my mother's womb. I will give thanks
to Thee, for I am fearfully and wonderfully made;
Wonderful are Thy works, And my soul knows it
very well.*

(Psalm 139: 13,14)

Consider this scenario: A pregnant teen-
ager comes to a Crisis Pregnancy Center
(CPC). She is frightened and desperate.
Not wanting to be alone, she receives permission
to have her friend in the room as she completes
the basic questionnaire and talks with the counselor. Before completing the questionnaire, she
blurts out: "What's it like to have an abortion?"

The counselor, in a gentle and non-graphic manner, explains the medical procedure and asks if she

311

has discussed her options with anyone. At this point, her friend jumps to her feet, standing in anger in the face of the counselor and snarls: "I know this place! You will try to talk her out of her right to choose! Well, let me tell you, I had an abortion and it didn't bother me!" Her anger is more than threatening. At that moment, all the training and prayers that supported the counselor come to the fore. Not backing away from this face to face encounter, the counselor calmly and with compassion, replies: "You have to believe that lie in order to live with the deed, don't you?"

Immediately the angered friend's entire countenance changes. Tears come to her eyes and in a now quiet voice she says: "No one ever said that to me before." Turning to her friend, putting her arms around her, she counsels her friend to carry her baby to term and not abort as she had done.

A fanciful story? No way! This is an account of a true story that occurred at the CPC in El Cajon, California, some years ago. The counselor was my beloved wife, Barbe.

Abortion has always been living the lie of convenience except when the *life* of the mother is in question. Ever since that fateful day of 22 January 1973 when the Roe v. Wade decision of the Supreme Court descended upon the pre-born in America, the issue of life versus death has resulted in about 42 million abortions, murder in the womb. This number represents well over thirty-six times the number of Americans killed in battle in all the wars fought by our country. Unbelievable? Please tally the following number of killed in action (KIA) in the following wars:

Revolutionary War	25,324
Civil War	498,332
World War I	116,708
World War II	407,316
Korean War	54,246
Vietnam War	58,655
Total[1]	1,160,581
War on the Unborn	42,000,000

The well known adage that "liars figure and figures lie" cannot be applied here. The truth is overwhelming. The planned and executed deaths of the pre-born can only come from a society and culture that has abandoned the Word of God. God is most clear in His Word that He is the One Who gives life. He knows each child in the womb. Consider Psalm 139:13,14, Isaiah 49:1, Jeremiah 1:5, Galatians 1:15, and Ephesians 1:3,4. Throughout Scripture the will of God for His beloved, pre-born and born, is life. Otherwise, why even speak of life? In no way has God sanctioned murder and that is exactly what abortion is.

"But how," you ask, "can it be otherwise?" The answer is simple, yet sickeningly real. The Supreme Court of our nation has ruled in the Roe v. Wade decision that the fetus is a non-person with no rights at all in any stage of pregnancy. The only person in a pregnancy that has rights is the mother with her undeniable right to privacy. In her right to privacy, she has been given the option of choice, either life or death, for the unborn child in her womb.

The unborn child is termed as a "Product of Conception" (POC), a "glob," a mass of tissue and blood inside her body. This is an explanation given by abortion counselors to women while they are making the decision to abort when they ask: "Is it a baby yet?"

This is deception at its height. In the New Testament, the Greek noun for an unborn child is the same as the noun used to denote an infant or a child older than an infant. In the Greek, it is *brephos*. It is the noun used to describe Jesus, unborn and born in Luke 1:41 and 1:44 (unborn), and in Luke 2:12 and in Luke 2:16 (born). It is also used in Luke 18:15; Acts 7:19; 2nd Timothy 3:15; and in 1st Peter 2:2. In no way does our God regard an unborn child or babe as a mere mass of tissue which can easily be discarded as a glob. The child *is* a product of conception! It *is* a child! Even the use of the word, "fetus," as used by pro-choice advocates, is a semantic cover-up. Fetus is a Latin word, meaning: "young one."

The words "pro-choice" and "pro-life" have been dominant words on the American scene since that fateful day of 22 January 1973. Their use polarizes both church and society. They determine sides in a "Civil War" going on today which is centered on the battlefield of the worth and value of human life. Dobson and Bauer make this evaluation:

> Not coincidentally, the issue of abortion most resembles the other issue that led our forefathers to literally take up arms against each other—the question of slavery. In many crucial ways, abortion and slavery are not merely similar issues.—they are the same.[2]

Demonstrations showing face to face confrontation between pro-life and pro-choice activists have filled our television screens. But have you noticed one distinctive feature in these demonstrations? One side shows irate anger and hatred toward anyone who would attempt to block their freedom of choice. The other side has a countenance of loving compassion and concern for both the mother and the unborn. One has to be almost blind to miss the difference in the facial countenance of both groups. If the face is the mirror of the heart, as many claim, then we have seen the face of the *god of this world* revealed, a face of anger, murder and spiritual destruction.

Indicative of this countenance is the loss of moral and spiritual values. When liberal protestors dem-

315

onstrate against the death penalty for murderers judged guilty by courts of law, and then condone the death penalty for the innocent in the womb, moral and spiritual chaos rules the day. Some commentators, columnists, and authors define this "Civil War" as the most controversial social issue of our time. It is so much more than a social issue. It is a theological issue which has temporal as well as eternal consequences.

The temporal consequences are both evident as well as hidden. The evident consequences are the millions of deaths of the unborn, the number of which is never disputed by those of the pro-choice persuasion. As well, abortion becomes the platform from which to ride the tide toward infanticide, the killing of infants outside the womb, and euthanasia, the extermination of the aged "who have become burdens" to both family and society. Dr. Jack Kevorkian is a leader in this endeavor toward "mercy killings." Peter Singer of Princeton University also echoes this theme.

Then, add to all this, the impact abortion has on morality and spirituality. The unwanted consequence of teen sex, such as pregnancy, venereal disease, and emotional dysfunction, can be glibly dismissed as mere physical intrusions. Sex without consequences becomes an established norm from which attacks on honesty, responsibility, and God's Word are launched. Morality becomes whatever is relevant to the individual. The goal lines and sidelines of morality are blurred in "belly button" ethics. Spirituality disappears when God is abandoned as the Creator of all life.

The not so evident consequences, hidden beneath the surface, hit the woman the hardest, so it seems. More often than not, the male can walk away from abortion as having been granted financial relief and possible forced marriage reprieve. But can he? There remains, no matter how deep the denial, the fact that a murder has been committed, a life denied the right of birth. In my ministry in civilian churches and in the Navy chaplaincy, I have counseled men who wish they could reverse the abortion they demanded or did nothing about. I was able to hold out to them the forgiveness which only the Lord can grant to penitent hearts.

The woman has the most difficult burden to bear. No matter what Planned Parenthood or other pro-abortion counselors have said to try to convince her that a "glob," or a product of conception, is all that is in her womb, deep within she instinctively knows better. The maternal instinct has been intricately woven into the fabric of her being by God, an instinct governed by hormones so strong that she cannot fully deny it, try as she may. It is when this instinct surfaces from the hidden depth of her life, combined with the reality of what she has "chosen" to do, that a traumatic burden too heavy to bear alone, comes to the fore.

This burden can take many avenues of expression: intrusive, spontaneous thoughts and images, nightmares, flashbacks that make her feel as though she were actually re-experiencing the abortion, distress when exposed to events that symbolize or resemble the abortion experience (trigger events), anniversary reactions, and suicidal thoughts. These flashbacks, like a latent disease about to erupt, are real and are known as post-traumatic stress disorder (PTSD) or post-abortion syndrome.

Post-abortion syndrome has no time limit. It can hit days, months, or years after the abortion. Its criteria is identical to the post-traumatic war syndrome experienced by combat veterans like myself. When the reality hits concerning what abortion has done to her child in the womb, a woman can be swept by guilt and regret into the depths of depression. The trauma of abortion surfaces unannounced, just like the trauma of war.

It is oppressive, like a weight around all of life. It does not evaporate. Planned Parenthood and abortion activists cannot make it disappear. They are helpless in the face of the lie they have helped create. Nothing they say or propose alleviates the burden. Their words are like chaff blowing in the wind. Their only counsel is to "compassionately" assure her that she has done the right and best thing for herself and her "fetus." Abortion activists avoid calling the product of conception a "baby." "Fetus" represents a non-life entity, an easily disposable bodily intrusion. Certainly this cannot be in harmony with God's revealed plan of abundant life in His Son, Jesus, and in His perfect Word, the Holy Scriptures, for all of life.

If per chance, the reader has experienced, or is now experiencing post-abortion syndrome, seek the counsel of your pastor, who, hopefully, is committed to Scripture as the true Word of God. As well, find a crisis pregnancy center that will work with your pastor or priest in the healing process. Yes, there is healing, but it comes only from God, not through the fanciful ruminations of those committed to abortion. My beloved, Barbe, has been a post-abortion group facilitator since 1981 and has seen healing take place, but only in and through God's Means of Grace which point to Jesus Christ as the Healer, the Savior.

The eternal consequence of abortion is physical death of the unborn and spiritual death of those who abort and those who encourage and perform the act. However, the day of God's grace has not ended and those who truly seek the Lord's forgiveness for the killing of the unborn will receive God's mercy. This is the promise that can be realized only through new life in Jesus Who bore the weight of all sin for every one of us sinners. I dare say that almost 99 and 9/10th percent of clergy have had or still do have opportunities to counsel those who come to them with the guilt and grief of abortion heavy upon their hearts. Thanks be to God that abortion guilt and grief can be addressed and forgiveness proclaimed in and through Jesus and His sacrifice on Calvary's cross.

One of the most famous of all the abortionists, Dr. Bernard Nathanson, came to new life in Jesus and embraced Christianity. As an abortionist, he had performed over 60,000 abortions. Today he is one of its fiercest foes. Realizing that a society's ethical and moral climate is revealed in its treatment of the weak and defenseless, he stopped performing abortions. With ultrasound technology well established, he saw first hand what was going on in the womb during the abortion procedure. Colson and Pearcey describe the following:

> He asked a colleague who was performing several abortions a day to put an ulrasound device on a few of his patients and, with their permission, tape the procedure.
>
> Nathanson knew quite well what happened in an abortion. Yet when he saw abstract concepts

transformed into vivid images—when he actually witnessed tiny bodies being torn limb from
limb—he was startled and revolted. Even more
sickening, the ultrasound showed the babies trying to wiggle away from the suction apparatus.
One twelve-week fetus continued to struggle
even after it had been severely maimed, opening his mouth in what looked horrifyingly like a
scream of fear and pain.[3]

Nathanson made the tape of this twelve-week
fetus into a film entitled, *The Silent Scream,* a
monumental work that even abortion activists
had to admit showed the taking of human life.
The evidence was crystal clear. It was murder in
the womb.

Abortion murder can also be administered
through a non-surgical/medical abortion, abortion by a pill, usually for early pregnancies before the seventh week period following conception.
The pill has been named Mifepristone or Mifprex
(RU-486). It works by blocking the effect of proges-
terone, a hormone that is essential for a pregnancy
to continue. Some times an injection of Methotrex-
ate is used instead of the pill. Two days after receiving Mifprex, the woman returns for a dose of
Misoprostol, a drug originally used to treat peptic
ulcers. G. D. Searle & Company, which developed
Misoprostol, has refused to sanction its use for in-
ducing abortions due to the lack of safety for off-
label use. This drug induces uterine contractions to

expel the conceived child. Usually within four days the fetus or developing child is expelled in death. If not, a surgical abortion is performed. The mother delivers her tiny dead baby at home, usually alone. The danger of hemorrhage and possible death of the mother is a real and threatening possibility. This procedure is not simply "popping a pill!"

Abortion murder occurs not only in the womb, but also in the birth canal in the procedure known as dilation and extraction (D and X). It is more commonly referred to as "partial birth abortion" by pro-life advocates and is performed late in the pregnancy. In this procedure, the uterus of the mother is dilated, an unnatural and potentially dangerous procedure in itself. Using ultrasound to locate the baby's feet, an instrument is inserted into the womb to grasp the feet for removal as the baby has not yet turned headfirst to be delivered. With the legs and body outside the birth canal and the head still in the birth canal, medical scissors are thrust into the back of the skull, opening access to the brain which is then suctioned out, collapsing the skull, affording delivery of a dead child. If the child had been killed outside the birth canal it would be murder.

The legality of this procedure radically changed on 4 June 2003 when the U. S. House of Representatives by a two-thirds vote (282–139), joined the Senate, approving a ban on partial-birth abortions.

> The bill (H.R. 760) legally defines a partial-birth abortion as any abortion in which the baby is delivered alive until "in the case of breech presentation, any part of the fetal trunk past the navel is outside the body of the mother," or if the baby is delivered head first, "the entire fetal head is outside the body of the mother," before being killed.

> H.R. 760 would allow the method if it was ever necessary to save a mother's life.[4]

However, the very day this ban was passed three federal lawsuits were filed in Nebraska, New York, and California granting injunctions until the cases can be heard in court. Federal judges in San Francisco and Omaha have limited the scope of evidence government attorneys can present thus making it an uphill battle to defend the ban.

Some ten months later, on 13 April 2004, in a New York courtroom Dr. Kanwaljeet Anand, a famous neonatal pediatrician and pain expert, gave his testimony. John Dawson reports:

> Dr. Anand took the stand in the morning and testified for hours that unborn children can feel pain even more vividly than adults or even

infants. He said that by 20 weeks fetuses have developed all the nerve and brain functions to feel pain, but none of the coping mechanisms that help infants and adults deal with the sensation. According to Dr. Anand's research, handling the fetus in the womb, delivering the child up to its head, slicing open its skull and sucking out the brains would all produce "prolonged and excruciating pain to the fetus."

The evidence for fetal pain is not new—Dr. Anand studied expressions of pain in unborn and neonatal children as early as the 1980s— but the legal argument is novel. Unlike previous legislative attempts to ban partial-birth abortion, Congress used a fetal-pain argument to rally support. If a fetus does feel pain as early as 20 weeks into pregnancy, it bolsters Congress' ethical argument for banning the procedure. And in the courtroom it humanizes the unborn child in a way that the pro-life legal community has never been able to do.[5]

The delay in enforcing the ban could take years to resolve.

In spite of judicial activism the abortion issue is being shown for what it is—murder. Not even pointing to "back alley abortions" can be presented as a legitimate reason for the "safety" of abortion clinics. Nathanson helped torpedo that myth when he admitted the statistics published on "back alley abortions" showing large numbers were inflated in order for abortionists to make quick and easy money.[6] In Chicago, when Nathanson was interning at Michael Reese Hospital before the Roe v. Wade Supreme Court decision of 1973, there was a drinking song sung by the gynecological interns:

> There's a fortune . . . in abortion
> Just a twist of the wrist and you're through.
> The population . . . of the nation
> Won't grow if it's left up to you,
> In the daytime . . . in the nighttime
> There is always some work to undo.
> Oh, there's a fortune . . . in abortion
> But you'll wind up in the pen before you're through.

> Now there's a gold mine . . . in the sex line
> And it's so easy to do,
> Not only rabbits . . . have those habits
> So why worry 'bout typhoid and flu?
> You never bother . . . the future father
> And there are so many of them, too.
> Oh, there's a fortune . . . in abortion
> But you'll wind up in the pen before you're through.[7]

The "not so silent merger" of the world into the life of the Christian Church cannot be covered up or hidden when it comes to abortion. This is most evident in liberal denominations where a word game is played. Instead of using the word "abortion," a softer descriptive term is embraced. It is the word "choice." After all, are not Americans free to choose?

We live in a free country and are only restrained by law, so when the highest court in our land no longer deems abortion to be illegal, the flood gates of choice are opened wide.

Choice becomes the right choice, even the choice to murder the unborn. Liberal denominations, impressed by the Roe v. Wade decision, turned not to the Word of God for direction, but to the prevailing, sin-filled culture for their direction. They set a course that can in no way be considered Christian. Could it be that these liberal "mainline" denominations are unaware of their culpability in enabling "the fruits of abortion" to fester long after the event? Their unwillingness to address the consequences of choice that lead to abortion is evidence that to do so would be an admission they have supported a lie unto death.

Liberals will argue vehemently that the sin lies with orthodox denominations who embrace the inerrant and infallible Word of God as truth. It is their prejudice, their intolerance which causes the problem. The so-called "religious right" are out of step with the prevailing culture and in order to be relevant to that culture they must change, or else be ignored, or laughed at as being obsolete, old-fashioned, and not with it.

Liberal "mainline" denominations like cabooses on trains follow the engines of change. They are not

326

at the forefront, but merely along for the ride, believing the power of the world should propel theology. In utter amazement they look at the absurdity of the inflexibility of those denominations where Holy Scripture is held to be the true Word of God. Once more the issue has deeper roots than abortion or homosexuality. The issue is the historical-critical method of biblical interpretation wherein biblical scholars, under the full influence of 18th century reason, claimed their right to judge, rule, and interpret Scripture according to their academic fancy. It is still the question of authority as seen in Chapter 3.

When the prevailing culture is blended into varying theologies that are barren of God's authority in His Word, the concoction that emerges has little semblance to Christianity, although the name is retained to add appealing flavor to the blend. Rather than take on a culture and a society wherein abortion has been legalized, liberal denominations have thrown in the towel. After all, with God's authority neutered in their biblical interpretations, the way for liberal theology has already been paved. Physical and spiritual death line their roadways.

Support for choice has not been exclusively in the liberal camp. Unfortunately, there are clergy whose denominations condemn abortion by choice as sin and murder, yet knuckle under to the pressure of the culture. They believe to do otherwise would mean alienating members in the congregation who have opted for abortion. A classic example is a prominent Lutheran Church-Missouri Synod clergyman in a large congregation in Orange County, California, who preached a pro-life sermon one Sunday. As he stood at the church door greeting the worshipers, he was accosted by an irrate, tearful woman claiming he was insensitive to take on the issue of abortion in church. She vowed never to return again. Instead of using the woman's pain, expressed in anger, as an opportunity for concerned pastoral care, this pastor made a vow never to preach pro-life sermons again. Unfortunately, this is a true story told to my wife by a pastor whom she had approached to enlist his support for the lives of the unborn. She was turned away.

On the front cover of the Winter 2001 issue of *Life Date*, a publication of National Lutherans For Life, appears these words:

ABORTION: A Matter of the Heart

Refusing to talk about abortion in our churches forfeits the opportunity to "speak to the heart" of those who have had abortions and to share with them the only source of forgiveness, healing, and hope that can really make a difference . . . the Gospel of Jesus Christ.

Indeed our silence on the issue can unintentionally reinforce what so many post-abortive women already feel. "This sin is too big to be forgiven."

Spineless clergy, sadly enough, are in Christian churches that confess Scripture as the true Word of God. The *god of this world* has numbed them to inaction, compromise, and silence on the life issue. If clergy will not stand for life, but turn their backs on the murder of the unborn so as not to offend, how can they claim to be men of God? Their posture is one of advantageous spiritual surrender and betrayal. Just maybe the liberal winds of theological deconstruction have filled their sails, making their determination not to offend, their way of doing ministry. Post-abortive victims are in almost every Christian congregation. Will their shepherds allow the wounded sheep to suffer in torment? If the clergy refuse, or are unable, to deal with the sanctity of life, all other issues, causes, or programs are moot. An active pro-life stand is more than a cause or a program. It is a home mission field ripe for the harvest of souls.

THE LUTHERAN, in its 7 March 1984 edition, echoed the tenor of Protestant liberalism in regard to abortion. Joy Bussert, then a pastor in the Lutheran Church in America which became The Evangelical Lutheran Church in America, wrote an article entitled: *Can abortion be life-giving?* Naturally, her position was strongly pro-choice with reverence to be shown toward the mother and against a "pro-fetus" stance. The child in the womb was made to appear that he or she had stature and acceptance only if certain social, emotional, and financial conditions had been met. Bussert maintained:

> For many women the decision to terminate a pregnancy can be an expression of reverence and concern for life, not only for her own life but also for the quality of life of the fetus or future child. Since women often intuitively know when they can or cannot care for a child, the termination of an unwanted pregnancy is often an expression of serious concern for life, so serious that a woman is not willing to bring into the world a life for which she cannot adequately care.

> Clearly, reverence for life means that every child has the God-given right to be brought into this world under conditions conducive to love. Love of life does not mean that society should maximize the number of children born. It means that society can love children best by not having so many that some must be deprived of adequate love and attention, or, worse yet, even abused.[8]

The above words reflect the essence of the pro-choice position of liberal denominations. Please read them once more and try, if you can, to equate them with Psalm 139:13–16; Job 31:15; Deuteronomy 30:119, and Colossians 1:16[9] Bussert and other liberal theologians and clergy seem intent on setting the parameters for life, a prerogative that rests solely with God. Are there still any questions in your mind as to *who* wants to rule the Church and the world?

My wife, Barbe, wrote a rebuttal to Bussert's article, but *THE LUTHERAN* returned the copy with the explanation that they had already dealt with the other side of the issue which they certainly did, in a pro-choice way. Barbe sent the same rebuttal to John Cardinal O'Connor in New York, a dear friend from the days I served under him in Washington, D.C. when he was Chief of Navy Chaplains. Graciously, he asked for permission to quote Barbe's words. Guess it depends on a theology of God, rooted in the absolutes of Holy Scripture, or a liberal man-made theology of creation management.

Beverly Wildung Hanson, a liberation feminist who was quoted in the last chapter, brings to the abortion issue a common social and relativistic view that attempts to overhaul the realm of procreation. This view has been widely acclaimed and admired by liberal feminist, theological architects. She explains:

> . . . a feminist theological approach recognizes that *nothing* is more urgent . . . then to recognize that the entire natural-historical context of human procreation has shifted. We desperately need a desacralization of our *biological* power to reproduce, and at the same time a real concern

for human dignity and the social conditions for personhood and the values of human relationship. And note that desacralization does not mean complete devaluation of the worth of procreation. It means that we must shift away from the notion that the central metaphors for divine blessing are expressed at the biological level to the recognition that our social relations bear the image of what is most holy.[10]

If this isn't the shifting of the focus of liberal theology away from God and onto man, excuse me, onto persons, what is? It represents making unholy what God set in motion as His holy gift of procreation for all mankind. It takes God out of procreation, our God who alone can give life, and make "social relations" among humans, no matter what they may be, *holy*. The agenda of feminine liberationists is to deconstruct God as Father, Son, and Holy Spirit and put in His place contorted ideologies which attempt to convince society that not only is pro-choice the only acceptable choice, but a holy one at that.

What is most confusing is the oppression issue which undergirds all of liberation theology. What can be more oppressive than the killing of the unborn in the womb or partially out of the birth canal? Sadly, liberationists view it as choice, not as oppression. Since the unborn child is not viable until the birth has fully taken place, they maintain with the help of the courts, that oppression has not taken place. This is their way out of facing and dealing with the murder of the unborn.

James B. Nelson writes about a Roman Catholic theologian by the name of Daniel Maguire who determined to acquire a meaningful view of what abortion is about. Maguire obtained permission to make visits to a local abortion clinic so as to see for himself. Nelson reports:

> He sat in on problem pregnancy counseling sessions and was struck by how vacuous the slogans of the debate are in the face of these concrete, living, human dilemmas. He held in his hand the plastic bag with the product of an abortion, and later reflected, "It was impressive to realize that I was holding in the cup what many people think to be the legal and moral peer of a woman, if not, indeed her superior . . . . I have held babies in my hands and now I held this embryo. I know the difference . . . . We are more sensitized to embryos than to the women who bear them . . . (and) until we open our affections to enlightenment here, we will none of us be wise."[11]

Wisdom unto death. The inability of this theologian to understand the issue so as to tip the scales of life toward the mother, even when her life is not in danger, reveals the commonly accepted mind-set of a liberal culture in regard to viability. The unborn are viewed as worthless blobs of developing flesh and blood that have no right to life until birth suddenly conveys on them that right. Otherwise, they can be wrapped in plastic and discarded in the trash or else have their broken body parts sold to industry for cosmetics or pending medical research.

As has been presented, the merger of the world in and with the Christian Church has been the intrusion of the secular on the sacred. Consequently, liberal denominations led by theologians who have elevated their authority as superior to God's authority, have nothing to say to the world which presents the spiritual and moral side of any issue, such as homosexuality or abortion. They have stripped themselves spiritually naked before the absolutes of God's law and gospel in Scripture. What they propose as theology is "manology," ideologies normed by a culture in revolt against God. They join the sinful chorus of this world and sing a tune composed by the *god of this world,* the words of which echo spiritual death. The spiritual SARS virus infects again!

Already named in this work have been liberal "mainline" denominations who affirm abortion as acceptable "choice" to be leveled on the unborn or partially-born. The Rev. Dr. James Lamb of Lutherans For Life, provides a more inclusive list, but not totally inclusive of those denominations which support abortion as choice. The front runners are members of the "Religious Coalition for Reproductive Choice" (RCRC). Lamb identifies them:

> RCRC comprises more than 40 national organizations from 18 denominations, movements, and faith groups. They include the Episcopal Church, Presbyterian Church (USA), United Church of Christ, United Methodist Church, Unitarian Universalist Association, and the Conservative, Humanist, Reconstructionist, and Reform movements of Judaism. According to their website, they believe that "Abortion can be a moral, ethical, and religiously responsible decision."[12]

The Christian Church must never abdicate its loyalty to God and to His Word, His love message in Jesus. It must always be specific because God's truth is always specific and always loving. It must not turn in the winds of culture. Nor dare it bend and flee in the face of sinful persecution. God's truth is always uncompromising, absolute, because it is His truth, not man's. His truth has never been proven wrong. Ignored, yes. Attacked as out-dated, yes. Deconstructed and reconstructed as many foreign truths, yes. Never, however, proven to be a celestial fairy tale. The precious gift of God through His Means of Grace has been given to the Christian Church for abundant spiritual life which is eternal. There is always the issue of accountability, and this the Christian Church cannot escape. God has so revealed. Please remember that our God never promised salvation to His beloved by means of social change.

Not even a former "most powerful person in the human world" can place a new spin on the acceptability of abortion. Barbara Olson shows how former President William Jefferson Clinton attempted to do so in the military. She reveals:

> Bill Clinton's feminist cheerleaders and the abortion lobby had to wait only two days into the Clinton presidency before a memorandum was issued allowing abortions on U. S. Military bases overseas, another reversal of Regan and Bush.[13]

Perhaps the biggest blow to abortion by any President since Roe v. Wade was carried in a 31 January 2002 Associated Press release by Laura Meckler. There, she describes the major redefinition of the pre-born from a "fetus" to an "unborn child." She reports:

> WASHINGTON - The Bush administration handed abortion opponents a symbolic victory Thursday, classifying a developing fetus as an "unborn child" as a way of extending prenatal care to low-income pregnant women.
>
> The plan allows states to extend health insurance to fetuses—or even embryos—from

the moment of conception by enrolling them in the State Children's Health Insurance program.

Health and Human Services Secretary Tommy Thompson said the goal was to quickly get more women prenatal care, which greatly increases the chances of delivering a healthy baby. "How anybody can turn this into a pro-choice or pro-life argument, I can't understand," Thompson said.

Activists on both sides of the issue did just that.

"This will strengthen the right-to-life philosophy," said Lou Sheldon, chairman of the Traditional Values Coalition, . . . Abortion rights supporters agreed, saying the change could help lay groundwork establishing the rights of a fetus and therefore outlawing abortion . . . . "It undermines the whole premise of Roe v. Wade by giving legal status to a fetus from the moment of conception," said Marcia Greenberger of the National Women's Law Center. She and others compared it to the legislation supported by the White House making it a crime to harm a fetus during an assault on its mother. "There's a pattern here to establish fetal personhood," said Kim Gandy, president of the National Organization for Women. "At this point you establish a fetus as a person under law, then even first trimester abortion becomes murder, and the Bush administration knows that."

Bush has offered regular encouragement to anti-abortion forces. He telephoned encouragement last week to anti-abortion marchers on the anniversary of Roe v. Wade. "Everybody there believes, as I do, that every life is valuable, that our society has a responsibility to defend the vulnerable and weak, the imperfect and even the unwanted, and that our nation should set a great goal—that unborn children should be welcomed in life and protected in law," he told them.[14]

The pro-choice advocates, have for the moment, had the pro-death rug pulled out from under them. I write "for the moment" as the battle still rages and has yet to see a final conclusion. However, to have the definition of a child in the womb be changed from a mere developing fetus to an "unborn child" is devastating to the pro-choice coalition.

This new definition, along with the "delayed" 4 June 2003 ban on partial birth abortion, challenges and attacks the Roe v. Wade decision which placed full autonomy upon the mother in her right to privacy to decide the fate of her child in her womb. Stay tuned because the Bush administration's classification of a fetus as an "unborn child" is having the same effect as when it was discovered that the earth revolved around the sun and not visa versa. It is a life revolution! The fetus is an unborn child! To kill that unborn child in abortion will stand as murder, which it always was and always will be.

A tumultuous decision now faces liberal denominations who have supported the pro-choice agenda. Do they continue in their march toward the death of the unborn via unbridled abortion, or do they come to their senses and see, in regard to life, that what God has decreed in His Word is true? Do they care about the spiritual lives of their people who have been victims of the abortion myth that the unborn can be held at the mercy of convenient choice, even unto death? The wounded by abortion abound in their congregations and liberal pastors have been co-conspirators of death.

How long will the pied pipers of death through abortion continue to sound cadence for their denominations? The question hovering over liberal denominations is: "When will you see the truth of God for all of life as it is revealed in God's Holy Word?" Ideologies can not cut the mustard. When challenging God's truth they can only crumble in dust and decay.

Be assured that man does not have the final word. Those denominations which will remain true to their "death march" on the unborn, will experience their own death march. God's beloved people will not be confused and deceived forever! Our God will not sanction or allow it. The light of His truth for all of life cannot be extinguished! His Word in Scripture tells us so.

Spiritual healing through God's Means of Grace, His Word and Sacraments, is the only remedy, the only abiding eternal verity for healing for casualties of abortion, precious souls of God who have danced to the enticing melody of "easy solutions for unwanted pregnancies." Easy is not of God. Life is! Physical life and eternal life! Our God is in both arenas!

NOTES

1. 1982 World Almanac.
2. James Dobson and Gary L Bauer, op. cit., 140.
3. Charles Colson and Nancy Pearsey, *How Now Shall We Live?* (Wheaton, Illinois: Tyndale House Publishers, Inc., 1999), 221.
4. 4 June 2003 news release from the National Right to Life Committee (NRLC) Washington, D.C.
5. John Dawson, *WORLD*, 24 April 2004, 24.
6. Bernard N. Nathanson and Richard N. Ostling, *Aborting America,* (Pinnacle Press Book, 1981, reprint), 197.
7. Ibid., 16.
8. Joy Bussert, "Can abortion be life-giving?" in *THE LUTHERAN,* 7 March 1984, 13.
9. Other pertinent Scripture passages: Job 10:8–13; Isaiah 44:24; Jeremiah 1:5; Galatians 1:15; Ephesians 1:3, 4; and Proverbs 24:11, 12 apply.

10. Beverly Wildung, op. cit., 288.
11. James B. Nelson, op. cit., 117.
12. James I. Lamb, *LifeDate,* Winter 2002, 2.
13. Barbara Olson, op. cit. 79.
14. Laura Meckler, San Diego Union, 31 January 2002, "Mothers Coverage," an Associated Press release.

CHAPTER 11

Ecclesiastical Megalomania

Again, the devil took Him to a very high mountain,
and showed Him all the kingdoms of the world, and
their glory; and said unto Him, "All these things
will I give You, if You will fall down and worship
me." Then Jesus said to him, "Begone, Satan! For
it is written, YOU SHALL WORSHIP THE LORD
YOUR GOD, AND SERVE HIM ONLY."

(Matthew 4: 8–10)

If you lived before the Second World War, you were acquainted with churches which served their ethnic oriented communities. Families with German, Danish, Norwegian, or Swedish backgrounds belonged to Lutheran Churches. Those of British and Scottish heritage tended toward the Episcopal, Presbyterian, and Methodist Churches; while the Irish, Italian, and Polish folk were usually Roman Catholic. Protestant churches were normally smaller in structural size and in membership than those which were situated in Roman Catholic parishes or areas which had been established by their parent diocese. Most congregations carried little or no debt. Minimal new church construction took place.

All of this drastically changed following that war. The American church scene followed the charging societal rush of the 1950s and 1960s from the cities to the suburbs and conversely from the farms to the urban and suburban areas. New freeways and roads crisscrossed the landscape. Faster air and rail travel shrunk the miles between population areas. Housing developments emerged almost as fast as rabbits can procreate. Shopping malls became the rage and the post-war boom was on. Profit became *king* as business and its sunshine blessing, *prosperity*, dawned once more upon this blessed land.

Following a step or two behind were the churches, because where the people go, so go the churches. New sanctuaries and educational buildings of many denominations rose in the midst of this societal explosion. Seeping into their thinking, their planning, were concepts of *size*, and *fund raising* to meet building debt, and *innovative programming* to attract members. The competition for new members was fierce. Suddenly, many churches became no different than their business counterparts. Their methods mirrored the market-place. Church business became a new kid on the block and entrepreneurs of varying stripes were willing to act as consultants. "How to do books" about church growth were now appearing in religious supply catalogues. Success, as measured by the world, became the driving force. Almost overnight the church was not measured by its faithfulness to God and His Word, but by its size and profitability.

How do I know about this? Simple. I was in the midst of this whirlwind in the late 1950s and early 1960s as a newly-called pastor to a Lutheran congregation in Pennsylvania with 300 members which grew to almost 1300 in 1965 when I answered my nation's call to active duty in the U.S. Navy as a chaplain. Hatboro, Pennsylvania, had been founded before the Revolutionary War and derived its name from its hat making business for the soldiers of George Washington's army. When I arrived in 1956, it was still a sleepy, wonderful village filled with ordinary folks who made their livelihood from their small businesses and professions. The family doctor even made house calls! Some building of new homes was taking place, but nothing like what occurred from the early 1960s to the early 1980s. In early American history, the village had been a one day carriage or horse ride from Philadelphia to New York on a famous road known as York Road. Today it adjoins the urban mass of that city of brotherly love even though it likes to keep the tag of "suburban."

Yes, I witnessed this societal whirlwind of change in its inception and was so caught up in it that its newness challenged me to drive for success for my congregation. I admit I enjoyed the numerous "pats on the back." Of course, along the way, there were some "major pats" that were on the lower posterior side. This is a good balance for pastors to have. It brings reality to the fore as well as to the rear. Had Vietnam not erupted as it did in 1965 and had I not been in the Naval Reserve where I was moved by God's call to military ministry, I might have remained in the civilian ministry.

After almost back-to-back tours of duty in Vietnam, one with Destroyer Division 212 and the other with the 11th Marine Corps Regiment, First Marine Division, I returned to San Diego, California, in the early 1970's when I could relate once more to the changes that were happening in civilian churches. What was more than an undercurrent which I had experienced in my civilian ministry was now "surfing big time" and was breaking upon the shores, and even beyond the shores, in civilian denominations. Now, it had a name. It was called "The Church Growth Movement." What I thought was huge at that time has grown even bigger as it still captivates churches of almost every denomination. I view it today as "The Trojan Horse" of ecclesiastical megalomania (churchly mania for grandiose worldly status—my definition). It is also a major magnet for the demise of Christian spirituality.

346

What is deceiving about it lies in its tie to the admonition of the Risen Lord in Matthew 28: 19, 20: "Go therefore and make disciples of all nations, baptizing them in the name of the Father and the Son and the Holy Spirit, teaching them to observe all that I commanded you; and lo, I am with you always to the end of the age." No sane Christian would ever dispute this great commission from our Lord. The trouble emerges in the method of carrying out the Lord's command.

When one studies the Church Growth Movement, there can be no denial that it is a method. As a method, it is tied to business practices and strategies which are advertised to bring growth and success. As a method, you will never find it proclaiming doctrinal theology, for that would narrow the gap of its use. As a method, it does not proclaim both God's Law and Gospel. Instead, as a method, it focuses upon sociological and psychological strategies which have had great success in the business world. Simply put, it understands the church market and then applies techniques which will insure growth. It spotlights both the ways of the world and the animal heat of humans to make churches grow. No one can dismiss hard work in the name of the Lord, but church growth is more than a human dimension of numbers engineering and profitability.

347

Os Guinness rightly strikes the keyboard notes by which the Church Growth Movement is tuned and motivated when he points to

> the centrality of the church, the priority of mission, the possibility of growth, the necessity of speaking to outsiders, the acknowledgment of culture and cultures, the instance on real results, and the wisdom of using the best insights and technologies proffered by the key disciplines of the human sciences.[1]

What really stands out in the Church Growth Movement is how well it blends in with and compliments the historical-critical method of biblical interpretation. We have seen how this method has replaced the authority of God's Word with the authority of liberal biblical scholars. The Church Growth Movement denies God's proven method of spiritually growing His Church through the Gospel Word of God and the Sacraments. "God, get out of the way! We'll take over!" has become the cry of church growth devotees and gurus. The ways and means of the marketplace are extolled as the best tools for Christian Churches to realize numerical growth and financial solvency. It becomes more than obvious than not that the very essence of God's means of growing His Church has been abandoned for a quick fix.

When theologians in liberal seminaries and liberal pastors in both liberal and conservative denominations follow the historical-critical method of biblical interpretation, they have already provided fertile ground in which the Church Growth Movement can easily be accepted and employed. Failing to honor the authority of God's Word, any method or idea for human success in the church can roar or sneak in and take up residence. It can make the Christian Church comfortable and appealing, user friendly, to the degree that it deconstructs the Church in an effort to reconstruct the Church.

The reality of human sin is down-played, for after all, guilt is not a happy encounter in a post-modern world where everything is held to be "relative," where there are no boundaries for right or wrong. When this occurs, there remains no biblical foundation upon which to build.

Ad infinitum and also *ad nauseam* (without end and to a sickening degree) I have heard lay members who are prominent business people extol the Church Growth Movement as logical. Of course many of the concerns of the Church Growth Movement are logical, but are they THEO-logical? This is exactly what the Church Growth Movement is not. It is not centered upon God and His Word and Sacraments, but upon man, using techniques and processes of the business world in sociological and psychological ways so that it appears to be logical to those in churches who have had their thinking and energies directed to the marketplace throughout the work week. If it brings results there, why not "use" them in the church?

The answer is simple and obvious. Only God can make His Church grow and Holy Scripture is most clear about how He bestows growth—through the hearing and believing of His Word, His love message in Jesus. Spiritual growth is always of God, not of man. Luke in Acts 6:7 clearly states: "And the word of God kept on spreading; and the number of disciples continued to increase greatly in Jerusalem, and a great many of the priests were becoming obedient to the faith." Paul, in Romans 10:17 writes: "So faith comes from hearing, and hearing by the word of Christ." Nowhere in Holy Scripture will you find contradictions to these passages as God's way of growing His Church.

One of the distressing elements of the Church Growth Movement is to make worship entertaining and fun for a television conditioned culture. Then, small amounts of biblical food can be fed, but never in an offensive way. Not wanting to ruffle the feathers of a relative minded post-modern society, Christianity is then presented in a sugar-coated manner, easily digestible. The aim is to make comfortable and entertaining the walk from the world into the church, to make it as unobtrusive as possible. Where, then, is the distinction between the church and the world? Have they merged?

A church in Southern California where Barbe and I once held membership, discontinued using any semblance of confession of sins in their worship along with an abandonment of absolution of sin for the penitent. When I protested and asked, "Why?" I was told: "Because we do not want to offend those outside the church who wouldn't understand. We want to reach these people." Obviously the subject of sin was offensive, a thorny subject too strong for the unchurched to handle. My identity as a sinner in need of God's forgiving grace was being ignored. My protests were finally honored as I centered upon dishonesty to the doctrine of the church as well as their non-consideration of the worship needs of those who were already members and who expressed their spiritual need for confession and absolution.

Another "cute" rendition was to modify the confession of faith or belief so that it could be acceptable, if possible, not to the people within the church, but once more, to those outside the church whom they wanted to *entice* to join their membership. In most instances it seemed that even a Muslim or a Hindu could easily join in their confession of faith which was dominated by the winds and currents of pluralism. What a subtle spiritual minefield the Church Growth Movement has laid!

The Christian Church, if it is to be the Christian Church, must always have its heart set on the

351

objective of new lives for old, spiritually equipping God's people through both Word and Sacraments to be able to live God-blessed lives here on earth and with God for all eternity. Certainly church growth is a factor, but it must adhere to God's way of growing His Church, not according to the mandates and techniques of the marketplace which emphasize the return factors of size, profitability, and accommodation to products that sell no matter what may be the compromises that are imposed. Spiritual growth within churches easily becomes compromised and becomes one of the first symptoms of the SARS spiritual virus. Then, the very spiritual heart of congregations falls prey to spiritual cardiac arrest.

It should not be forgotten that the Church Growth Movement not only changes the character of the church, but also redefines the role of the pastor, the under-shepherd of God. In this movement, he or she becomes a C.E.O., the chief executive officer, who oversees the operation and keeps all the parts well-oiled and working. The scripturally ordained office of preaching, teaching God's Word, and administering the sacraments is compromised with the pastoral side of ministry focusing upon making people feel good and comfortable in their sin, so as not to offend. As well, the one-on-one contact of the pastor with the hurting, the sick, and those who have strayed from God, easily slips from the pastoral agenda. The shepherd of the flock loses spiritual identity as a servant of God for the eternal spiritual life of God's beloved. How easy it is for liberal and some orthodox clergy to become seduced and wed to the *god of this world* by this method which promises astonishing, verifiable numerical results—results that have no bearing upon the spiritual life of congregations committed to this method.

You may question: "Where and when did this Church Growth Movement really begin?" The real answer must always point to the *god of this world* who used good and well-meaning theologians for his purpose. A stalwart pioneer in this movement is Donald McGarven and some of his associates at Fuller Theological Seminary in Pasadena, California. Good intentions, apart from the authority of God's Word for growth, will always yield a mixed-bag and that is exactly what the Church Growth Movement is, a mixed bag. Substantiating this claim is David F. Wells who writes the following about McGarvan:

> First, McGavran was not theologically oriented. His thinking was quite pragmatic and results-oriented. He argued, for example, that the only barriers to conversion were social, such as class and ethnicity—and that they were not theological in nature at all; remove these barriers and conversion would follow as naturally as water running downhill. This unintended advocacy of a form of faith stripped of theological content has made

Church Growth technique completely vulnerable to the intrusions of modernity, because it filters out the transcendent features of the Christian faith that constitute its best defense against the relativizing dogmas of modernity.[2]

In this work I have discussed ecumenism and pluralism. Both find a solid fit in the Church Growth Movement. In ecumenism, we saw that there was no consensus regarding the need to teach doctrine—a major conciliation of the Church Growth Movement. What fits one will fit all! It also resembles the Social Gospel theology of the 1870s in America when in some Protestant churches the preaching and teaching would emphasize "Life, not doctrine." The aim of this movement was to redefine or recast the meaning of Christianity in ethical terms. It was another attempt at reconstruction of biblical theology so that the major aim of Christianity was human progress, a by-product of Christianity, not its central theme of salvation through Jesus.

In pluralism, we saw a jumble of religions as co-equal wherein the substance of God's revelation in Jesus Christ for mankind's salvation was neutered, as Jesus was merely one of the bunch, just another banana on the tree of religion. Pluralism in the Church Growth Movement attempts to do exactly that. God and His love message in Jesus plays second fiddle to numbers. His love message in all of Scripture is submerged, so as not to offend. Oh, yes, there is preaching on scriptural themes, but very rarely proclaiming the exclusive working of the Holy Spirit, through the Means of God's Grace, to evoke faith and spiritual life in the people of God. God takes a back seat to man's sociological, psychological, and administrative ways of growing the church. Thus, when a new found "man-made idea" for church growth emerges, it is made to explode as a God-given gift, a new, fantastic saddle on which to ride to ecclesiastical glory.

In Chapter 3, I wrote about objective and subjective truth. Here is another example. The objective truth of God's power to grow His Church is substituted for the subjective power of human thinking and action to accomplish what "God" apparently couldn't do, grow His Church according to man's expectations.

Don Cupitt, an English Anglican priest and well known writer walks in the footsteps of the Church Growth Movement as he centers in upon the merits of subjectivity in theology. After a glowing defense of subjectivity, he reveals why he takes his subjective position because "it has given us the chance to make and finish our selves and our world by our own historical action."[3] And this is exactly what the Church Growth Movement wants to accomplish—growth by "our historical action"—our physical sweat and ingenuity—with God's Holy Spirit being a thankful spectator and fan, a non-participant in the action.

355

The late Rev. Dr. Robert David Preus had this to say to the Christian Church in 1953 when the Church Growth Movement was in its embryonic stage:

> The church of God must be content to remain a struggling, militant minority. This it has always been and always will be. God will have it no other way . . . . Remember, our rightness or wrongness, our success or failure, will never be measured by counting noses, but by something which will stand forever and will judge men in the last day, the Word of God.[4]

Can there be any other criterion, especially when "megalomania" is defined by Webster's Dictionary as "A mania for great or grandiose performance; a delusional mental disorder that is marked by infantile feelings of personal omnipotence and grandeur." Now, please tell me where this fits in regard to Jesus, the Lord of His Church, as God's suffering servant, which Isaiah 53:3–5 proclaims. Read and see! It is only through Jesus that you and I can ever be spiritually alive! Only through Jesus can His Church grow and He has provided the Means: His Word and Sacraments!

NOTES

1. Os Guinnes, "Sounding Out the Idols of Church Growth," in *No God but God,* ed. Os Guinness and John Seel, (Chicago: Moody Press,1992), 153.

2. David F. Wells, *God In The Wasteland*, op.cit.,70, 71.
3. Don Cupitt, *After God*, (New York: Basic Books, 1997), 67.
4. From Robert David Preus, In Memoriam, 1924–1995, in *LOGIA*, vol.V, (Epiphany 1996) No. 1, 3.

CHAPTER 12

Conclusion: Only One Way!

For indeed Jews ask for signs, and Greeks search for wisdom; but we preach Christ crucified, to Jews a stumbling block and to Gentiles foolishness, but to those who are called, both Jews and Greeks, Christ the power of God and the wisdom of God.

(Ist Cor. 1: 22–24)

The German theologian Wolfhart Pannenberg has written:

. . . the Protestant main line churches are in acute danger of disappearing. I expect they will disappear if they continue neither to resist the spirit of a progressively secularist culture nor try to transform it.[1]

Pannenberg adroitly predicted in 1994 what we are seeing in this new millennium as the result of "the not so silent merger of the world with the church." A progressively secularist culture under the headship of the *god of this world* has woven barren theological threads together to make up the fabric of liberal theology. The pattern which emerges depicts the battle plan—the destruction of Christian spirituality.

In Operation Iraqi Freedom, we saw the battle plan begin by attacking command and control targets, the nerve centers from which offensive and defensive strategies flow. God's enemy has used this tactic with cunning brilliance since the Enlightenment of the 18th century. Not that he didn't use it before that time, but we have seen the ripeness for this tactic being employed once man's reason in the service of subjectivity ascended in power among theologians. Then, God's command and control, which is His authority, can be assaulted. What you have read in this work has been the many-pronged theological attacks against God's authority in His Word. Once the Word is left in ruins, the Sacraments of Baptism and The Lord's Supper also fall. Christian spirituality vanishes because its foundation, God's Means of Grace, has been divested of power.

This is what has happened in the liberal, "mainline" denominations. They have lost God's power to effectively address both God's Law and Gospel to their members. God's Holy Spirit refuses to be in the employ of "diversity" and "inclusiveness," twin pillars of spiritual mashed potatoes, upon which the *god of this world* attempts to erect a "culturally correct" theology without the authority of God. This "new found" theology of culture overflows with incompleteness, double-talk, confusion, and deception. It is a complete "left" turn away from God's revealed truth in Holy Scripture, really a conglomeration of "methods of ideologies" rather than a Christ-centered theology of Word and Sacraments.

As I was completing research for this work at Pacific Lutheran University in Tacoma, Washington, a university endorsed by the ELCA, I checked out a few books from the library. Standing behind the check-out counter was a beautiful coed, wearing a maroon T-shirt with words emblazoned in white which read: "My object in life is to piss on the radical right."

Her written and bold statement provoked some immediate questions. First, I asked if what she was wearing signified that she is for abortion? Her answer was: "Yes, I believe it is the right of freedom of choice." I then asked: "Do you know what the Bible reveals about life?" The answer was: "No." This answer led to my next question: "Do you believe that Holy Scripture is the authoritative Word of God?" "No," she replied, "because there are a lot of errors in it." "Have you studied God's Word to come to that conclusion?" I asked. "No." she replied. From my library card she knew that I was a pastor and her manner became quiet and withdrawn.

There stood a young university student who is being schooled in liberal ways by a "Christian" university, a trendy post-modern phenomena. Softly, I said to her: "I love you as a child of God and I am concerned for you and your generation that has little or no biblical foundation in the Word of God. Please read Psalm 139 concerning life and please read and study God's Word because He loves you." Her eyes followed me as I left and heavy upon my heart was the soul of this precious child of God for whom my prayers have not ended. Sadly, her education in a supposedly Christian university, mirrors our progressively secularist culture and as such, represents an incomplete education. She is young and I am sure our God hasn't finished the work of His Holy Spirit in her life. The final chapter in her precious life has not as yet been written.

The above story is not an isolated case within our world today. It represents crippled spirituality which abounds *ad infinitum* to the delight of this world's *god*. This is because the great theological divide which developed in Semler-like fashion within liberal Christian denominations, has planted poisonous spiritual roots within these denominations. The means for this to be accomplished resides in the historical-critical method wherein man's authority supercedes God's authority. John F. Walvood has it right when he maintains:

> . . . the relationship of verbal inspiration to scriptural authority is the crux of all Christian theology and provides a principal which bifurcates all theological systems as resting either in divine inspiration or in human judgments.[2]

In simpler language, Walvood is saying that the crucial issue in Christianity is whether or not God inspired the Holy Scriptures to be written as His authoritative Word. Walvood points to a bifurcation, a dividing into two branches, so that theological systems fall into one of two camps—either into the authority of the divine inspiration of His Word—or human judgment, or opinion by scholars influenced by the Enlightenment of the 18th century. It is the great theological divide that Semler initiated when he tried to find what was and what was not the Word of God in Holy Scripture—the seed bed of the historical-critical method—the source of fractured spirituality. It is fractured because it tries to bear the name "Christian" without the unquestioned *authority* of God's Word as inerrant and infallible.

A quick review in *bullet* fashion provides the evidence through which the *god of this world* has worked to bring spiritual ruin upon the lives of

Christians under the influence of liberal theologians whose work has impregnated "mainline" denominations.

- Being free "to do theology," liberal theologians influenced by the historical-critical method of biblical interpretation attempt to take the authority out of God's Holy Word in Scripture. Elevating their opinions as truth, they fashion a post-18th century authority of reason—human man in control—an "antiquated" Word of God at their academic mercy. The casualties: God's beloved who were and are influenced by such human reason which follows the cultural flow of human reason and living, the seedbed of spiritual death.

- Ecumenism is embraced at the expense of scriptural, doctrinal truth which God's Word teaches and proclaims. "Unity in diversity" becomes the objective.
  Driving the force of ecumenism are the "twin dynamos:" *peace* and *justice.*
  Liberation theology rules the roost. Like pluralism, the world's survival is "top banana."

- Pluralism becomes the means for circling the wagons of the world's religions, hopeful that some elixir of truth will emerge which will avert world destruction through war or other devastating means. Jesus is made to appear as one of many solutions in a grab-bag of mixed religious possibilities.

- Evolution, through a combination of chance and natural selection, an unproven theory, is attractively fashioned to cancel God's creation as intelligent design by an omnipotent Creator.

- Process theology views the world in a "process of becoming" in which God is along for the ride as a passenger. Eternal change rules the day.

- The community of believers usurps final authority to reinterpret Scripture in order to find truth for "post-modern" living. God's truth no longer can be found in an "archaic" book. His authority has expired. The community of believers arise as new "spiritual" architects.

- Education in liberal Christian colleges, universities, and seminaries is ringed with empirical doubt, swimming in diversity, to the extent that God in Scripture has to be deconstructed in order to be reconstructed according to what a post-modern academic culture can accept as believable. In non-

Christian schools of "higher learning," God is the enemy of liberated bellybutton morality. Scholars create synthesis as their "god." Evolution rules the sciences and Christian truth becomes the "target of opportunity."

- "Oppressive" constraints imposed by a Christianity committed to the truth of God's Word must be changed. God must now be portrayed as a "She," with Jesus regarded as a male oppressor. Homosexuality is viewed as a normal life-style. Same-sex marriage moves onto the legal and ecclesiastical horizons. The authority of sexual hedonism is unleashed in a growing number of "mainline" Christian denominations. Liberation theology becomes the engine for change within these denominations.

- Abortion is condoned as the legal right of "choice." The sanctity of life is not accorded to "products of conception" within the womb. Indeed, life has lost the sanctity God bequeathed to all life in His magnificent creation.

- Methods of church growth via marketplace strategy are appropriated as more effective than God's way through His Means of Grace. Christian spirituality is sacrificed for the sake of numbers.

These twisted and bare threads of theologies and methods, not under the authority of God's Word, have become the non-spiritual fabric of liberal denominations in which they wrap themselves. Yes, "An enemy has done this!"

Their paths to truth, essentially spiritual minefields, have been littered with human opinions and judgments which have brought spiritual death to unsuspecting people of God. As their non-scriptural theologies continue to roll out as productions of fanciful opinions, they are painting themselves into a corner from which only God can rescue them. The Christian faith has always been about rescue as proclaimed by God in both Law and Gospel. The world and its liberal denominations are confronted in a decisive word of divine judgment in Scripture (Law). They are also confronted by a decisive word of redemption flowing from Christ's death on the cross for all sinners (Gospel). It is the working of the Holy Spirit through God's Word which creates faith. True Christian spirituality blossoms and grows God's way: through His Means of Grace. There can be no other way!

In Chapter 1, I wrote about the "Parable of the Tares among the Wheat," in Matthew 13:24–30, which vividly reveals that "An enemy has done this!" There is another truth in the parable which we must never allow to slip from our hearts and minds. Easily it can be missed. The first portion of verse 30 contains words too often by-passed by those of us who want to attack and wipe out offenses against our God and His Word by human effort. We want to take transformation responsibility upon ourselves, a transformation to which Pannenberg pointed. Those authoritative parable words of the parable are: "Allow both to grow until the harvest . . ."

They are hard words for those of us who see how the world has merged with liberal denominations, and in some instances with liberal congregations within conservative denominations. They are not words of tolerance, but words of Godly wisdom. Our God is in control and the harvest time will arrive at His bidding. It is all in God's perfect timing as has been everything else of His creation, even our lives wherein we have experienced new lives for old.

Certainly this does not mean surrendering to the enticing ideologies of liberalism. In no way does it mean that we need not witness to those our God has placed around us with the truth that Jesus is Lord and Savior and that the authority of God's Word in Holy Scripture must always stand as the foundation for all Christian doctrine. To do less than that would make us unfaithful servants of God and it is in the context of servanthood, Christ living within us as Lord and

Savior, that true Christian spirituality is lived to the neighbor to the glory of God.

As one who served in combat with the United States Marine Corps in Vietnam, I know well the motto of the Corps: "Semper Fidelis" or just plain "Semper Fi," *always faithful.* The individual Marine is never called upon to win the battle by himself. He is part of a unit: a squad, a platoon, a battery, a regiment, or a division. He is called to be faithful in carrying out his mission to his "band of brothers," to his country, and to his God. The Marine knows he stands against a known enemy. And this is exactly what God inspired St. Paul to communicate to the Christians in Ephesus and to us, in Ephesians 6: 10–12:

> Finally, be strong in the Lord, and in the strength of His might.
>
> Put on the full armor of God, that you may be able to stand firm against the schemes of the devil.
>
> For our struggle is not against flesh and blood, but against the rulers, against the powers, against the world forces of this darkness, against the spiritual *forces* of wickedness in the heavenly *places.*

The Marine also knows his armor, just as the Christian knows his or her spiritual armor: Truth,

Righteousness, The Gospel of Peace, The Shield of
Faith, The Helmet of Salvation, and The Sword of
the Spirit which is The Word of God. Ephesians
6:14–17 is most clear in the naming of God's spiritual armor, for the battle is spiritual. What follows in the next two verses regarding prayer and
petition reveals St. Paul following the words of
his Master, Jesus, Who in Matthew 5:44 defines
His spiritual plan of battle for Christian lives:

> But I say unto you, love your enemies, and
> pray for those who persecute you . . . .

And in Luke 6:27:

> But I say to you who hear, love your enemies,
> do good to those who hate you . . . .

Look at those verbs, those action words:
"love," "pray," and "do good!" They are words of
Christ's power for our lives. When they become
alive in us, as God's Word directs and attests,
God's Holy Spirit will direct His love action of
power in our lives wherein we stand as His faithful witnesses. There is that word *faithful*—the
"Semper Fi" of the Christian Church. Our God
does not call us to win the battle by ourselves,
but He does call us to stand fast for Him in the faithfulness which He provides. Be assured that while
God calls us to be faithful witnesses in the midst of
the heat of this spiritual battle, the outcome or the
harvest is never in doubt. It is in good hands!

For too many years the "not so silent merger" of the world with the Church has been unfolding and it has not yielded spiritual blessings. In our human impatience, we are prone to ask: "When will it end?" Then comes the assurance which only our God can give. The "harvest time" *will* come and that harvest will be by the final action of God. It will be God's way, the only way!

NOTES

1. Wolfhart Pannenberg, "Christianity and the West: Ambiguous Past, Uncertain Future," *First Things*, (December 1994), 23.
2. John Walvood, *"The Pragmatic Confirmation of Scriptural Authority"* in *"The Bible - The Living Word of Revelation,"* ed. Merrill C. Tenny, (Grand Rapids: Zondervan Publishing House, 1968), 182.

Soli Deo Gloria!

To order additional copies of

N^{The}ot_{So}
Silent
Merger

Have your credit card ready and call:

1-877-421-READ (7323)

or please visit our web site at
www.pleasantword.com

Also available at:
www.amazon.com
and
www.barnesandnoble.com

Printed in the United States
23650LVS00002B/178-210

9 781414 102412